ALAHAN
AN EARLY CHRISTIAN MONASTERY
IN SOUTHERN TURKEY

edited by Mary Gough

The Early Christian monastery at Alahan occupies a terrace high in the
mountains of Isauria in southern Asia Minor. Constructed in the second
half of the fifth century AD, its remains include three churches, a
baptistery, a colonnaded walkway running the full lenght of the site, and
several subsidiary buildings. One of the churches (the earliest) was cut into
the rock of a natural cave, the other two, constructed of fine ashlar
masonry, are of extremely advanced architectural design, richly decorated
with lively relief-sculpture of the highest technical calibre, and
extraordinarily well preserved; the East Church, with its central tower
and squinches, is virtually intact except for its roof. The complex was
almost certainly funded by the Emperor Zeno (474-491), who was a
native of the region, as part of a larger programme for Isauria, and it
stands as the finest achievement of native Isaurian stone-masons and
sculptors, before their diaspora in the civil wars which followed Zeno's
death, to seek work abroad, in Syria, Palestine, and elsewhere. Alahan is a
key site in the history of Early Byzantine architecture, half a century
before the great achievements of Anicia Juliana and Justinian in
Constantinople.

The site was excavated and studied by Michael Gough in a series of
campaigns from 1955 to 1972, but publication was delayed by his early
death in 1974. The full report has been completed by his collaborators,
and, after an introductory section on the site, the excavation, inscriptions,
and chronology, there follow catalogues of the coins, pottery, and small
finds, and a long and fully illustrated architectural description. The
volume is concluded by a discussion of the place of Alahan in the
development of Eastern monasticism.

Contributors

Gerard Bakker
Jonathan Coulston
Mary Gough
Martin Harrison
Michael M. Sheehan, CSB
Paolo Verzone
Caroline Williams

STUDIES AND TEXTS 73

"ALAHAN,
AN EARLY CHRISTIAN
MONASTERY
IN SOUTHERN TURKEY,,

Based on the Work of Michael Gough

EDITED BY

MARY GOUGH

PONTIFICAL INSTITUTE OF MEDIAEVAL STUDIES

ACKNOWLEDGMENT

This book has been published with the help of a grant
from the Canadian Federation for the Humanities,
using funds provided by the Social Sciences
and Humanities Research Council of Canada.

CANADIAN CATALOGUING IN PUBLICATION DATA

Main entry under title:
Alahan : an early Christian monastery in Southern Turkey

(Studies and texts, ISSN 0082-5328 ; 73)
Bibliography: p.
Includes index.
ISBN 0-88844-073-1

1. Alahan Manastiri (Turkey).   2. Christian antiquities - Turkey.
3. Monastic and religious life - History - Early church, ca. 30-600.   4. Turkey -
Antiquities.   5. Excavations (Archaeological) - Turkey.   I. Gough, Michael.
II. Gough, Mary, 1914-   III. Pontifical Institute of Mediaeval Studies.
IV. Series: Studies and texts (Pontifical Institute of Mediaeval Studies) ; 73.

DS156.A46A5 1985   939′.29   C84-099018-9

Pontifical Institute of Mediaeval Studies
59 Queen's Park Crescent East
Toronto, Ontario, Canada M5S 2C4

PRINTED BY UNIVERSA, WETTEREN, BELGIUM

Michael Gough had decided that his book on Alahan should be dedicated to everyone who had worked there and in particular to the Turkish workmen and craftsmen who had been with him during all his years of excavation at Alahan itself and at other sites in the same area.

This book has the same dedication.

Contents

PART THREE

LIST OF MAPS

LIST OF FIGURES

List of Plates

The following abbreviations are used to indicate the photographers:

AF	Dr Alison Frantz	MG	Michael Gough
DC	David Cheshire	OA	Bay Oktay Acer
EAR	Dr Elisabeth Alfoldi-	PV	Prof. Paolo Verzone
	Rosenbaum	SH	Sonya Halliday
GB	Gerard Bakker	St.H	Dr Stephen Hill

Preface

It is necessary that there should be a short preface to this book in order to explain how it comes to be written in this form.

The late Michael Gough studied, thought about and worked at the monastery of Alahan over a period of some twenty years[1] and undertook a final Study Season there in 1973. A month or so later he started work on a definitive publication of the site, just about a week before his untimely death. It seemed important that the publication of Alahan should go on, even after the death of the excavator, and it was decided that several especially qualified scholars should be invited to write different sections of it under the general editorshp of the undersigned. They agreed to do so and this volume is the result.

It need scarcely be said that the writers of this book, Mr. Bakker, Mr. Coulston, Professor Harrison, the Reverend M. M. Sheehan and Dr. Williams have had a very difficult task. Although almost all had worked at Alahan only Mr. Bakker had expected to be called upon to write about the monastery and even he had always envisaged doing so in close collaboration with Michael Gough himself. Thus not only have they had to do the normal work of interpreting and recording the archaeology and the monuments but also have had to make research into the notes, published articles and lectures of the excavator written and promulgated over a very long period. That they have done so is a considerable achievement and students of Early Christian archaeology owe them a debt of gratitude for the erudition and patience that they have devoted to the work and for their generosity in finding time to complete it. Particular thanks must be expressed to them by the editor for their willing, kind and continued co-operation with her. Professor Verzone comes into a different category from the others and must be thanked separately for his contribution; his monograph on Alahan appeared in Turkish in 1955 and in Italian in 1956[2] and, when the editor approached him to find out where she might obtain a copy of the latter, he kindly presented her with one and

---

[1] The sequence of periods of study and excavation at Alahan is given below, p. 225.
[2] *Alahan Manastiri mimarisi üzerinde bir inceleme* (Istanbul, 1955); *Alahan Monastir: Un Monumento dell'arte Tardo-Romano in Isauria* (Turin, 1956).

also offered a short article on his visit to Alahan before the excavation started. It appears at the end of this volume.

Before his death Michael Gough had composed a general scheme for his Alahan book and written a rough and incomplete introductory chapter. The scheme of his book was the first of "first drafts" and would surely have been modified as the work progressed just as it has been modified here. It has, though, given useful guidance as to the weight and value which he himself attached to the various aspects of the site and, largely, his plan has been adhered to. The introductory chapter (Chapter 1) appears here just as it was written; added to it, however, is a brief general description of the monastery which had not been included in the original manuscript before it was broken off. It is very likely that Michael Gough would have included such a description had he had time to do so. From the first and main part of this chapter the reader will gather, tantalisingly, that the book which he planned would have been much wider in scope than it was decided to make this one. He had become increasingly interested not only in Alahan itself but also in the whole surrounding countryside, in the relations of the monastery with other religious foundations in the area and in the road systems than linked them. He had been working for some time on this line of research and had published two articles in connection with it.[3]

From the first chapter, therefore, the reader can learn some of Michael Gough's thoughts about the topography of the Alahan district. What he cannot learn is how the aesthetic values of the various features of the monastery might have been treated, although it is certain that the architectural and artistic trends and fashions which must have influenced the planning and building at Alahan, together with the way in which Alahan, in turn, influenced other monasteries and churches, both local and further afield, would have been extensively considered and that the excavated artifacts would have been discussed in the same context. Also, much more lenghty speculation than has been given here would have been devoted to the circumstances which led to the original foundation of the monastery, to its importance during its *floreat* and to the reasons for its abandonment and later re-occupation.

Thus, this book is quite different from the one which Michael Gough might have written; the writers were not asked (and, indeed, it would have been impossible for them) to try and reproduce his opinions and

---

[3] "The Emperor Zeno and some Cilician Churches," *Anatolian Studies*, 22 (1972), 199-212; "Notes on a Visit to Mahras Monastery in Isauria," *Byzantine Studies/Études byzantines*, 1 (1974), 65-72.

speculation. They have, as they could not fail to do, introduced historical and organisational speculation of their own but, on the whole, this has not been based on stylistic comparison nor has the excellence or otherwise of the architecture, the sculpture or the artifacts been seriously discussed. This book is designed to be a handbook to Alahan Monastery, a collection of carefully researched facts and informed comment on these facts. The wide field of review and comparative examination must be left to future Early Christian archaeologists.

An additional difference between this book and the one which Michael Gough planned scarcely needs to be pointed out. His book, if not entirely written by him, would have been a homogenous whole, the excavator's final report and final conclusions on his excavation. This volume, however, should rather be regarded as a series of monographs each dealing with a different aspect of Alahan. For this reason the reader may notice a certain multiplication of the same information although in each case the information is given from a different viewpoint.

The principle on which this book has been organised should be clear from the Table of Contents. In Part One, Chapter 1 locates Alahan on the map and this is followed by a General Description of the Monastery which should enable the reader to find his way about the site and to identify the various buildings; Part One, therefore, should answer the question "where?" Part Two is designed to answer the question "when?" based on the assembled answers to the question "what?" and is divided into three chapters. The first deals with the background history of the period in general and the dating and chronology of Alahan in particular, and is supported by epigraphic, numismatic and small find evidence in the form of lists and also by Chapter 3, the Catalogue of Pottery and Glass. Chapter 5 also supports Chapter 2 but is, of necessity, very long as it gives an exhaustive description of Alahan's architecture and architectural sculpture which are the monastery's glory and main claim to fame; we also find here a detailed technical argument as to the sequence of construction and the changes in planning that took place while the construction was in progress.

In Part Three, Chapter 6, the Reverend M. M. Sheehan in dealing with the organisation of the monastery sets out to give some answers to the question "why?" Why, for ecclesiastical or domestic reasons, a building was located where it has been, why an expansion may have been undertaken and why some special feature may have been put in a particular place. Although many "why?" questions remain unanswered and may remain so for ever, this chapter makes a most illuminating conclusion to the main part of the book.

Professor Verzone's Appendix describes the site and his visit to it before any excavation had taken place; from it and also with reference to his monograph, it can be seen how able were his deductions at a time when only parts of some of the buildings could be studied. It is impressive that so much of his theory has later been substantiated.

The list of those to whom thanks are due for making the appearance of this volume possible is long indeed. In his Introduction Michael Gough had already sketched out some paragraphs of acknowledgments; they are, of course, as relevant to this book as they would have been to his and it seems appropriate that they should be given here rather than later. He wrote:

> My debt of gratitude to persons and institutions is very great and it is logical to express my first thanks to the Director[4] and the staff of the Turkish Department of Museums and Antiquities whose active and effective aid has allowed me to work for so long at Alahan. I am grateful, too, to the successive Government Representatives whose tact and experience have greatly helped me. I must also thank our old friends from Mut and the surrounding villages who have worked on the excavation, whose skill and industry have greatly contributed to its success and whose friendship has helped us to find at Alahan a second home; some first joined us nearly twenty years ago. We have been fortunate, too, in the watchmen who have guarded the site and acted as guides to the ever increasing number of visitors.
>
> No less than my debt of gratitude to Turkey and her people is that which I owe to the British Institute of Archaeology at Ankara for consistent support of my work and to the Canada Council for continuing that support with characteristic generosity. I have been encouraged, too, over the years, by the financial aid of individual subscribers to the expenses of the excavation, by the Reid and Russell Trusts and by my Canadian sponsors at the Pontifical Institute of Mediaeval Studies and the Royal Ontario Museum. It is thanks to the sustained interest of all of these that Alahan Monastery has come to life again.
>
> It would be invidious to single out individual members of the archaeological teams who have worked so patiently and loyally with me on the site for so many years; British, Canadians, American, French, they can be numbered by the score. Architects, however, are an exception and I must mention Gerard Bakker, whose plans and many of whose photographs illustrate the text,[5] and also Robert Wylie whose engineering

---

[4] The late Bay Hikmet Gürçay.

[5] It is likely that, in subsequent drafts of his Introduction, Michael Gough would have mentioned earlier in the chapter that it was planned that Mr. Bakker should write on Alahan's architecture. If not, he might have chosen to do so here. What is certain is that, wherever it occurred, the acknowledgment would have been in the warmest terms.

skill was the mainstay of our restoration work. I would like also to mention our conservationists, Susan Bakker, Marjorie Hutchinson and Anne Searight.[6] As always, I feel especially grateful to my wife and my debt to her cannot be met or measured in formal thanks.

In this present volume it is simplest to make acknowledgments in chronological order, that is, from the acceptance of the idea of a "new" Alahan publication. Thanks must first be made, therefore, to the then President of the Pontifical Institute of Mediaeval Studies, the Reverend E. A. Synan and to Dr. A. D. Tushingham the then Chief Archaeologist of the Royal Ontario Museum for their initial and continued encouragement to the editor and to the institutions they represented for academic recognition of her and financial help. Gratitude must also be expressed to the Canada Council for their financing both of a Study Season in 1975 and of the preparation of the manuscript. The General Director of Museums and Antiquities in Turkey, the late Bay Hikmet Gürçay, and his staff readily and kindly accepted the editor in her new role; the Directors of the Museums at Konya and Adana gave facilities for work on the Alahan material lodged with them; the Representative assigned to the Study Season integrated well into the team and officials in Mut, particularly those in the Forestry Department, gave advice and help when the final work at Alahan was undertaken, the setting up of a fence around the entire complex. The Director of the British Institute of Archaeology at Ankara gave the hospitality of the Hostel, as well as advice and support to the editor and her associates when they were in Ankara. To all of these she is very grateful.

The list of friends and scholars who, when they heard that a book on Alahan in a new form was being written, offered to help the editor with knowledge and experience is equally long, the gratitude equally great. As Michael Gough wrote in a different context it is invidious (and, indeed, would take too long) to mention all names but those of Dr. Alison Frantz, Professor Cyril Mango and Dr. Joyce Reynolds must not go unrecorded.

The majority of the photographs used to illustrate this book were taken by Mr. Bakker or by Michael Gough. Others, however, were taken at various times and by different people, as follows. Dr. Elisabeth Alföldi-Rosenbaum worked with Michael Gough at Alahan in 1961 as official photographer to the excavation and turned over all her photographs and negatives to him at the end of the season. Mr. David Cheshire visited Alahan with a BBC team in 1972 and kindly volunteered to put all his

---

[6] Now Anne Macdonald.

photographs at Michael Gough's (and later the editor's) disposal. Dr. Alison Frantz stayed at Alahan while the 1970 excavation was in progress and also generously offered the use of her pictures, as did Miss Sonya Halliday and Dr. Stephen Hill who visited the monastery after the excavation was completed. Professor Verzone sent some of his own photographs with his article. Bay Oktay Acar, in 1976 the official photographer to the Museum of Archaeology at Konya, took the pottery photographs. The editor would like very much to thank all the above and also Mr. David Barwick for the skill and interest that he showed in preparing the photographs for publication.

It is difficult to express gratitude to so many people and institutions not only for their help but also for the warmth and sensivity with which it was invariably offered and given. In these few paragraphs an inadequate attempts has been made to do so.

MARY GOUGH

Part One

PLATE 1. – Alahan Monastery: General view from west to east

1

Alahan Monastery and its Setting in the Isaurian Country Side

Michael Gough

After enjoying the hospitality of the city (Karaman) for three days, and touring and sightseeing as much as we were able, we said farewell to all our friends, and travelled south for four hours until we came to Şeyh Deresi, which is a narrow rocky valley. We passed this, and came in five hours to Seki Yaylasi, which is the boundary of the *sancak* of Silifke. There was not a soul at this Yayla, and we travelled over roads that were entirely untended until, in the thirteenth hour, after the sun had set, we unloaded our bedding in an insecure thicket, and together with our servants commended ourselves to God's hospitality. Praise be to Him, on the next morning we arrived safely at Alaca Han, a small hostelry founded by Ya'kub Khan [a member of the Karamanoğlu dynasty, but apparently known only to Evliya Çelebi]. On the far side of this *han*, and to the left, on a steep rock that reaches to the very sky, there is a castle of Takyenos. Nobody lives there, but it is a very strong castle, a fortress of vast prospect, that stands even now as if it had just left the architect's hands. It must once have been a very prosperous city.

Between the aforementioned *han* and the castle itself are more than ten thousand stone chests made of white marble. The carcases of infidels lie in them – but sure knowledge of this rests with God. As for their date, according to the inscriptions on them, which are in Greek, they date from some 630 years after the Hejira of the prophet.[1] I traced out the letters closely, as the farrier fits shoe to shoe, and when I arrived in Jerusalem, I got the priests there to read them to me. They said that these were tombs of men who professed faith in our Lord Jesus.

---

[1] I am told by Dr Mackay that a more revealing rendering of the latter part of this sentence would be "from the Hejira of the Prophet back to their date is about 630 years." *Editor*.

> On all four sides of the castle there are hundreds of thousands of caves in
> the rock, in each of which there is marble working such that not even a
> master stonecutter of the present day would be competent to touch his pick
> to it. It was given to the people of that time to enchant the rocks, so that
> they carved every stone as if it were a work of the wood-carver Fakhri, into
> flowers and interlaces in the Greek fashion, so fine that a man stands
> stupefied in amazement at the sight of them. This is something that deserves
> a visit.[2]

This passage, the first known to refer to the monastery of Alahan in
Isauria, was written just over three centuries ago (1671-1672) by Evliya
Çelebi, the Turkish traveller whose *Seyahatname* was the first and only
Baedeker of Asia Minor known to his contemporaries. No doubt, both
before and after his time, other Turkish travellers had seen and admired
the place and one at least, who visited Alahan in 1952, was impressed by
its magnificence and actually echoed the early chronicler's words. "This is
a place that certainly should be seen," said he.

The first account of the monastery by a European was written by
Count Leon de Laborde,[3] who described the ruins as he saw them in 1826
with a refreshing enthusiasm and a lively disregard for accuracy. More
than sixty years later an English cleric, A. C. Headlam, published a plan of
the monastic complex, detailed in the case of the well preserved church at
the east end of it, together with a descriptive article which still remains a
fine example of meticulous scholarship.[4] His work first brought Alahan,
(under the *soubriquet* "Koja Kalessi"), into public notice, and the singular
architectural distinction of the East Church almost immediately sparked
off a fierce controversy, which even today still smoulders on. The fiercest
opponent of Headlam's views on the East Church was the brilliant, if
eccentric, scholar Josef Strzygowski;[5] nowadays, however, modern
argument has been more concerned with the dating of the separate
elements of the monastery than with the architectural problems that so
much inflamed Strzygowski.

The end of the Second World War saw an increase of popular and
scholarly interest in the archaeology of Asia Minor, an interest fostered

[2] Pierre A. MacKay, "The First Modern Visitor to Alahan," *Anatolian Studies*, 21
(1961), pp. 173-174.

[3] Leon de Laborde, "Église d'Aladja dans le Taurus," *Revue archéologique*, 4 (1847-
1848), pp. 172-176.

[4] A. C. Headlam [with W. M. Ramsay and D. G. Hogarth], *Ecclesiastical Sites in
Isauria (Cilicia Trachea)*, Society for the Promotion of Hellenic Studies, Supplementary
Papers 1 (London, 1893), pp. 9-19.

[5] Josef Strzygowski, *Kleinasien, ein Neuland der Kunstgeschichte* (Leipzig, 1903; rpt.
New Rochelle, NY, 1980).

and encouraged by the Turkish authorities in Ankara and by individual Turkish scholars whom foreign archaeologists of my generation will always remember with gratitude, affection and respect. By 1948 Headlam's pictorial record of Alahan had already been much enlarged and improved upon by Denis Wright, then Acting British Consul at Mersin.[6] In 1952, on the 9th September, I myself first saw the monastery which has occupied so much of my time and thought over nearly a quarter of a century. In those days Alahan looked just as it did in 1954 (the year before any excavation had begun) when George Forsyth Jr. wrote a particularly apposite description of the site from the point of view of a visiting scholar. It has a fresh enthusiasm which cannot be matched. He wrote:

> One of the unforgettable moments of my trip was that which I experienced when, after clambering up pine clad slopes, I first saw this famous church, glowing with tawny warmth in the morning sun and beckoning to me. Its situation, high on the shoulder of a mountain, is magnificent, and the monastic group clings to the rocky contours, giving the impression of a Christian Delphi.[7]

In 1955, each expedition being at the time quite unaware of the other's activities, Professor Paolo Verzone with a team from the Technical University of Istanbul, arrived at Alahan at almost the same time as I did with assistants from Britain. Our respective publications also appeared almost simultaneously, by far the more comprehensive being Verzone's monograph which appeared first in Turkish, to be followed by an Italian version in 1956.[8] This work was the most important and extensive study of the whole monastery (as opposed to those of the East Church alone) which had appeared up to that time and is still very valuable as a scholarly and accurate account of the site before excavation. In that year, 1955, I undertook a sounding at the west end of the complex and established that a large building there was a church, as Verzone had conjectured. Alahan now was attracting more interest since the new road between Karaman and Mut made the monastery relatively easy of access. In 1957 Mme Nicole Thierry published a short article on the place under its old, but now correctly spelt, name of Koca Kalesi, and in 1962 she wrote an interpretation of some of the sculpture, having then adopted the more

---

[6] Denis Wright, "The Lost Monastery of Alahan: Christian Remains in Roman Cilicia," *Illustrated London News*, vol. 208 (5 Jan. 1946), pp. 24-25.

[7] George H. Forsyth, "Architectural Notes on a Trip through Cilicia," *Dumbarton Oaks Papers*, 11 (1957), p. 228.

[8] Paolo Verzone, *Alahan Manastırı mimarisi üzerinde bir inceleme* (Istanbul, 1955); *Alahan Monastir: Un Monumento dell'arte Tardo-Romano in Isauria* (Turin, 1956).

generally accepted title of Alahan Manastırı.[9] The site has been discussed by many scholars since then but from 1961 onwards the responsibility for excavation has been solely mine.

From the time of Evliya Çelebi at least, Alahan monastery has impressed the visitor no less for the beauty of its natural setting than for its awe-inspiring architecture; as this book is concerned not only with monastic buildings and appointments but also with archaeological evidence for the day to day life of a religious community of the fifth and sixth centuries a description of the surrounding countryside is here relevant.

The modern traveller who uses the highway from Konya (Iconium) to the Mediterranean coast by way of Karaman (Laranda) and Mut (Claudiopolis) (see Map 2) may still sense the scenic grandeur of his course though the romance of the old road, which, now disused except for local traffic and following a natural and uninhibited way around mountain contours and along river valleys, is unforgettable by those who have used it in real earnest.

Konya, though not naturally endowed with the advantages of an un-disputed capital like Istanbul, must always have been the cultural centre of the great plain to which it gives its name. It was certainly the obvious site for the chief city of the Selcuk Sultanate for the fertility of its soil, and its pleasant orchards and gardens must have given the ancient Konya, as they do to its modern successor, a charm and individuality all its own. South of the city the road runs through newly irrigated fields of wheat and barley with a chain of hills, dominated by Hasan Baba mountain, closing in from the western side and the impressive dark mass of Karadağ brooding over the eastern horizon. In that part of the plain are the sites of Çatal Hüyük and Can Hasan, two of the most ancient excavated sites of the Near East.

The last great oasis of the Konya plain is that of Karaman the city where Turkish was first declared the official language of the ruling dynasty, the Karamanoğullari, over six centuries ago. Between Konya and Karaman, a distance of 106 kilometres the Turkish Forestry Department has planted acacia trees on either side of the road and Karaman itself looks from the distance very like an open park until the castle, the houses and the new silo come into view. Karaman once left behind, however, the traveller senses a change of scenery that becomes increasingly marked as the road climbs gradually towards the Taurus range.

[9] N. and J.-M. Thierry, "La Monastère de Koca Kalesi en Isaurie," *Cahiers archéologiques*, 9 (1957), pp. 89-98; N. Thierry, "Notes sur l'un des bas-reliefs d'Alahan Manastiri, en Isaurie," *Cahiers archéologiques*, 13 (1962), pp. 43-47.

The ascent is not very steep but after a few kilometres the plain gives way to rugged limestone with rough scrub, dwarf oak and the occasional stone pine as the main vegetation. The soil is much eroded by mountain streams which carry it down to a fairly narrow valley which is, consequently, fertile and cultivable. In one of these richer patches stands a fine Karamanoğlu *han*, some 30 kilometres or so south of Karaman and, in the past, this distance would very probably have amounted to a single day's journey. The old road plunges straight into this valley and then goes upwards again to follow a contour to Geçimli a further 20 kilometres south. From that point, almost exactly below the mountainside on which Alahan monastery was founded, it follows nearly the same course as the modern road to Mut. The engineers who constructed this modern asphalt highway generally avoided the valleys, preferring a more direct route across higher but more rugged country. As has been said, the two roads more or less coincide just below Alahan; they also meet, briefly, at the Sertavul Pass, some 1,600 m above sea level, where they cross the Taurus.

Beyond the Sertavul pass the whole scene changes dramatically. Southward is the valley of the Gök Çayı, the northern arm of the Göksu (Kalykadnos), which it joins southwest of Mut before entering the sea not far from Silifke (Seleucia). Throughout its lower reaches the river is bounded by mountains; to the north by the Taurus chain, to the south by the last range before the downward slope to the Mediterranean. Very prominent, as seen against the southern skyline, is the profile of Mahras Dağ, a lone flat-topped mountain which dominates the view from Alahan Monastery itself as from the cluster of houses at the foot of the Alahan hill. Mahras had its own monastery, less grandiose than Alahan but enjoying a site almost as magnificent, and a sharp-eyed monk of either establishment might well have been able to pick out the buildings of the other.[10]

The first sight of Alahan has been described very often and always with enthusiasm even by the tourist who has had to climb the steep slope on foot in July or August and Professor Forsyth's account is, perhaps, the most lyrically graphic. Excavation has revealed the regularity of the monastery's plan, the nature of the various buildings which comprised it and (possibly most important for its proper appreciation) restored the level

---

[10] Michael Gough, "Notes on a Visit to Mahras Monastery in Isauria, *Byzantine Studies/Études byzantines*, 1 (1974), pp. 65-72. See also R. M. Harrison, "The Monastery on Mahras Dağ in Isauria," in *Yayla. Third Report of the Northern Society for Anatolian Archaeology* (Newcastle upon Tyne: Department of Archaeology, University of Newcastle upon Tyne, 1980), pp. 22-24.

of the Colonnaded Walkway which was the monumental link between the Basilica at the west end of the complex and the wonderfully preserved "Koca Kilise," called hereafter the East Church, "glowing with tawny warmth" more than 130 m to the east of it. Not long ago the way to the site was little more than a track used by villagers and their animals on their passage to and from the summer pastures in the upper Taurus; now, however, a winding earth road makes an approach by car possible if not easy. The total ascent is no more, vertically, than 300 m above the present road between Karaman (the ancient Laranda) and Mut (Claudiopolis), from which latter Alahan is 21 kilometres distant, but the distance to be traversed is nearly 2 kilometres.

The cretaceous limestone, never far from the surface in the wild Isaurian countryside, is generally well watered. Except during the high summer, usually hot and dry, rainfall is considerable and the pockets of earth which accumulate in hollows on the slopes allow the growth of conifers, junipers and dwarf oak as well as numerous small shrubs, herbs and flowers including asphodel, thistles, red and yellow poppies and, in the spring, cyclamen and a miniature delphinium. Of the more exotic fauna the leopard and ounce are now extinct while ibex, moufflon and wild boar have retreated to the more remote mountains. Bears and wolves, however, still come down to the valleys in search of food during the winter months. At Alahan itself the hare is reasonably common while the ubiquitous red squirrel with a dark stripe down his back is thought something of a pest but is usually left unmolested. Curiously enough the squirrel does not appear on mosaic floors of the Early Christian period, when animals and birds were specially popular with artists in the Levant and North Africa, though the partridge (*keklik*), quite common in the Taurus twenty years ago but now shot almost to extinction, is a sculptural motif at Alahan almost as characteristic of the monastery as is that of the fish.

St. Basil, the father of coenobitic monasticism, would have approved the choice of Alahan as suitable for a religious community. Headlam certainly appreciated this fact in quoting the saint's famous letter describing his own retreat near the shore of the Black Sea. The English translation is unhappy but the indulgent reader will perhaps forget the mangling of Basil's Greek with the reflection that any sort of rendering is better than none.

> What need is there to tell of the sweet-smelling earth or of the breezes from the river? Others might admire the multitude of flowers and singing birds but the monk has no leisure for such thoughts. The chief praise of the place is that it nurtures what to him is the greatest gift of all tranquility.

Peace is of the essence of Alahan monastery but there are practical considerations too that influenced the choice of site as there must be for any human settlement, especially for one in an inhospitable environment. First of all there is a plentiful supply of water to serve the community and this was also piped down for the lay settlement below. Second in importance, perhaps, was protection from the prevailing north wind (*poyraz*) provided by the natural configuration of the cliff overhanging the ledge on which the buildings were founded. Last was its easily defensible position (an important consideration in a wild province like Isauria) and the existence of a prosperous *mansio* at the foot of the hill at the first staging post northwards from Claudiopolis.

There is another pass from Karaman to Mut of some antiquity. It is by way of the village of Dağ Pazarı, site of an ancient city that was only re-occupied by Turks from Bulgaria in the nineteenth century. The description by Sir William Ramsay of this second road[11] was based on an account supplied by Colonel J. D. H. Stewart and remained accurate until only a few years ago, when a new approach was made to Dağ Pazari by the construction of a branch road from Karabağ on the present main road between Karaman and Mut. Why Ramsay ignored the evidence of Leake,[12] de Laborde[13] and his own near contemporary A. C. Headlam[14] for the Kalykadnos valley route, even then far easier than the northern alternative via Dağ Pazari, is a mystery; all the more so in view of his admission that "ruins are mentioned by Leake at a khan on the road from Mut to Laranda; but at the present day there is not even a village on the road." In fact, Ramsay was totally confused and his footnotes prove that he knew nothing of the road travelled by Leake and the others. However, even Headlam thought that de Laborde had exaggerated the extent of the ruins, including the *han*, at the foot of the hill or that the buildings had been much destroyed since the French savant's day. He was probably right, for although we know that the ancient *mansio* was at least about 1,500 m² in area, that there were public buildings including a church, as well as private houses and storage depots, we had time to make a thorough investigation and Headlam had not. Leake provided further circumstantial evidence in his statement that "... some ruins ... were reported to us as existing towards the village Malıya, half an hour to the

[11] W. M. Ramsay, *The Historical Geography of Asia Minor*, Royal Geographical Society, Supplementary Papers 4 (London, 1890).

[12] W. M. Leake, *Journal of a Tour in Asia Minor* (London, 1824).

[13] Laborde, "Église d'Aladja."

[14] Headlam, "Ecclesiastical Sites."

north west; the native who had promised to guide us to them failed."
Malıya (modern Geçimli) still exists and, what is more, our twentieth-
century guide did not fail us and led us by a most vertiginous path to
"some ruins" which turned out to be the rock cut monastery named Al
Oda, of which wall paintings and part of a floor mosaic have been
recorded.[15] Other late Roman or early Byzantine ruins are visible in a few
places south of the Sertavul pass and the new highway actually cuts into a
(probably) Byzantine building. Unfortunately the settlement has not yet
been properly examined owing to the rapid development of modern
housing in the area.

Near Alahan and Geçimli pottery and coinage confirm the antiquity of
this route through the Taurus and there is epigraphic evidence for a
definitive land settlement thereabouts in the time of the Tetrarchy. Four
inscriptions carved on rock faces and thus immovable all bear the name of
Diocletian and his colleauges. All are situated in the general Alahan-
Geçimli area, a fact which perhaps serves to rationalise the association by
Evliya Çelebi of Alahen monastery with Takyenos (Diocletian).[16] Local
boundaries were being fixed in Diocletian's day and his memory may well
have survived in the conservative recollection of the countryside. It has
been said that in the nineteenth century a villager in the New Forest
would still point out the spot where "the old king" (i.e., William Rufus)
met his death.[17]

The simplest way in which to describe the monastery site is to make a
guided tour on paper exactly as a guided tour over the ground would be
made, building by building, feature by feature, as they are encountered by
any visitor on a slow walk from one end of the complex to the other. The
site lends itself to this sort of informal description and it is hoped that it
will give a vividness and an actuality which will enable a reader (the
"visitor") to see the monastery in his mind's eye before he studies it in
detail.

It has already been explained that Alahan is 300 m above the main road
and that the ascent to the monastery is steep and can be made either on

---

[15] Michael Gough, "A Church of the Iconoclast (?) Period in Byzantine Isauria,"
Anatolian Studies, 7 (1957), pp. 153-161.

[16] MacKay, "First Modern Visitor," p. 174.

[17] Michael Gough's introductory chapter ends here. The following few pages have
been added in order that a reader may be familiar with the plan of Alahan and the names
which have been given to buildings and areas before embarking on the detailed
discussions given in later chapters.

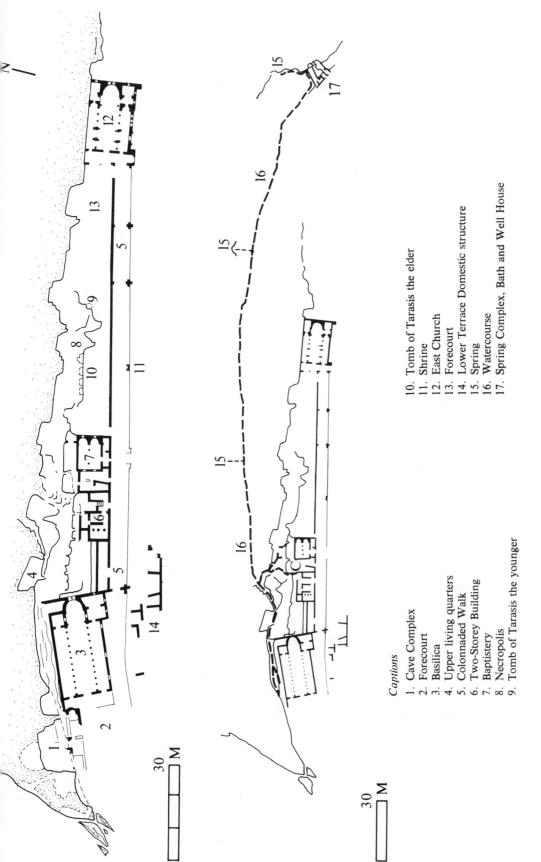

Captions

1. Cave Complex
2. Forecourt
3. Basilica
4. Upper living quarters
5. Colonnaded Walk
6. Two-Storey Building
7. Baptistery
8. Necropolis
9. Tomb of Tarasis the younger
10. Tomb of Tarasis the elder
11. Shrine
12. East Church
13. Forecourt
14. Lower Terrace Domestic structure
15. Spring
16. Watercourse
17. Spring Complex, Bath and Well House

FIGURE 1. – General Layout of the Alahan Site

foot or by car. However, by whatever means this ascent is made, the impression on a visitor when he reaches the top is likely to be one of wonder. Wonder at the grandeur and extent of the buildings which stretch away to the right, and wonder, as he turns back towards the road up which he has come, at the magnificence of the wide views over the valley of the Göksu, to Mahras Dağ on its far side and to the ranges of the blue Isaurian hills beyond. A moment or two is needed to catch breath.

The monastery (see Fig. 1) lies on a narrow ledge on the mountain side some 250 m long and about 30 m wide and roughly oriented; on the north side, the visitor's left as he looks along the ledge, is a low cliff, some lengths of which have been made sheer by quarrying that served the double purpose of creating space for a building and providing material with which to construct it. To the south, the right, the ground falls away steeply but a retaining wall was built along the length of most of the complex and the surface of the ledge was levelled within it by a rubble infill. On this ledge nearly all the monastery was built, a flat, if narrow, surface having been attained in a difficult way in a difficult terrain. The surface of the ledge rises gently from west to east.

When a visitor has drawn breath, ceased to peer along the ledge or gaze at the view, he will probably look at what is immediately in front of him, at a natural outcrop of rock which curves outward from the cliff (Pl. 5). It was here that the first monastery was established, its founders developing a series of natural caves in the rock to create chambers with inter-communicating passages and stairways; this feature is now called the Cave Complex. The limestone has bleached and weathered over the centuries to a pale dun colour; where it is sheltered from sun and weather it tends to be a darkish grey and it takes many years of winter rain and snow and burning summer sun to fade it through brownish and orangey shades (Professor Forsyth's "tawny" is the best word) [18] to the near white that it sometimes is today. These changes in the colour of the stone give Alahan much variety and add greatly to its natural and man-made beauty. One cave in the Complex, presumably originally very large, was greatly developed and contained three storeys and two churches, as well as several other chambers. The church at ground level (Pl. 6) has an easily recognised plan and is known as the Cave Church; the existence of the second, above it, has only been established by its apse, which is cut into the rock above the apse of the Cave Church itself.

At this point the visitor is probably standing on the largest flat open area of the site, the Forecourt, which in the past was paved. The Forecourt

[18] See above, p. 5, note 7.

served as a sort of atrium to the Cave Church and, as will be perceived on turning to the right, also as an atrium to the Basilica, the first building on the monastery ledge. Plate 1 gives a very good representation of what is now to be seen although, as the photograph was taken from a point on the cliff above the Forecourt, the general plan is there more apparent than it is at ground level. Now, a visitor will, undoubtedly, move eastward and is likely to step through and over the narthex of the Basilica which is not easy to recognise at first view (but its position can easily be seen in Plate 1). In short, he is likely to make straight for the great doorway, the Evangelists' Door, now just two jambs and a lintel, that is the central door of the three that pierce the west facade of the Basilica (Pl. 7, 19-22). Here he will be certain to linger in order to observe and admire the remarkable sculpture on the doorway itself and also the fragments of the Basilica's entablature that are now grouped around it (Pl. 10-18). The church has an apparently simple three aisled plan (Pl. 9) with an interior apse with a three tier synthronon terminating the central aisle, the side aisles ending in pastophories. The subtilties of the east end, however, and the way that carved screens were set up on the stylobate columns that divide the aisles are not immediately easy to grasp; still less, on first view, can one theorise as to the elevations and probable roofing design.

On proceeding eastward along a path on the outside of the Basilica's south facade there will be an opportunity to glance upwards towards the tumbled gold and dun face of the cliff, where patches of green show where vegetation has found some pockets of earth in which to root itself, and to notice several cells or chambers which have been cut into it. These may be picked out by the rock cut steps which lead up to them and by the very noticeable holes cut for their roof beams. These rooms (Pl. 65) are thought to have been monk's living quarters, used when the Cave Complex became too small or too public.

The east facade of the Basilica, on the left, coincides with the start of the retaining wall on the right, and here the path becomes a definite walkway, the Colonnaded Walkway, so called because there is abundant evidence, both from columns in situ on the retaining wall and from fallen voussoirs, that a roofed colonnaded ambulatory was designed to stretch from this point to the east end of the wall. The doors of the next building along the ledge open on to the Colonnaded Walkway and during the excavation this building was generally known as the hospice, because the division of its interior into comfortable living quarters, storage rooms, kitchen and so forth, suggested that it may have been used to house the more important visitors to the monastery. As this use, however, could never absolutely be established the more prosaic title of Two-Storey Building is now used. It is a plain building, undecorated, and a visitor is unlikely to spend long enough time here to be conversant with the separate rooms and their assumed functions, the way in which the upper floor was reached and the theory as to its roofing (Pl. 61-64). Unlike the Basilica, where a few portions of masonry were visible above ground before excavation, this section of the ledge was completely buried by earth and stone falls.

The next building to be seen, as a leisurely progress from west to east continues, leaves no doubt at all as to its purpose. It was, unequivocally, a Baptistery, twin aisled and with a sunken cruciform font at the west end of the northern aisle and a one tier synthronon in the apse to the east (Pl. 50-52). It has a very simple narthex, lying on the same east to west axis, which is entered by a door from the Walkway in its south facade (Pl. 56) directly opposite the door into the Baptistery proper. The font, ingenious and complete, is the main attraction here; steps on each arm of the cross lead down to their intersection where there is a drain leading to a conduit, and water is led in by a little aqueduct in the rock cut north wall of the building. There was a small three legged altar table in the bema and the apse was decorated with painted plaster, some fragments of which still remain.

The Grave Area comes next and the fact that it was a specific area is hard, at first sight, to understand. The main graves, including those with the important Tarasis inscriptions[19] (Pl. 2, 3) are easy enough to spot but the very important doorway from the Walkway, just east of the Baptistery, that leads into the area is less so. It is harder still to appreciate that the Walkway was bounded here on its northern (left hand) side by a high wall which supported the inner length of its roof, the outer being taken (as throughout the length of the Walkway) by the colonnade (Pl. 57-59). At one point, almost exactly opposite the grave of Tarasis the First (although in the past neither was visible from the other because of the high north wall) a little Shrine is set between the columns (Pl. 60). A visitor may consider whether this siting was intentional or just a coincidence.

All this time, however interesting or beautiful have been the various features inspected, the eye is inevitably drawn to the large building at the end of the ledge. This is the Koca Kilise, the Great Church, which originally gave its name to the whole complex, which was never buried by rock or earth falls, which still stands to roof height and which, before excavation, was the only recognisable building on the site. It is now known as the East Church and is entered by one of three doors in its

---

[19] See below, Chapter 2: A "The Inscriptions," pp. 22-24.

western facade (Pl. 32, 35-40). There was originally a narthex, but this is the only part of the building now to have fallen into ruins and disappeared. After the bright sunlight and glare without, the interior of the East Church – cool, lofty and complete (although roofless) – comes almost as a shock; it takes a moment or two to adjust to looking upward through the shadows and to seeing a building very nearly as it was first planned to be seen. The church is three aisled (Pl. 49), with a centralised tower (Pl. 33, 34), and there is a three tier synthronon in the apse at the end of the central aisle (Pl. 45), pastophories at the ends of the side aisles. The "singular architectural distinction"of the East Church has already been touched on by Michael Gough and the subject is dealt with in depth later in this book; a first-time visitor, however, will immediately be aware of the importance of the central tower and also cannot fail to notice the difference between the disposition of sculpture in this building and of that in the Basilica. In the latter it is exuberant and abundant; capitals, entablature, stylobate and screens are all decorated in a flowing and handsome style. In the East Church the embellishment is more restrained and is confined to specific areas; a great deal of it is executed in the same style as that of the Basilica (Pl. 38, 39) but in some cases more use has been made of the drill (Pl. 44, 46). When one gets to know each building well one can debate which, in the past, was the more striking: the Basilica, florid and vast and designed to be admired from the outside as well as from within or the East Church, with an exterior often described as "fortress like" (Pl. 31), its only outside decoration confined to the west facade, but with so sophisticated a plan and such disciplined and delicate interior sculpture. It has been said that the Basilica can be described as one of the last truly Roman buildings in the region while the East Church, inward turning and confined, might be one of the first really Byzantine ones. The latter notion is reinforced by the fact that between the Grave Area and the East Church are a series of domestic rooms, kitchens, a bakery and possible refectory (Pl. 66, 67) which are very private (unlike similar rooms must have been in the Cave Complex) separated as they are from the relatively public Walkway by the high north wall.

We have now reached the end of the ledge but not quite reached the end of the monastery complex. Well beyond and above the East Church, with access by means of a steep path, is the Spring Complex, Bath and Well House. Here a natural cave was improved and built up to form, on the left hand, a very small but complete one-person bath, with a tiny furnace room, a minute but real hypocaust and a tank from which hot water could be dipped and used (Pl. 68, 71). The Alahan bath is a far cry from the great municipal *thermae* or the luxurious private baths in rich houses, but, except that there are no plunges or areas for repose, it is built and arranged on the same principle and in it a very good, cleansing and refreshing hot bath could have been taken. The further part of the cave, separated from the bath by a spur of natural rock, is called the Well House; here it is always cool and dark and in the innermost recesses there is a masonry cistern, fed from the same spring that serves the bath. It is thought that this chamber was used as a storage place for perishable food – a larder (Pl. 69, 70).

Anyone who spends even an hour at Alahan will certainly think about water. Where did it come from? Was there enough? How was it distributed And how, finally, was it disposed of? Some of the answers are simple; there is plenty of water which came from at least three springs all of which, given a little time and work, could still be usable today. The Bath and Well House spring is a notable one; there is another nearby slightly to the west; and another further to the west still, above (to the north of) the cliff. Still functioning, on the path that leads up past Alahan to the summer pastures of today's villagers and used by them, is a fourth spring; this was the main source of water for the excavation until superseded when the Bath and Well House spring was dug out, and was also, no doubt, used in the past. Water was distributed by aqueducts cut into the ground and stone faced (Pl. 72) and later carried by rock cut channels across the cliff face from which further ducts led into the various parts of the monastery. Very nearly all areas had their own water supply; it can almost be said of Alahan, as of to-day's hotels, "running water in every room."

Supply of water at Alahan was not too difficult a problem; disposal of it was a much greater one, as not only had used water to be run off but also rain water and snow melt had to be channeled and taken away too. This operation must have been a challenge to the builders, a challenge to which they responded, as otherwise some of the structures and certainly the retaining wall would not stand today. On retracing his steps from east to west a visitor will now have time to look down to an area which previously he may not have noticed. This is the Lower Terrace, below (to the south of) the Two-Storey Building and the Basilica. Here a number of rather roughly constructed rooms, thought to be workshops and "utility rooms," were revealed together with a complicated system of drainage channels which were linked to conduits from the buildings above (Pl. 73, 74). It is noteworthy that a high proportion of the few artifacts found at Alahan were discovered in these drains as well as a quantity of pottery fragments; it would seem that a considerable volume of water was disposed of here, a volume sufficient to carry small articles with it.

As a visitor prepares for the descent from Alahan, the thought uppermost in his mind may still be one of wonder, as it was when he first saw the monastery; but now it may not only be on account of the beauty of the scenery or the splendour of the ecclesiastical buildings. Having seen the carefully devised living quarters, the water system and other domestic appointments, he may also wonder at the pertinacity and sense of fitness which determinated those who lived here to arrange their everyday lives in such an orderly and civilised fashion.

MAP 1. – Eastern Mediterranean

MAP 2. – Alahan Region

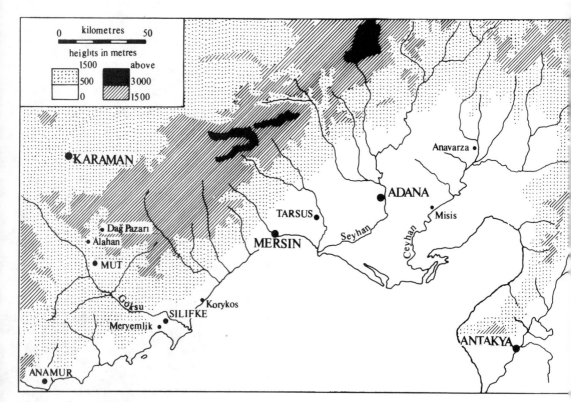

MAP 3. – Central Southern Turkey

Part Two

2

The Inscriptions and Chronology of Alahan

Martin Harrison

The significance of Alahan depends closely on a fairly precise dating of its first settlement, structural development, and length of occupation, and on its regional context. Although the detailed mapping of ancient sites and roads in the region, which will provide this context, is for the future, Michael Gough's investigations at Alahan did provide important new dating evidence, and the present chapter is an attempt briefly to review this and other evidence. While none of the evidence by itself is conclusive (stratification and sealed material were unfortunately minimal), taken together it is remarkably consistent, and the ascription of at least the major part of the building programme (including the East Church) to the reign of the Emperor Zeno (474-491) can be accepted with confidence.

A. The Inscriptions

Eleven inscriptions were recorded at Alahan during the excavations; a twelfth, on the north wall of the narthex of the Baptistery, was observed,

I am grateful to have been invited to contribute to the final report on Michael Gough's work at this most important site. I first saw Alahan in 1955 as a member of that first excavation team, but my primary task then was to dig the cave church of nearby Al Oda and I only worked at the main site for one week, while a fire in the cave's stratified deposits of goat-dung burnt itself out (Michael Gough, "A Church of the Iconoclast (?) Period in Byzantine Isauria," *Anatolian Studies*, 7 [1957], p. 157). I owe a great deal to Michael Gough's enthusiasm and encouragement both then and subsequently, for he opened my eyes to Byzantine studies and to Anatolia. Mary Gough generously put all the excavation notebooks and inventories at my disposal, but I have not found in them conclusive stratigraphic information, and it is clear from the record that in this one sense the site was unrewarding. What little there was of stratification is described in the various preliminary reports.

but no letters could be read. Two of the inscriptions provide valuable information, including dates, and their texts are reproduced here with short discussions. The other inscriptions, for the sake of completeness, are also listed here.

1. The inscription on a rock-cut sarcophagus (see Plate 2):

> + [ἐνθ]άδε κῖτε τῆς μακα-
> ρίας μνήμης Ταρασις ὁ κτίσας τα ἀπα[ντη]-
> τήρια, τελευτήσας μηνὶ Φεβρουαρίου
> τρισκεδεκάτῃ ἰνδ(ικτιῶνος) πεντεκε-
> δεκ[ά]της μετὰ τὴν ὑπατίαν Φλ(αυίου)
> Σευ[η]ριανοῦ Φλ(αυίου) Δαγαλαίφφου
> τῶν λαμπρ(οτάτων), ἡμέρᾳ τρίτῃ πρώ-
> τῃ < τῃ > ἑβδομ[ά]δι τῶν ἁγίων
> νη < σ > τεῶ[ν] +

This inscription was discovered by Michael Gough and was published by him in "Some recent Finds at Alahan (Koja Kalessi)," *Anatolian Studies*, 5 (1955), pp. 115-117; cf. also G. E. Bean in P. Verzone, *Alahan Manastırı mimarisi üzerinde bir inceleme* (Istanbul, 1955), pp. 37-39, and in the Italian version, partly updated, *Alahan Monastir: Un Monumento dell'arte Tardo-Romano in Isauria* (Turin, 1956), pp. 52-54.

Lines 2-3: ὁ κτίσας τὰ ἀπα[ντη]τήρια. This is a gloss, outside the *tabula ansata*, presumably added to distinguish this Tarasis from Tarasis the Younger (see **2**, below), at the same time as (or after) the latter's epitaph was inscribed nearby (which may have been considerably later than that of the elder Tarasis).

The death of Tarasis the Elder, the subject of this inscription, was on 13 February 462. Thus the inscription establishes the existence of ἀπαντητήρια at Alahan by 462. The word, which is very rare, appears to mean "rest-houses" and to have some sort of official connotation.[1] Gough's original suggestion was that it might refer here to an official rest-house constructed at the ancient site below the monastery and beside the modern Karaman-Mut road. Although there was certainly a road (and a *han*) here in the seventeenth century,[2] there is some doubt about the

---

[1] Cf. Michael Gough, "Some Recent Finds at Alahan (Koja Kalessi)," *Anatolian Studies*, 5 (1955), p. 117; T. B. Mitford, "Some New Inscriptions from Early Christian Cyprus," *Byzantion*, 20 (1950), p. 153. The root of ἀπαντητήρια, however, is clearly that of ἀπαντάω (I meet); could the word here refer to a meeting-place or church?

[2] Cf. P. A. MacKay, "The First Modern Visitor to Alahan," *Anatolian Studies*, 21 (1971), pp. 173-174 which deals with Evliya Çelebi's visit in 1671-1672 to Alaca Han, the inn on the Karaman-Mut road below the monastery ruins.

importance of this route in antiquity, when the main road from Laranda
(Karaman) to Claudiopolis (Mut) went via Coropissus (almost certainly
Dağ Pazarı).[3] In any case, however, it does seem possible, as Gough
recognized, that the word ἀπαντητήρια might have been applied to
accommodation designed specifically for visitors to the monastery rather
than for benighted passers-by, in which case the rest-houses referred to
would presumably be within the monastery itself and might indeed be the
so-called Two-Storey Building.

2. The inscription within a niche above a rock-cut sarcophagus (see
Plate 3):

> \+ ἐνθάδε κατάκιτε
> Ταρασις δίς, γενόμενος
> πρεσβ(ύτερος) καὶ παραμονάριος
> παροικήσας ἐν τῷ τόπῳ
> τούτῳ ἀπὸ ὑπατίας Γαδα-
> λ[α]ίππου ἰνδ(ικτιῶνος) ιδ´ ἕως ἰνδ(ικτιῶνος) vacat
> ὑπατ[ί]ας vacat, ζήσας τὰ
> πάντα ἔτη vacat

This was discovered by Laborde in 1826 and was published in his
"Église d'Aladja dans le Taurus," *Revue archéologique*, 4 (1847-1848),
p. 175, as well as in *Corpus Inscriptionum Graecarum*, vol. 4 (Berlin,
1877), n° 9259; A. C. Headlam, *Ecclesiastical Sites in Isauria (Cilicia
Trachea)*, Society for the Promotion of Hellenic Studies, Supplementary
Papers, 1 (London, 1893), pp. 24-25; Michael Gough, "Some Recent
Finds at Alahan," pp. 115-117 and pl. IX(c); G. E. Bean in Verzone,
Alahan Monastir, pp. 51-52.

The inscription is the uncompleted epitaph of Tarasis the Younger who
was presumably the son of the Tarasis recorded in the first inscription
(above, **1**). He became priest and παραμονάριος and lived at Alahan from
461 to a date for which spaces were left but which was never filled in. He
may indeed have lived at Alahan for a very long time. We cannot,
however, be sure that he died there, and the unfinished epitaph may be
evidence that he did not do so.

---

[3] On the *Peutinger Table* the road from Iconium (Konya) to Seleucia (Silifke) goes by
Coropissus and Claudiopolis (Mut); Laranda (Karaman) is omitted, but must have lain on
this route. For a résumé of Michael Gough's work at Dağ Pazarı, see S. Hill, "Dağ Pazarı
and its Monuments – A Preliminary Report," in *Yayla, Second Report of the Northern
Society for Anatolian Archaeology* (Newcastle upon Tyne, 1979), pp. 8-12.

The precise meaning of παραμονάριος is elusive. Headlam suggested "guest-master," but usage of the word seems rather to imply guardianship or administration of church buildings.[4] In view of the great building programme, which (it is argued) took place mainly under Zeno (474-491) and at which Tarasis the Younger may thus have assisted, the position of παραμονάριος may have been one of considerable responsibility.

A silver reliquary, which is said to have been found in a church at Çirga, an upland village some 40 km southwest of Mut, and which has two representations of St. Konon, carries "a pricked inscription which must post-date the manufacture of the box. It should almost certainly be transliterated ὑπὲρ ἀναπαύσεως τοῦ μακαρ(ί)ου Ταρασης δίς.[5] It seems probable that this is the Tarasis son of Tarasis who had come to Alahan in 461, and it supports the suggestion that, although he had prepared a tomb for himself at Alahan, he died elsewhere.

3. In the East Church at the central west doorway, graffito on the inner face of the south jamb, with a cross below (see Figure 2.3):

IΦ +
ΘEOΔO
HONΩ

Letters 1.25 to 2 cm. Cf. G. E. Bean in P. Verzone, *Alahan Monastir*, p. 51, inscr. n° 1.

4. In the East Church on the window-divider in the narthex (see Figure 2.4):

KONON
HP *vacat* CAOPIOY

Letters 4.7 to 3.2 cm; the letter forms *HP* are in ligature.

5. In the East Church, an inscription on the upper moulding of the northeast pedestal (see Figure 2.5):

+EYXHAIΩA ...... +

---

[4] See the dictionaries of Sophocles, Liddell and Scott (9th ed., revised by Stuart Jones), and Lampe, s.v. The office is mentioned in connection with particular churches on two epitaphs at Korykos: *Monumenta Asiae Minoris Antiqua*, 3: *Denkmäler aus dem rauhen Kilikien*, ed. Joseph Keil and Adolf Wilhelm, Publications of the American Society for Archaeological Research in Asia Minor (Manchester, 1931), p. 186 item 590 and p. 191 item 638; on the latter the deceased is also designated πρεσβύτερος.

[5] Michael Gough, "A Fifth Century Silver Reliquary from Isauria," *Byzantinoslavica*, 19 (1958), 244-250; this inscription is on p. 248.

Letters 5 to 5.5 cm. See M. Gough, "Excavations at Alahan Monastery, Third Preliminary Report," *Anatolian Studies*, 14 (1964), p. 187 where he suggests a possible restoration as + Εὐχὴ ἁ Ἰωά[ννου πρεσ] + .

6. In the Baptistery, in the eastern part of the so-called narthex, "... on three separate, but adjacent blocks is a rustic inscription reading + Ἔνθα χ < α > τάχιτη Λέον." (Gough, "Third Preliminary Report," p. 189.)

7. In the Cave Church, there is a fragmentary painting on plaster, possibly a large ornamental cross. "To the top left of the rectangular frame are the letters $\overline{IC}$, the normal abbreviation of the name Jesus; to the right, the $\overline{XC}$ which would complete it has broken off, though a trace of the horizontal bar above the letters may be seen." (M. Gough, "Alahan Monastery, Fourth Preliminary Report," *Anatolian Studies*, 17 [1967], 44 and pl. IXb.)

8. In the tomb west of that of Tarasis the Younger (see Figure 2.8):

ωΔE vacat + Θ

Letters 3.8 to 4.5 cm.

9. On the cliff behind the grave area (see Figure 2.9):[6]

+ NEωNAKA

Letters 2.7 to 9.5 cm. See Headlam, *Ecclesiastical Sites*, p. 25, nº 8. Νέων ἀβα would be Neon the Abbot, or Neon son of Abas (or of Akas?); or should we read ΔKA, i.e., δεκανός ?

10. On the cliff behind the grave area (see Figure 2.10):

ΚΙΤΙCΑΟ ...

Letters 2.5 to 5.1 cm.

11. On the cliff behind the grave area (see Figure 2.11):

+ [.]ωΠωΚΟ	i.e., + [τ]ωπω (?) χο[ι]-
NωΓωΓω	νω Γωγω-
NIOY	νιου

Letters 4.4 to 6.7 cm. See Headlam, *Ecclesiastical Sites*, p. 25, nº 10.

---

[6] The files passed to me include comments, which I have gratefully incorporated here, by Prof. C. Mango and Miss J. M. Reynolds on this inscription and on nº 11.

FIGURE 2. – The Inscriptions

B. The Coins

The monastery at Alahan yielded 113 coins, which are catalogued in Chapter 3 and which can be briefly summarized as follows:

5	Turkish
1	11th century (Anonymous – *DOC* 3.2: Class B, AD 1030/35-1042)
1	7th century (Constans II – *DOC* 2.2: 75d, AD 655/656)
32	6th century, including Anastasius I (latest is of Maurice – *DOC* 1: 178, AD 586/587)
46	4th and 5th century (pre-reform)
26	Illegible, but presumed to be 4th and 5th century
1	3rd century
1	2nd century

The sixth-century coins are, with only one exception (a pentanummion), folles and half-folles. This suggests that the fourth and fifth-century pieces, which are small and generally very worn, continued to serve as small change during at least the first half of the sixth century. The relatively large number of fourth and fifth-century coins found at Alahan does not therefore of itself confirm fourth and fifth-century occupation, but it does support the other evidence.

The fourth and fifth-century series include coins of the Constantinian house, with a concentration towards the end of the fourth century and the beginning of the fifth (Theodosius I and Arcadius), and perhaps a smaller concentration about AD 450. Coins of Anastasius I (10) include 8 from a small hoard, but individual coins of Justin (3), Justinian (7), Justin II (9), Tiberius II (1), and Maurice (1) do imply continuity of occupation from the beginning of that century to at least AD 586. The coin of Constans II is, however, isolated and by itself has no implications for the state of Alahan in the seventh century; that it may in fact not be irrelevant is indicated by the fact that the site has produced a fair amount of seventh-century pottery.

C. The Pottery

Approximate dates of manufacture can be assigned to imported late Roman fine wares (see Figures 3-9). Although these, amounting to some two score vessels, account for only a small proportion of the pottery recovered (as Dr. Williams in her catalogue of the pottery in Chapter 3 observes), they do span the period from the early fifth century (perhaps earlier) to the early seventh (perhaps later). Catalogue item **1** may indeed belong to the fourth century, and items **12** and **15**, comprising seven vessels, are of the seventh. The solitary coin of Constans ii in AD 655/656, found in the Cave Church, perhaps here acquires a context. Six vessels imitating African Red Slip forms, must, on the basis of dates for their models, similarly belong to the seventh century.

A late Roman date for the prevalent and important so-called Monastic Ware (see Plates 75-89) was proved in 1972 by excavation of the Lower Terrace. Here, in a complex of sewers and water-tanks, there were abundant finds with some stratification. Spiral-burnished ware was found in contexts together with Monastic Ware and both together with late Roman C, Miscellaneous Fine Wares, and fifth and sixth-century coins. Precision is impossible, but the general contemporaneity is clear. Quantities were considerable, and two much later coins here, one of the eleventh century and the other Turkish, and both from the topsoil, may be disregarded for this purpose.

Medieval glazed sherds from the site are fragmentary and generally unstratified. They are probably attributable to the Basilica's secondary phase, which may be as late as the Selcuk period; a number of these sherds were found in the Basilica before secondary walls were dismantled and in the courtyard to the west. None, however, appears to have been sealed by the secondary building, which may thus antedate the occupation attested by this pottery.

D. THE SMALL FINDS

The catalogue of small finds constitutes an interesting and useful monastic assemblage; it does little, however, to refine the chronology (see Figures 11-13). N° **2** (the steatite cross) is probably medieval, as is perhaps also n° **18** (the iron fragments); the rest reflect the fifth and sixth-century main period of occupation. N° **8** (the ring stone with Pegasus in intaglio) may perhaps refer to the slaying of the Chimaera by Bellerephon, a scene which appears to have entered the Christian repertory. For wick-holders (n° **10**) compare now other examples excavated at Anemurium.[7] The lampstand (n° **17**) is a fine piece, characteristic of the Early Byzantine

---

[7] J. Russell, "Byzantine *Instrumenta Domestica* from Anemurium: The Significance of Context," in R. L. Hohlfelder, ed., *City, Town and Countryside in the Early Byzantine Era* (New York, 1982), pp. 133-154, esp. note 14.

period. The bronze spatula (n° **14**) is of cosmetic or medical use.[8] It may seem peevish to regret that we do not have the monastery's silver treasure, with date-stamps and niello inscriptions;[9] these would have provided a *terminus ante quem* for the monastery's foundation, and (perhaps) an indication of the monastery's life-span.

E. THE BUILDING SEQUENCE

The terrace upon which the monastery was built is largely man-made, having been obtained by quarrying back into the hillside and by building out the revetment for a covered walkway (see Plate 1). It is difficult today to visualise how the hillside must have looked before quarrying began, except perhaps in the undeveloped area of the tombs.

The narthex of the Basilica is curtailed at its northern end to respect the partly rock-cut apse of the Cave Church, which therefore antedates it (see Figure 19, p. 157). The question then arises as to why the Basilica should have been constructed on an evidently cramped site, rather than, say, a short distance to the east. One theoretical possibility is that the area to the east (that of the Two-Storey Building) was already built upon, or at least earmarked for building. Another is that the Basilica's undercroft, which could not be examined but to which there was external access by a low-level doorway in the church's south wall, was in fact a crypt preserving an earlier shrine – like the cave church of St. Thekla at Meryemlik, whose entrance is similarly placed in relation to the great church which was later erected above it.

The Basilica (Plate 9) was remarkably elaborate in both design and decoration. The east end, with bema entered by a triumphal arch and with well-articulated side-chambers which are broader than the aisles and open to the bema, is sophisticated in conception, anticipating development of the tripartite transept. The scale of the church, which had galleries, was

---

[8] Cf. M. Gill, "The Small Finds," n°s 448-449 in R. M. Harrison, *Excavations at Saraçhane in Istanbul* (Princeton: Princeton University Press, forthcoming); also A. G. Gilson, "A Group of Roman Surgical and Medical Instruments from Corbridge," *Saalburg-Jahrbuch*, 37 (1981), pp. 5-9.

[9] As, for example, the silver treasure from the Holy Sion monastery in Lycia, divided between Dumbarton Oaks and the Antalya Archaeological Museum: N. Fıratlı, "Un trésor du vi° s. trouvé à Kumluca en Lycie," *Akten des VII Internationalen Kongresses für Christliche Archäologie, Trier ... 1965* (Vatican City and Berlin, 1969), pp. 523-525; Dumbarton Oaks, *Handbook of the Byzantine Collection* (Washington, DC, 1967), pp. 18-20; Ernst Kitzinger, "A Pair of Silver Book Covers in the Sion Treasure," in *Gatherings in Honor of Dorothy E. Miner*, ed. Ursula E. McKracken, et. al. (Baltimore, 1974), pp. 3-17.

considerable, and its decoration astonishingly rich. The architectural sculpture, internal and external, figured and ornamental, is of the highest artistic and technical calibre (see Plates 10-30). The bold iconographic scheme of the West Portal (see Plates 19-22) and the spirited deployment elsewhere of birds, fishes, and dolphins are masterly.

The East Church, with its central tower over the nave, presents a more tightly knit scheme. Externally stark, it has rich sculptural detail both within the narthex and in the main body of the church. The decoration of the corbels in the narthex and of the principal doorways (Plates 36 to 40) is in many respects (e.g., vinescrolls, fishes, wreath-borders, palmettes, modillions) close to that of the Basilica. The principal capitals too, although more developed than those in the Basilica, have a form of acanthus sprig (resembling superimposed V's) which occurs on modillions there. Although the churches appear at first sight to be so different in conception, it seems likely that the two programmes were consecutive. Differences in architectural form are perhaps at least partly explicable in terms of differing function.

The Walkway, from the south side of the Basilica to the narthex of the East Church, was evidently begun from the eastern end and never completed. That the same sculptors were involved here, too, is implied by the decoration of the Shrine (Plate 60), which has a number of links with both buildings, and by the familiar fishes carved upon a pier base. The Colonnade, running westwards from the East Church, had reached a little over half-way, when work was apparently suspended. There is some evidence that the Baptistery too may never have been completely finished.

It was normal practice in antiquity for the detailing of fine architectural sculpture to be carried out on blocks which were already erected in place. We should thus expect the sculptors to have moved in when the masons had finished the task of construction (and probably before they had moved the scaffolding). Decoration of the Basilica might thus have been carried out *pari passu* with the construction of the East Church, and the decoration of the latter *pari passu* with the construction of the Baptistery and the Walkway.

F. The Historical Context

The historical context has recently been discussed by Mango and Gough in two important articles.[10] Mango has shown that Isaurian masons and

[10] C. Mango, "Isaurian Builders," in *Polychronion. Festschrift Franz Dölger zum 75. Geburtstag*, ed. Peter Wirth (Heidelberg, 1966), pp. 358-365; Michael Gough, "The Emperor Zeno and some Cilician Churches," *Anatolian Studies*, 22 (1972), pp. 199-212.

architects are attested at the monastery of St. Sabas near Jerusalem in 501, at the monastery of St. Symeon on the Wondrous Mountain near Antioch in 541-551, and at St. Sophia in Constantinople in 558, and he observed that they evidently enjoyed a high reputation as construction-workers. Whence came this reputation?

Forsyth had pointed to similarities between the East Church at Alahan, and churches at Dağ Pazarı, Korykos, and Meryemlik (near Silifke).[11] The Isaurian Emperor Zeno (474-491) is known to have founded a church at Meryemlik, and his reign, when Isaurian influence ran high, must have left its mark.[12] Previously Isauria had been largely characterized by barbarian brigands, and after Zeno's death it was racked for most of a decade by a particularly savage civil war (492-498), which must have precluded constructive development till long after its close.[13]

Gough developed these arguments, introducing architectural and excavational evidence from Alahan and Dağ Pazarı, and adding the suggestion that the frequent introduction of the *paradeisos* into the mosaics of this region might be understood as a reference to Zeno's *henotikon*.[14]

Coastal sites in Cilicia Tracheia were accessible in late antiquity, and Egeria, for example, was able to visit Meryemlik from Tarsus in 394 on her way from Antioch to Constantinople by way of the Cilician Gates.[15] The rugged hinterland, however, was a different matter, and these wild mountains, normally remote, emerged briefly into the limelight only in the second half of the fifth century.

[11] G. H. Forsyth, "Architectural Notes on a Trip Through Cilicia," *Dumbarton Oaks Papers*, 11 (1957), pp. 223-236.

[12] Evagrius Scholasticus, *The Ecclesiastical History*, 3.8, ed. J. Bidez and L. Parmentier (Amsterdam, 1964), p. 108 l. 2; Zeno's church is designated μέγιστον τέμενος and is thus probably the great basilica with the crypt rather than the "domed church." As at Alahan, however, only a short time may have separated the basilica from the church with its central tower, and a context must be found for the proliferation of the latter in this province.

[13] E. W. Brooks, "The Emperor Zenon and the Isaurians," *English Historical Review*, 8 (1893), pp. 209-238, esp. pp. 231-238. The arguments of Mango, "Isaurian Builders," for a diaspora of Isaurian masons in the troubled times after Zeno's death were reinforced by Stephen Hill, "The Early Christian Church at Tomarza, Cappadocia," *Dumbarton Oaks Papers*, 29 (1975), pp. 151-164, who proposed (p. 163) that the church at Tomarza and others in Cappadocia were the work of exiled Isaurians early in the sixth century; Hill has carried this reasoning further in his "Sarı Kilise," in *Yayla, [First] Report of the Northern Society for Anatolian Archaeology* (Newcastle upon Tyne: Department of Archaeology, University of Newcastle upon Tyne, 1977), pp. 16-20.

[14] Gough, "The Emperor Zeno," pp. 199-212.

[15] *Itinerarium Egeriae*, 23.1-8, ed. A. Franceschini and R. Weber, CCSL 175 (Tournai, 1965), pp. 66-67.

In the reign of Leo (457-474), an Isaurian chieftain, whose name is generally taken to have been Tarasikodisa Rousoumbladiotes but who was almost certainly known as Tarasis, the son of Kodisas and man of Rousoumblada, came to Constantinople, became head of an imperial guard (of Isaurians), changed his name to Zeno, married the Emperor's daughter Ariadne, was posted to major military commands, and succeeded to the throne in 474.[16] Isauria was a power-base for Zeno, a region to which to repair in time of troubles and a place to which to banish political enemies; and it was to benefit financially from confiscations during his reign.

The period of Isaurian ascendancy began under Leo and ended, abruptly, with Zeno's death in 491. The Basilica and East Church at Alahan were closely related, and it is a reasonable hypothesis that funds dried up, when the Walkway was only half-complete, in 491. It seems reasonable, moveover, to suppose that the two churches were close in time, and that we should therefore look for an active building period of, say, up to two or three decades, which terminated abruptly in 491. Tarasis the Elder, who is (by an addition to the inscription 1) described as "the man who founded the rest-houses," died at Alahan in 462.[17] Tarasis the Younger survived him and may indeed have remained at Alahan throughout Zeno's reign, in charge of the building programme. Whether he remained until 491 cannot be known.

It has been noted above (and is demonstrated in detail by Mr. Bakker below) that (a) there are close sculptural similarities between the Basilica and the East Church and (b) the East Church is the later of the two buildings. Whereas the Basilica is especially remarkable both for its sculptural decoration and for the elaborate plan of its eastern end, the East Church is chiefly notable for the superimposition of a central tower with

[16] On the name, see my "The Emperor Zeno's Real Name," *Byzantinische Zeitschrift*, 74 (1981), pp. 27-28; for the narrative, J. B. Bury, *History of the Later Roman Empire from the Death of Theodosius I to the Death of Justinian* (London, 1923), vol. 1: chapters 10 and 12, and Brooks, "The Emperor Zenon."

[17] Although Tarasis was a fairly common name in Isauria (cf. Ladislav Zgusta, *Kleinasiatische Personennamen* [Prague, 1964], n° 1508), it is perhaps surprising that it should be the name both of the "founder of the rest-houses" whose grave appears to have been the focus of the developed monastery plan, and of the emperor, to whose patronage that development can probably be ascribed. If we ask why Alahan should have received this patronage, we might suggest either that the emperor sought simply to honour the memory of his homonym or that Rousoumblada, where Zeno was born, was at or near Alahan. The proximity (15 km) of a comparable church at Dağ Pazarı (Coropissus?), within whose territory Alahan presumably lay, might be thought to imply that this small region had some particular claim on the emperor.

squinches upon an oblong nave. Both churches exhibit a mastery of materials and design, and both convey a sense or originality which points to the fifth century rather than to the sixth; this is admittedly a subjective impression but one which cannot entirely be disregarded.

If a sixth-century date for the East Church were entertained, then *either* it would have to lie at the beginning of that century in the immediate aftermath of the civil wars and separated by them from the construction and decoration of the Basilica under Zeno, *or* it would be somewhat later in that century (but hardly before the reign of Justin ı [518-527]), and the Basilica too would then presumably be post-war. Both hypotheses, however, are open to strong objections: for it is as inconceivable that the similar sculptural decoration of the two churches be separated by the war and its aftermath which, as has been shown, saw the mass exodus of Isaurian masons to Syria and elsewhere, as that the Basilica's tetramorph relief, with its spirited and original composition which is flanked by Archangels trampling demons, be a work of the sixth century; this figured sculpture surely belongs to an early and formative stage in Byzantine iconography.

The most reasonable hypothesis, and surely the correct one, is that the major building period was from about the middle of the fifth century to about 491. This satisfies both the archaeological evidence (pottery, coins, inscriptions) and the historical (opportunities under Zeno, none immediately thereafter), and it provides acceptable contexts for the sculptural initiatives of the Basilica and the architectural initiatives of both churches. Alahan's East Church and Isaurian churches on a similar plan, all with central tower over the nave, thus belong to the reign of Zeno and represent an important stage in that Early Byzantine architectural development, which led to the centrally planned Constantinopolitan basilicas of St. Polyeuktos (524-527) [18] and St. Sophia (532-537), [19] and,

[18] R. M. Harrison and N. Fıratlı, "Excavations at Saraçhane in Istanbul. First Preliminary Report," *Dumbarton Oaks Papers*, 19 (1965), pp. 231-236; "... Second and Third Preliminary Reports," *ibid.*, 20 (1966), pp. 223-238; "... Fourth Preliminary Report," *ibid.*, 21 (1967), pp. 273-278; "... Fifth Preliminary Report," *ibid.*, 22 (1968), pp. 195-203. The full report on these excavations was submitted for publication to Dumbarton Oaks in 1981. A possible association with St. Polyeuktos of the churches at Meryemlik and Alahan was noted by R. Krautheimer, *Early Christian and Byzantine Architecture*, 2nd ed. (Harmondsworth, 1975), p. 258.

[19] The importance of St. Sophia as a basilica with a central dome on pendentives was admirably analysed by J. B. Ward-Perkins, "The Italian Element in Late Roman and Early Medieval Architecture," *Proceedings of the British Academy*, 33 (1947), pp. 163-183. This remains an important study, although much relevant Anatolian material was not available at the time. In the light of new discoveries, both in Anatolia and in Istanbul, the time is ripe for a detailed review of the whole problem.

collaterally, to the roughly contemporary triconchos churches in Lycia.[20]

---

[20] R. M. Harrison, "Churches and Chapels in Central Lycia," *Anatolian Studies*, 13 (1963), pp. 117-151. If, as seems likely (ibid., p. 150), the Church at Karabel is to be identified with the Sion monastery built early in Justinian's reign, the fifth-century dating proposed above for Alahan receives further support. The plan of Karabel, with a central dome on pendentives, is considerably more advanced than that of Alahan's East Church and those associated with it, and yet Lycia seems generally to have been much more remote than Cilicia.

3

The Pottery and Glass at Alahan

Caroline Williams

In the catalogue which follows, the first number given is that assigned to the piece both in the text and in the figures. Every vessel is drawn except where otherwise stated; if a photograph has been included, a reference to the plate number is also given.

Some of the material is no longer available except in drawings. This has resulted in an absence of descriptions for fabric and surface treatment in a few cases. Reference to relative quantities must be treated with some caution since I have only the sherds that were kept upon which to base them.

D	diameter at rim (cm)	H	height (cm)
DB	diameter at base (cm)	LV	location on vessel
FS	findspot	NA	information not available

A. Late Roman Tablewares

Under this heading are grouped sherds of the standard imported Late Roman fine wares, African Red Slip, Late Roman C and Cypriot Red Slip,

My very special thanks are due to Mrs. Michael Gough who unfailingly provided me with help and encouragement in the difficult task of preparing for publication a body of material with which I had not worked during the actual excavations. The staff of the Archaeological Museum in Konya was generous with time and assistance during my stay in June 1975 to study the pottery now stored there. I owe my thanks for most of the drawings to Anne Macdonald and Susan Bakker; a few were done by me. Since three hands were involved in the preparation of the profiles, no acknowledgement for individual drawings has been made; space does not permit and it is no longer possible to assign all of them to the appropriate hand.

The publication of the pottery is presented in a necessarily abbreviated form because of the changes in format decided upon after the untimely death of Michael Gough.

and of less well-documented fine red wares whose sources are unknown. The form numbers cited refer to the type-series developed for the first group by J. Hayes in his volume, *Late Roman Pottery*.[1] In the absence of chronological evidence from Alahan, the dates assigned to the forms by Hayes are given below. Descriptions of clay and surface treatment for the first three wares have been omitted for the sake of brevity. I refer the reader to Hayes' book where the details are fully published.

In contrast to the pottery assemblages of this period from coastal cities in the Eastern Mediterranean, African Red Slip, Late Roman C and Cypriot Red Slip do not predominate among the tablewares.[2] African Red Slip is the most common of the three being represented by twenty-six identifiable vessels and a handful of sherds while Late Roman C and Cypriot Red Slip are known from only a few examples each. Such numbers would seem to indicate that the arrival of these wares at Alahan was the result of chance rather than any systematic importation.

Alahan's inland location and social structure were probably both factors determining their rare appearance. Sea-borne trade carried these wares to cities on the Mediterranean coast[3] and it is in these cities that the largest markets for them were most likely to be found. The monastic community at Alahan would not in all probability have had either the funds or the inclination to acquire these luxury items from abroad. The vessels that did find their way here are possibly gifts from or forgotten possessions of pilgrims to the monastery.

The predominant tableware at Alahan is a fine red ware whose characteristic feature is spiral burnishing on the wall and floor (nº **16** "Spiral Burnished Ware"). It has not so far been attested in the literature from other sites in the Eastern Mediterranean, but since few pottery assemblages, especially from Turkey, have been documented, further evidence for this ware may appear in the future.

It is immediately apparent that the number of tableware vessels from Alahan is not large. Less than one hundred dishes, plates or bowls were found in the entire excavation and it must be supposed that in addition to the ceramic pieces described here, the community used wooden or metal vessels for eating.

[1] J. W. Hayes, *Late Roman Pottery* (London, 1972).

[2] Antioch-on-the-Orontes and Anemurium (Anamur) provide two good examples of the predominance of these wares during the period in question. See F. O. Waagé, *Antioch-on-the-Orontes*, 4.1: *Ceramics and Islamic Coins* (Princeton, London, The Hague, 1948). The Roman pottery from Anemurium is now being studied for eventual publication by the author; some of this material is presented in my "A Byzantine Well Deposit from Anemurium (Rough Cilicia)," *Anatolian Studies*, 27 (1977), pp. 175-190.

[3] Hayes, *Late Roman Pottery*, pp. 414-424.

African Red Slip

This ware is found at the site in all periods but fifth-century forms are less common than those of the sixth and early seventh centuries. Of the twenty-six identifiable vessels, seventeen are forms belonging to the sixth and early seventh centuries.

1 Rim, dish, Form 59, early fourth to early fifth century. D: impossible to determine. FS: Two-Storey Building, room c, level NA (1965). Figure 3.1.

2 Rim, bowl, Form 67, late fourth to late fifth century. Estimated maximum D: 36-38 cm. FS: Two-Storey Building, room d, level 1 (1965). Figure 3.2.
   Similar: Five rims. FS: Basilica, adjacent to door to undercroft, top-soil; Basilica, north aisle, topsoil (1967).

3 Rim, bowl, Form 70 (variant), first half fifth century (?). Estimated maximum D: 20-22 cm. FS: grave area northwest of Baptistery, topsoil (1962). Figure 3.3.
   No grooves or rouletting on rim.

4 Rim, bowl, Form 93A, ca. second half fifth century. D: 24 cm. FS: grave area northwest of Baptistery, topsoil (1962). Fig. 3.4.

5 Rim, bowl, Form 97, ca. 490-550. Estimated maximum D: 22 cm. FS: Two-Storey Building, room NA, level NA (1965). Not drawn.
   Similar: Three sherds, non-joining, probably from two other vessels. FS: Lower Terrace south of southeast corner of the Basilica (1967).

6 Rim, bowl, Form 99, sixth to early seventh century. D: 20 cm. FS: Two-Storey Building, room h, level 1 (1965). Figure 3.6.
   Similar: one base and one rim from different vessels. FS: Two-Storey Building, room h, level 1 (1965).

7 Rim, dish, Form 104A, ca. 530-580. Estimated maximum D: 34 cm. FS: Lower Terrace, drainage channel, topsoil (1972). Figure 3.7.
   Similar: four bases and two rims. FS: Lower Terrace drainage channel (1972) and grave area northwest of Baptistery (1962).

8 Rim, dish, Form 104B, ca. 570-600 (625 +). Estimated maximum D: 33-34 cm. FS: Lower Terrace, drainage channel, topsoil (1972). Figure 3.8.
   Similar: One base with a large stamped cross on floor (Hayes, *Late Roman Pottery*, Style E (ii), p. 280, fig. 57, no. 333). FS: Lower Terrace, topsoil (1972).

9 Rim, plate, Form 105 (variant), ca. 580/600 to 660 + . D: 32 cm. FS: Basilica, north aisle midway between pastophory and narthex, level 2 (1962). Figure 3.9.

Similar: One rim. FS: Lower Terrace drainage channel, topsoil (1972).

Eleven other sherds of African Red Slip were found but their condition is too fragmentary to permit an identification of form.

Late Roman C (Phocean Ware)

Late Roman C ware is poorly represented with only a handful of vessels of the very common Forms 3 and 10 being found. These forms were current in the Mediterranean region in the sixth and seventh centuries.

10 Rim, bowl, Form 3 E/F, late fifth to sixth century. Estimated maximum D: 20-21 cm. FS: Lower Terrace, baulk between drainage channels (1972). Figure 3.10.
Deeply impressed multiple rouletting on rim.
Similar: Two rims, Form 3 E/F. FS: Lower Terrace, topsoil, 1972. Two bases, Form 3 or Form 10. FS: Lower Terrace, topsoil, 1972.

11 Rim, dish, Form 10A, late sixth to early seventh century. Estimated maximum D: 25-27 cm. FS: Two-Storey Building, room h, east end, level 1 (1965). Figure 3.11.

12 Rim, dish, Form 10C, early to mid seventh century. Estimated maximum D: 28 cm. FS: NA. Figure 3.12.

Three sherds from the wall of one other unidentifiable vessel were also found. FS: NA.

Cypriot Red Slip

Only one vessel of the third common late Roman ware, Cypriot Red Slip, is represented. Its date can be anywhere from the late fourth to the early sixth century depending upon which form the base comes from.

13 Base, dish, Form 1 or 2, late fourth to early sixth century; also one body sherd. FS: Cave Church, topsoil (1965). Figure 3.13.

Imitation African Red Slip

Seven vessels imitating common African Red Slip forms were found. On the basis of the dates for their prototypes, all of these must belong to the seventh century. Five of the examples belong to a fairly well-known class called Egyptian "C" by Hayes.[4]

[4] Ibid., pp. 399-401.

14   Base, plate, imitates Form 104B or C, probably late sixth to seventh
century. FS: Basilica, north aisle, rainwater soakaway (1962). Figure
3.14.

Orange-red, fine-grained clay full of white lime particles, black and
red grits, very micaceous. No slip preserved. Flat floor with thick
wall, fairly low ring foot set inside the edge of the floor. Impressed
decoration of uncertain design set on floor inside the foot.
Similar: One base.

15   Dish, imitates Form 105, seventh century (Hayes' Egyptian "C"
Ware). D: 35 cm; DB: 16 cm; H: 4.8 cm. FS: Two-Storey Building,
room d, topsoil. Figure 3.15.

Light orange, gritty, coarse grained clay with many large lime
particles and dark grits. Misfired with a grey core. Slip is poorly
preserved, thin, dark red-brown.
Published: J. W. Hayes, *Late Roman Pottery*, p. 400, fig. 89a.
Similar: Three rims, one base and six body sherds representing at
least four vessels. FS: NA.

Miscellaneous Fine Wares

16   Dish, "Spiral Burnished Ware." [5] D: 32 cm. FS: Basilica, north aisle,
level 3 (1965). Figure 3.16.

Pink-brown clay, fine-grained, hard and well fired with a few small
lime particles. The slip is bright red, sometimes with a fairly good
glossy finish on the exterior although on poorer examples it is matt.
The interior is matt. The exterior and interior wall and floor have
concentric lines of darker red as the result of continuous spiral
burnishing while being turned on the wheel. The spiral burnishing is
not always carefully done and on more poorly finished examples
may appear only on the interior or the floor. Visible on the interior
are medium to large flakes of gold mica. Flat floor thickens at
outside edge where it joins the wall. The wall slopes gently outwards
narrowing towards the rim which is small, everted and sloped
upwards. Exterior wall has light, irregular wheel-ridging in some
cases.

---

[5] I have applied a purely descriptive term to this distinctive class of pottery in the
absence of any evidence for its source. The fact that it is the most common tableware at
Alahan, far outnumbering the African Red Slip, suggests a centre of production closer at
hand, perhaps in central Anatolia. The ware is not known to me from other sites or
published reports.

Similar: 55 sherds of the same ware representing at least 44 vessels. All have the same form. FS: Colonnaded Walk adjacent to Shrine; south of Baptistery; just east of Baptistery; Two-Storey Building, room h east and west ends; East Church, south aisle; Lower Terrace; other areas. A considerable quantity in all areas.

Discussion: The source and date of this ware are problematical. The site of Alahan does not provide any narrow chronological limits for it but establishes only that it is a late Roman ware of the fifth to early seventh century. It does not appear at all in the assemblage from the coastal Cilician city of Anemurium (modern Anamur), thereby supporting the possibility of a more local source somewhere in the interior of Turkey. The ware exhibits certain artistic connections that may have a bearing on its date although this type of evidence will remain only speculative until examples are published from closed contexts on other sites. The influence of African Red Slip and Late Roman C ware is apparent in the stamped designs which appear on the floor of one dish of this type. Two motifs are extant: the sole of a shoe and a decorated square. The former appears in slightly different form in Late Roman C ware in stylistic Group IIB which Hayes dates to the second half of the fifth century.[6] The square is part of the African Red Slip repertory and belongs to Style A (iii) dated to ca. 410-470.[7] Allowing time for importation and imitation in an Anatolian production centre, the stamped example of the ware would probably be late fifth or sixth century. The ware as a whole, however, may well have appeared earlier. The lack of any differences in the one form found argues against any lengthy period of production being represented by the finds from Alahan. Spiral burnishing is not a common decorative treatment on late Roman fine wares. It appears on African Red Slip Form 109 which is found in ca. 580/600 to mid-seventh century contexts. This late date makes it unlikely as a source of inspiration for the Alahan ware.

17 Rim, bowl (survival piece?). Estimated maximum D: 26 cm. FS: Basilica (found during removal of secondary wall, 1967). Figure 3.17.

Light red-brown fine grained clay breaks cleanly and has no visible impurities. The gloss is a mottled light brown to red-brown with an iridescent sheen. Thin-walled bowl with small everted rim, concave

---

[6] Hayes, *Late Roman Pottery*, p. 354, fig. 74, n° 29g.
[7] Ibid., p. 244, fig. 43, n° 92m.

on upper surface. The quality of the fabric and surface treatment and the thin-walled form all indicate an early Roman date for this piece.

18 Rim, bowl. Estimated maximum D: 22 cm. FS: Lower Terrace drainage channel (1972). Figure 3.18.

Light brown, well-fired hard clay with a few small white lime particles and dark grits. The thin, matt slip varies from light to red-brown. The shape appears to derive from Late Roman C Form 3.

19 Small pot. D: 4.1 cm; H: 8.4 cm. FS: Two-Storey Building, rooms f and g, level NA (1963). Figure 3.19.

Orange-buff clay, fine grained, hard and clean breaking. The most characteristic feature is its "peppered" appearance resulting from the large number of small to medium sized dark grits. The slip or wash is a bright red-brown applied evenly on the exterior but unevenly over the interior. Flat based small vessel without handles with a deep groove at junction of neck and body and two grooves at widest point on body.

Similar: One rim from another pot. In this case the slip has a slight purplish tinge with a metallic lustre.

20 Dish. D: 31.5 cm; DB: 22.4 cm; H: 5.4 cm. FS: Two-Storey Building, room f, level 1 (1963). Figure 3.20.

Clay and slip/wash as for **19** above. Flat raised base with groove on underside near the outside edge. Two grooves decorate the outside wall of the base. Flared curved wall ends in a plain hanging rim.

B. MONASTIC WARE[8]

A distinctive, homogeneous group of fine painted pottery constitutes the largest single class in the ceramic assemblage. The ware is attested at one other site, the nearby Dağ Pazarı.[9] The obvious Christian motifs apparent in many of the decorative types as well as its localisation at two neighbouring sites, one a monastery and the other containing three so far excavated churches (there may well be others, as yet unknown) justify the application of the term Monastic Ware.

The body-clay is medium grained with a distinctly gritty texture. The colour-range is buff to orange-red to light brown. The firing can vary from piece to piece with a resulting variation in hardness. The impurities

---

[8] I have retained the term first applied to this ware by Michael Gough.

[9] Personal communication from Mrs. Michael Gough. Sherds of the ware were found during Michael Gough's excavations at Dağ Pazarı.

most commonly present are medium to large-sized white lime particles and small dark grits. It is micaceous. The surface is not given a slip or wash before the painted decoration is applied. The paint is thin and matt and varies from red-brown to brown, sometimes taking on a purple or blackish tinge.

The vessels all belong to a few standard forms which range from open bowls to closed containers, thus covering all the needs of the monastic community for which the pottery seems to have been produced. The majority of vessels found fall into the category of closed shapes with sherds from bowls making up only a small fraction of the total.

The painted decoration is executed in a vigorous and forceful linear style. Although the designs are sometimes crude and lacking in artistic sophistication, the over-all effect is successful with the emphasis on the outline and the contrast between painted and reserved areas. The range of motifs is not extensive. Figured types include goats, birds, fish and stylized trees and fronds. The geometric motifs are for the most part based on spiraliform designs with dot-fringed circles or grouped dots being used as fillers. Everted rims of bowls are decorated with simple lines or more complicated patterns made up of intersecting lines.

The placement of the designs was accommodated to the shapes of the vessels. The floors of open shapes were decorated with a motif of vegetal type. A single tree was the most popular for this area. Continuous curvilinear designs appear on the shoulders of closed shapes. These designs took the form either of single figures repeated or of a running spiral.

The goats, fish and birds are the most interesting stylistically. There is no painstaking attention to detail in their drawing but by the utilization of simple linear dividers and subsidiary fillers, the body parts are articulated and the texture of the hair, feathers or scales is captured.

On many examples, often of less carefully levigated clay, the painted decoration is reduced to blotches or haphazard lines applied carelessly on the body. One fragmentary example exhibits impressed decoration forming a star-like pattern in addition to the lines and splashes of paint. Incised outlines were occasionally used to emphasize the outline created by the paint. No chronological significance can be assigned to these variations in treatment although in the absence of excavated sequences differences in the date of various types cannot be ruled out.

The most evocative Christian symbol used on the ware is the Greek cross. Four examples were found, all unfortunately of a fragmentary nature. The crosses were either simply outlined in paint or rendered by a combination of incision and painted highlights.

In one case only can it be said with certainty that no painted decoration was applied to a vessel of Monastic Ware. This occurs on the small cup (n° **25**). Many fragmentary plain sherds were found but they may well come from vessels having decoration.

Direct influence for the Monastic Ware pictorial style cannot be cited from contemporary pottery in the Mediterranean world. In general painted pottery is not common in the Roman period[10] and when it does occur it appears to be geographically limited. There are points of contact to be found in painted wares made in Egypt and Palestine in the same period, but these are limited to the choice of motifs such as fish and spiraliform designs.[11] Otherwise, there are no close stylistic affinities. It would seem rather that the Monastic Ware from Alahan is part of a widespread tradition of painting that saw local production for a limited market in some Mediterranean centres.[12]

The catalogue of Monastic Ware is presented in two parts. The range of shapes is given first and the various decorative types are illustrated separately in the second section. The motifs associated with each vessel form are listed with the forms. For the most part, complete shapes could not be reconstructed because of the fragmentary nature of the material.

21 Bowl. D: 18 cm; DB: 6 cm; H: 4.9 cm. FS: Lower Terrace, drainage channel (1972). Figure 4.21.
The clay is buff on the exterior with an orange core. Flat raised base, flaring wall and flat everted, slightly upturned rim.
Decoration: Zig-zag linear decoration on rim and single stylized pine tree on floor.
Similar: Five rims.

22 Bowl. D: 20 cm; DB: 7 cm; H: 5 cm. FS: Lower Terrace, drainage channel (1972). Figure 4.22; Plate 84.
The clay is orange-buff. A more open version of n° **21**.
Decoration: Parallel lines on rim and three large fronds on floor.

[10] See the list in Hayes, *Late Roman Pottery*, pp. 412-413.

[11] For example, fish on plates from Egypt – ibid., p. 413 and n. 3; fish on series of painted vessels found at Antioch in seventh-century contexts – Waagé, *Ceramics and Islamic Coins*, pp. 58-59 and fig. 36; spiraliform designs – Sylvester J. Saller, ed., *The Memorial of Moses on Mount Nebo*, 3: Hilary R. Schneider, *The Pottery* (Jerusalem, 1950), p. 32 fig. 2, n°s 2 and 4 and plates 146-147.

[12] A class of painted pottery specifically connected with a monastic community is noted by Schneider, *The Pottery*, p. 66. She is quoting Saller's opinion that the painted vessels may have been made for the pilgrims to the shrine or for the monks to use on special occasions.

23   Bowl. D: 14 cm; DB: 5.6 cm; H: 3.1 cm. FS: Lower Terrace, drainage
     channel (1972). Figure 4.23.
     A smaller, thicker-walled version of the above (n° 21) with less
     articulation between wall and rim.
     Decoration: Dots on rim's surface.
     Similar: Two rims and two bases with the same very thick floor.
     Three concentric rings are painted on the floor of one and on the
     other, two concentric circles between which are dots.

24   Basin. D: 40 cm; DB: 22 cm; H: 15 cm. FS: Two-Storey Building, room
     b, level NA. Figure 9.24.
     Flat base; straight flaring walls end in a small, plain everted rim; two
     horizontal handles.
     Decoration: Outside wall has lines of paint applied in random
     fashion. On the inside, the lines from a large cross running from rim
     to rim.

25   Cup. D: 7 cm; DB: 3.7 cm; H: 5.1 cm. FS: Lower Terrace, drainage
     channel (1972). Figure 4.25.
     Flat base, bulging wall and plain everted rim. No handles. Although
     the cup lacks painted decoration, the fabric is that of standard
     Monastic Ware.

26   Small pot. D: 6 cm. FS: Lower Terrace, south of Shrine, topsoil
     (1967). Figure 4.26.
     Globular body, plain everted rim.
     Decoration: Thick lines.

27   Rim, bowl (?). D: ca. 15-16 cm. FS: Lower Terrace, drainage channel
     (1972). Figure 4.27.
     Curved body ends in a slightly everted rim carefully scalloped on the
     inside edge.
     Decoration: Inside wall of rim bears a band of lightly impressed
     wavy combing and a single painted line. The combination of wavy
     combed decoration and painting is very uncommon. Four other
     body sherds having both elements were found.

28   Small pitcher. D: 4 cm; DB: 3.8 cm; H: 9.4 cm. FS: Living Quarters
     west of the East Church, level 2 (1963). Figure 4.28.
     Flat, raised base, pinched pouring spout.
     Decoration: Thick lines are applied in the same manner as on n° 26.

29   Small bottle. DB: 3.6 cm; preserved H: 7.4 cm. FS: Lower Terrace,
     drainage channel (1972). Figure 4.29.
     Flat raised base, globular body.
     Decoration: Primarily curvilinear bands somewhat carelessly
     applied.

30   Small jug or jar. DB: 5 cm; preserved H: 9 cm. FS: Basilica, south of south facade, level 1 (1967). Figure 5.30.

Heavy triangular low ring foot marked off by a broad groove on the outside. Globular body with shallow irregular ridging.

Decoration: Paint is splashed on in patches.

31   Base, jug. DB: 6.3 cm; preserved H: 11.3 cm. FS: Lower Terrace, drainage channel (1972). Figure 5.31.

Slightly coarser fabric than usual. Flat, slightly raised base, deeply ridged body, plain shoulder. No traces of handle on extant portion.

Decoration: On the shoulder there are lines that appear to be one element in the common running spiral design.

Similar: Common form. A large number of bases of the same type, ridged body sherds and plain shoulders with painted decoration or proportions that could come from this size of jug. The painted decoration on these is generally the running spiral but rows of fish, birds, etc. are also found.

32   Jug. DB: 10.6 cm; preserved H: 38 cm. FS: Colonnaded Walk adjacent to Pilaster Complex 3, level 2 (1965). Figure 9.32.

Flat base, slightly hollowed out in centre, biconical body, tall narrow neck with ridge at junction of neck and body, traces of handle attachment at widest point on body.

Decoration: Horizontal bands on body and neck, curvilinear patterns on shoulder.

Similar: Common form. Several bases of the same type as well as body sherds, handles and necks that are of the correct proportions to come from this form.

33   Rim, jug. D: 4.8 cm. FS: Colonnaded Walk, 10 m west of Pilaster Complex 3, topsoil (1965). Figure 5.33.

Narrow cylindrical neck, plain rim, round handle. Possibly from a jug such as n° **31**.

Decoration: Splashes of paint, no design.

Similar: Several rims.

34   Rim, jar. D: 15.4 cm. FS: East Church, south aisle, topsoil (1967). Figure 9.34.

Medium-high cylindrical neck decorated with fine grooves, traces of handle attachments below rim, thickened squarish rim, curved shoulder.

Decoration: Splashes and dribbles of paint applied in a careless fashion.

Similar: A few rims and body sherds which probably come from this type of large vessel.

35   Lid. DB: 7 cm; total H: 4.2 cm. FS: Two-Storey Building, room f, level
      1 (1963). Figure 5.35.
      Saucer-shaped lid with central knob and string-cut base.
      Decoration: Splashes of paint.
      Similar: One example.
      This is a very common shape for lids in the late Roman period and is
      found in a variety of fabrics. Cf. J. W. Hayes, "Excavations at
      Saraçhane in Istanbul: Fifth Preliminary Report; A Seventh-Century
      Pottery Group," *Dumbarton Oaks Papers*, 22 (1968), p. 207, fig. D
      n° 31, and 213, fig. G n° 107; G. F. Bass, ed., *A History of Seafaring
      based on Underwater Archaeology* (London, 1972), p. 155, fig. 22,
      from a seventh-century wreck. In the excavations at Anemurium
      over 50 examples of this form have been found in late Roman-early
      Byzantine fill deposits.

36   Fragments from a lantern or incense burner. FS: Lower Terrace,
      drainage channel (1972). Plate 78.
      Two fragments from the body of a large thick-walled (ca. 1.5 cm)
      object with trigular cut-outs. The shape of the openings is repeated
      on the body of the vessel by incised lines and painting.

   In addition to the classifiable sherds of Monastic Ware, a great mass of
body sherds, large and small handles and fragments of rims and bases
were found. Many of these exhibited interesting varieties of painted
decoration which are illustrated in the following section. From this large
body of fragmentary ceramic material it is evident that closed vessels
formed the overwhelming majority of the total. This fact further supports
the conclusion reached on the numerical evidence for imported tablewares that the monastic community must have utilized open vessels
manufactured from materials other than clay.

Decorative Types

37-45: Figured decorations.

37   Goat. LV: shoulder, closed shape. FS: Lower Terrace, drainage
      channel (1972). Figure 6.37, Plate 75.

38   Bird. LV: shoulder, closed shape. FS: Lower Terrace, drainage
      channel (1972). Figure 6.38; the type is illustrated on the sherd in
      Plate 88.

39   Bird. LV: shoulder, closed shape. FS: Lower Terrace, drainage
      channel (1972). Figure 6.39; the type is illustrated on another sherd
      in Plate 83.

40 Fish. lv: shoulder, closed shape. fs: Lower Terrace, south of south pastophory of Basilica (1972). Figure 6.40; the type is illustrated on another sherd in Plate 76.

41 Tree. lv: floor, bowl. fs: Lower Terrace, drainage channel (1972). Figure 5.41, Plate 79.

42 Tree. lv: floor, bowl. fs: na. Figure 5.42, Plate 82.

43 Fronds. lv: floor, bowl. fs: Lower Terrace, drainage channel (1972). Figure 5.43, Plate 81.

44 Greek cross in combination with rosettes. lv: shoulder, closed shape. fs: Baptistery, east of east facade, level 1 (1965). Figure 6.44.

45 Greek cross incised and painted. lv: ? fs: Lower Terrace, drainage channel (1972). Figure 6.45, Plate 86.

46-50: Geometric decorations.

46 Running spiral with dot fillers. lv: shoulder, closed shape. fs: Lower Terrace, drainage channel (1972). Figure 6.46; the type is illustrated in Plate 80.

47 Running spiral with subsidiary dot-fringed circles. lv: shoulder, closed shape. fs: Lower Terrace, south of south pastophory of Basilica (1972). Figure 6.47, Plate 85.

48 Concentric dotted semi-circles. lv: shoulder, closed shape. fs: Two-Storey Building, room e, topsoil (1963). Figure 6.48.

49 Curvilinear design. lv: ? fs: na. Figure 6.49.

50 Simple lines. lv: small handle. fs: Lower Terrace, south of south pastophory of Basilica (1972). Plate 87.

51-52: Gouged decoration. The technique of gouging out a pattern was very occasionally employed on Monastic Ware. Only a handful of examples were found of which the most complete exhibits the motif of a rosette within a circle.

51 Gouged rosette. lv: ? fs: Lower Terrace, south of southeast corner of Basilica, bedrock (1972). Figure 5.51, Plate 77.

52 Cross highlighted with paint. lv: ? fs: na. Plate 89.

C. Other Wares

Most of the material belonging to the kitchen-ware variety was very fragmentary. Complete profiles could rarely be recovered. A selection of the predominant forms and wares has been made. There is, in addition to the published material, a quantity of sherds among which there are few recurring or identifiable shapes. These have not been recorded.

In general the shapes are very simple. Bases from closed vessels are completely flat or slightly raised. Rims are plain, sometimes slightly thickened or everted. The majority of the body sherds are plain, with only a small number showing ridging. Only about a dozen sherds are found with grouped grooving or wavy combed decoration. The predominant body-clay is a hard, grainy light red-brown, full of medium to large-sized lime particles, dark grits and mica. This seems to be the standard "local" kitchen-ware fabric.

Cooking Pots

A large number of sherds were found belonging to the cooking-pot class. There are several varieties of rim. The body sherds generally bear fine ribbing. The clay is orange to orange-brown, grainy and full of small white lime particles and dark grits. It is fairly micaceous.

53   Cooking pot. D: 10 cm; DB: 8 cm; H: 18 cm. FS: Two-Storey Building, room h, level 1 (1965). Figure 9.53.
Flat base, ribbed round body, sharply down-turned rim overhanging the wall.
This is a common shape for cooking-pots in the late Roman period. Cf. H. W. Catling, "An Early Byzantine Pottery Factory at Dhiorios in Cyprus," *Levant*, 4 (1972), 47, fig. 29 n° P433, and 49, fig. 30 n° P210. Several examples have been found in the late fill at Anemurium including one from a closed context of the seventh century.

54   Cooking pot. D: 12.9 cm. FS: NA. Figure 7.54.
Upright rim, thickened and flattened on top. No ribbing on extant portion of wall.

55   Cooking pot. D: 12 cm; estimated H: 13.5 cm. FS: Two-Storey Building, room b, level 1 (1963). Figure 7.55.
Slightly thickened inturned rim, large vertical ring handle. Not common. Cf. J. Boardman and J. W. Hayes, *Excavations at Tocra 1963-1965. The Archaic Deposits II and Later Deposits*, British School of Archaeology at Athens suppl. vol. 10/Society for Libyan Studies (London, 1973), fig. 51 n° 2551 – level 2, seventh century.

56   Rim, cooking pot. Estimated maximum D: 12 cm. FS: Two-Storey Building, room d, topsoil (1965). Figure 7.56.
Plain, slightly thickened rim, ribbing on wall beneath.

57   Rim, cooking pot. D: impossible to determine. FS: Colonnaded Walk, 5 m west of Pilaster Complex 3, level 1 (1965). Figure 7.57.
Short everted rim with groove on outer surface, ribbing on wall.

58 Rim, cooking pot. Estimated maximum D: 13 cm. FS: NA. Figure 7.58.
Everted rim, tilting upward slightly, flaring out sharply immediately beneath rim.

59 Rim, cooking pot. D: impossible to determine. FS: Two-Storey Building, room h, topsoil (1965). Figure 7.59.
Everted rim, tilted upward; a variation of n° **57**.

60 Rim, cooking pot. D: impossible to determine. FS: Two-Storey Building, room d, level 1 (1965). Figure 7.60.
Small rolled rim, overhanging wall slightly at bottom.

Slipped Ware

A limited number of sherds of light orange-red clay full of white lime particles were found. A thin, matt, dark red-brown slip covers the exterior surface. This fabric appears to have been used entirely for closed shapes of jar or jug-type.

61 Rim, storage jar. Estimated maximum D: 12 cm. FS: Two-Storey Building, room h, topsoil (1965). Figure.7.61.
Heavy everted rim, flattened on top, rounded on outer surface; heavy oval ridged handle attached to neck below rim.

62 Rim, jug. D: impossible to determine. FS: Colonnaded Walk immediately west of Pilaster Complex 3, level 1 (1965). Figure 7.62.
Plain rim, bevelled on top; heavy oval ridged handle attached to rim.

D. MISCELLANEOUS FORMS

63 Mortarium. D: 31.6 cm; DB: 14.4 cm; H: 15 cm. FS: Two-Storey Building, room a, topsoil (1965). Figure 9.63.
Soft buff clay with many impurities. Flat base, steep walls, squarish rim with groove on top, spouted.

64 Rim, dish. D: 32 cm. FS: Colonnaded Walk, 3 m west of Pilaster Complex 3, level 1 (1967). Figure 9.64.
Very coarse, buff clay. Thickened upright rim decorated with an incised wavy line.

65 Pitcher. D: 8 cm; DB: 6 cm; H: 15 cm. FS: Basilica, north aisle west of north pastophory, level 1 (1963). Figure 7.65.
Dark grey coarse grained clay with many impurities. Flat, slightly raised base, globular body, ridge on neck.

66 Pitcher. D: 9 cm. FS: Spring Complex, furnace room, level 1 (1970). Figure 7.66.

Flaring rim, no neck, large angular handle joined at rim. Not a common form.

67 Rim, jar. D: 12.9 cm. FS: NA. Figure 8.67.
Heavy triangular rim, deep groove at junction of neck and rim.

68 Rim, jar. D: 10.9 cm. FS: Lower Terrace south of Shrine, topsoil (1972). Figure 8.68.
Variation of n° **67**. No groove.

69 Jug. D: 4.9 cm; DB: 6 cm; H: 18.2 cm. FS: Grave area north of Baptistery, topsoil (1962). Figure 8.69.
Coarse buff clay. Flat, slightly raised base, angular shoulder, tall neck widening slightly towards top, handle reconstructed, deep ridging on body and incised perpendicular lines on shoulder.
Similar: One vessel.

70 Pot stand. D: 13 cm; DB: 15.5 cm; H: 6.5 cm. FS: Two-Storey Building, room d, topsoil (1965). Figure 8.70.
Fine grained orange clay with a very gritty feel, full of small to medium-sized white lime particles and a few dark grits.
Similar: About 6 fragmentary sherds.

71 Unguentarium. D: 2.6 cm; DB: 1.5 cm; H: 18.2 cm. FS: Two-Storey Building, room h, topsoil (1965). Figure 8.71.
Fine grained, hard red-brown clay with a few white lime particles. No slip preserved. Flat base, fusiform body, short mouth, ridging on inside wall.
Cf. J. W. Hayes, "A New Type of Early Christian Ampulla," *The Annual of the British School at Athens*, 66 (1971), 243-248 where this vessel is cited on p. 247. Hayes dates this type to ca. 500/520-650 and suggests that their possible source may be Palestine. Their function would seem to be specifically Christian as containers for holy water and oil.

72 Sherd from the shoulder of a jar. FS: NA. (Known to the writer only from a photograph and from casts).
The clay is reported to be a gritty beige. Plain shoulder area bears stamped decoration. The body beneath the shoulder is grooved. The extant portion has three oval stamps, probably the impressions of finger rings. In each of the ovals is a standing, nimbed and draped figure, facing front. At least one of the figures carries an object in the crook of his left arm, possibly a staff or cross. The details of the figures are too indistinct to decide whether wings or folds of drapery appear at the back of each. The figures, if not winged, would represent Christ or a saint. Such robed figures with nimbus and large cross were a common stamped motif on African Red Slip pottery in

the sixth century. Cf. Hayes, *Late Roman Pottery*, pp. 264-267, fig. 51. Figures of saints were also a common motif on finger rings in the early Christian period; cf. O. M. Dalton, *Catalogue of the Finger Rings in the British Museum. Early Christian, Byzantine, Teutonic, Mediaeval and Later* (London, 1912), p. 19, n° 112; also n°s 116-121, 123 for standing and mounted saints. It is possible, too, that the impressions could have been made by wooden stamps utilized to create identification marks. For this class of object see H. E. Winlock and W. E. Crum, *The Monastery of Epiphanios at Thebes* (New York, 1926; rpt. New York, 1973), vol. 1, fig. 33 n° 22: a stamped impression in a sealing for a wine jar; the figure is identified as a warrior saint. For representations of Christian figures in Isaurian art of the fifth century, see Michael Gough, "A Thurible from Dağ Pazarı," *Anadolu Araştırmaları* (1965), pp. 231-235. (I thank Mrs. Michael Gough for this reference).

E. Amphoras

No complete example could be reconstructed. It is clear, however, that the sherds come from a common eastern Mediterranean type of the early Byzantine period[13] whose most characteristic feature is heavy irregular ridging on the body which varies from close set on the shoulders and near the base to broadly spaced and undercut in the central part. The clay is soft and has a very gritty feel; it is orange red and full of small and medium-sized lime particles and dark grits.

F. Lamps

There is basically only one type of ceramic lamp found at the site (see Figure 8.73). The clay can vary from a hard orange-buff grainy fabric to a coarser brown variety. Most are unslipped although a few examples have splashes of red-brown paint of the sort that characterizes Monastic Ware. The lamps are wheel made with a globular body, slightly raised base,

---

[13] The type is very common at Anemurium in the late Roman period. For examples from dated contexts, see G. F. Bass, "Underwater Excavations at Yassi Ada: A Byzantine Shipwreck," *Archäologischer Anzeiger*, 77 (1962), col. 546, fig. 6b; H. W. Catling and A. I. Dikigoropoulos, "The Kornos Cave: an Early Byzantine Site in Cyprus," *Levant*, 2 (1970), 47, n° 4 and plate xxixA. From a museum's collection, see T. O. Alpözen, "Bodrum Müzesi Ticarı Amphoraları," *Türk Arkeoloji Dergisi*, 22/2 (1975), 21, "Bizans Amphoraları" form 4 from Bodrum, Turkey.

knob handle and flat rim or raised ledge around the filling hole. Fragments coming from approximately thirty-one lamps were found.

G. MEDIEVAL POTTERY

A small quantity of sgraffito wares and plain glazed wares were found, often on or near the surface, in various contexts on the site. All the sherds were very fragmentary and no profiles could be reconstructed. The sherds do, however, indicate some reoccupation of the site in the twelfth to fourteenth centuries although the number of sherds dating from this period seems to indicate a minimal re-use of the area. Less than fifty sherds of these wares were either seen by the author or counted from notices in the excavation notebooks.

The sgraffito ware sherds exhibit an olive green glaze on the interior only. The glaze is black in the incised linear patterns. The fabric of these sherds is a very light red-brown, full of white lime particles and dark grits. Other sherds have glazes in various shades of green with brown and grey-black in the incisions. An unusual type is represented by three small sherds, non-joining but coming from one vessel, which have an egg-shell blue glaze on both the interior and exterior.

Glazed sherds were found in the following areas:

Cave Church;
Cave Complex;
Basilica: outside south facade, in secondary walls, in narthex, in interior adjacent to Evangelists' Door;
Colonnaded Walkway: adjacent to Pilaster Complex;[3]
East Church: south aisle;
Lower Terrace: southeast and southwest of Shrine and in drainage channel.

No one area showed a concentration of Byzantine sherds.

H. GLASS

It is impossible to present more than a small selection of representative pieces from the site. The assemblage as a whole is comparable to that coming from the late Roman-early Byzantine fill at Anemurium (Anamur). Published groups from the Eastern Mediterranean are not numerous but reference can be made to a few which include similar types.[14]

[14] See, for example, J. Napoleone-Lemaire and J. Ch. Balty, et al., *Fouilles d'Apamée de Syrie*, I.1: *L'Église à atrium de la grande colonnade* (Bruxelles, 1969), figs. 18 and 19;

The predominant colours are pale blue and pale green with amber and yellow vessels present in smaller numbers. Beaker and flask rims, bases from lamps and handles are the most common identifiable forms.

1   Rim, beaker. Pale blue/green. Figure 10.1.
2   Rim, beaker. Very pale green. Figure 10.2.
3   Rim, beaker. Pale blue. Figure 10.3.
4   Rim, beaker. Pale blue. Figure 10.4.
5   Rim, beaker. Pale green (?). Figure 10.5.
6   Rim, beaker. Pale green. Figure 10.6.
7   Rim, beaker. Pale yellow. Figure 10.7.
8   Rim, beaker. Pale yellow. Figure 10.8.
9   Rim, beaker. Pale blue. Figure 10.9.
10 Rim, flask. Pale green. Figure 10.10.
11 Rim, flask. Pale blue. Figure 10.11.
12 Rim, flask. Pale green. Figure 10.12.
13 Rim, mug. Pale blue. Figure 10.13.
14 Rim, mug. Pale blue. Figure 10.14.
15 Rim, mug. Very pale green. Figure 10.15.
16 Rim, bowl (?). Amber. Figure 10.16.
17 Base, lamp. Amber. Figure 10.17.
18 Base, "wine-glass" lamp. Pale blue. Figure 10.18.
19 Base, "wine-glass" lamp. Pale yellow. Figure 10.19.
20 Base, "wine-glass" lamp. Olive green. Figure 10.20.

H. W. Catling, "An Early Byzantine Pottery Factory at Dhiorios in Cyprus," *Levant*, 4 (1972), 75, fig. 41; P. Delougaz and R. C. Haines, *A Byzantine Church at Khirbet al-Karak*, University of Chicago Oriental Institute Publications, 85 (Chicago, 1960), Pl. 60 n[os] 21-23; P. Bagatti and J. T. Milik, *Gli Scavi del "Dominus Flevit" (Monte Oliveto, Gerusalemme)*, 1: *La necropoli del periodo romano*, Pubblicazioni dello Studium Biblicum Franciscanum, 13 (Jerusalem, 1958), figs. 34 (p. 145) and 35 (p. 147).

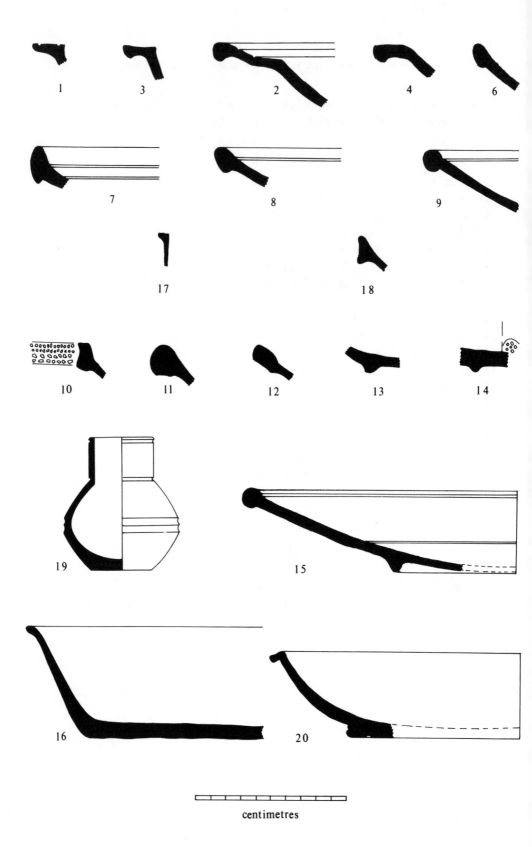

centimetres

FIGURE 3. – Pottery

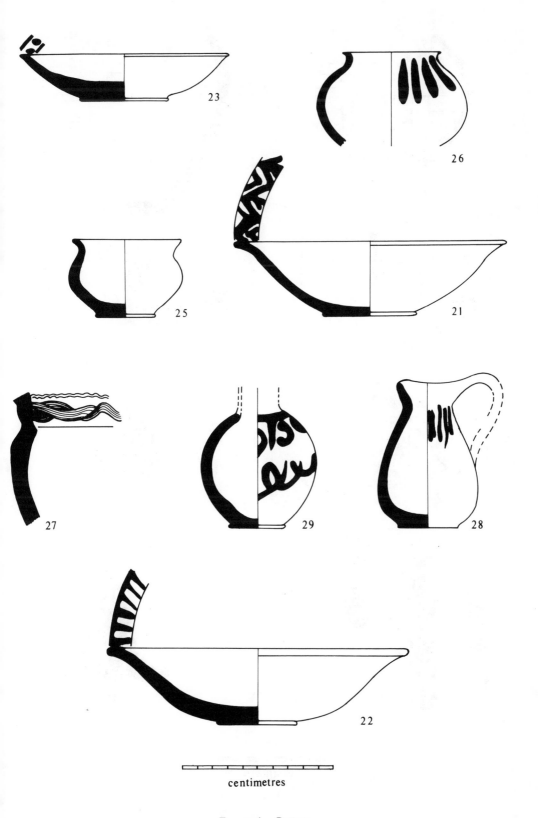

centimetres

Figure 4. – Pottery

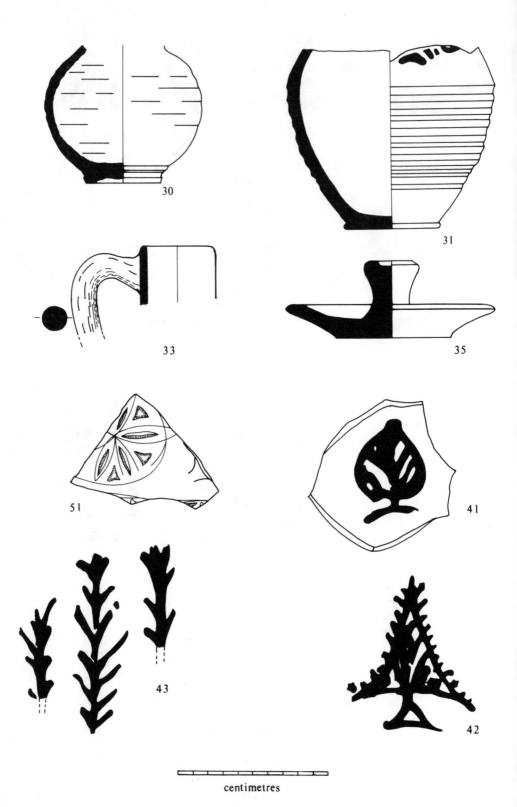

centimetres

FIGURE 5. – Pottery

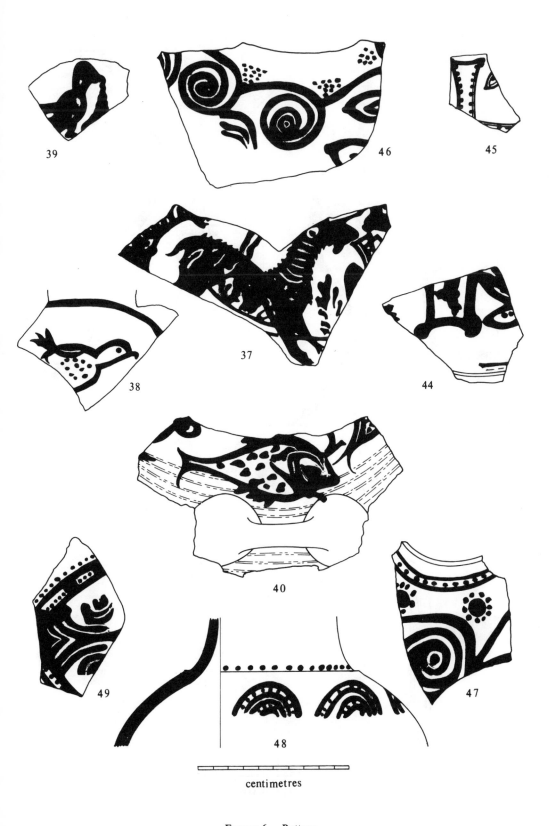

39

46

45

37

38

44

40

49

48

47

centimetres

FIGURE 6. – Pottery

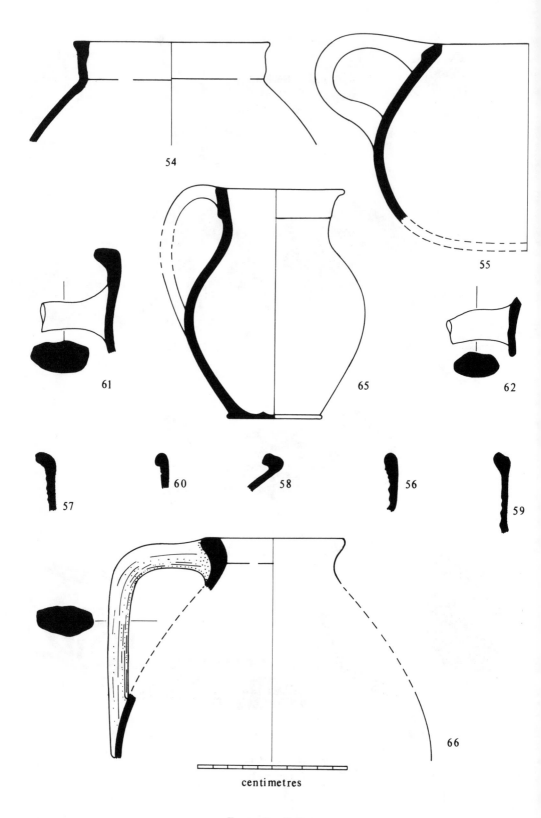

54

55

61

65

62

57

60

58

56

59

66

centimetres

FIGURE 7. – Pottery

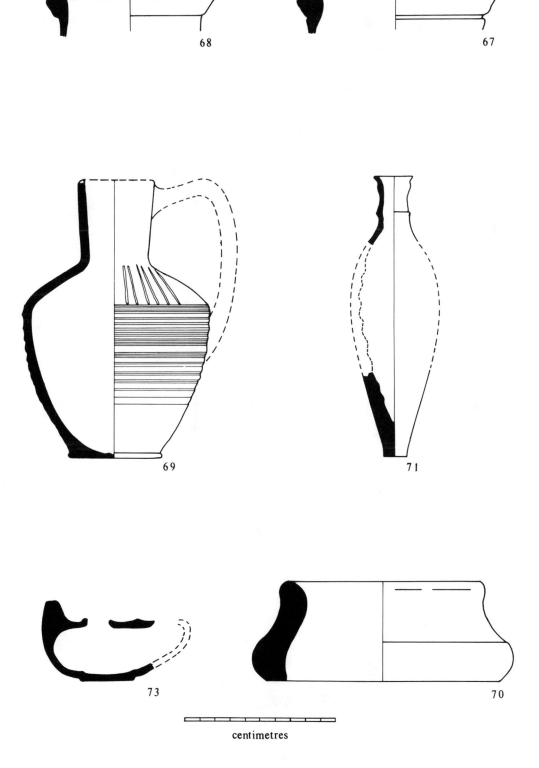

68

67

69

71

73

70

centimetres

FIGURE 8. – Pottery

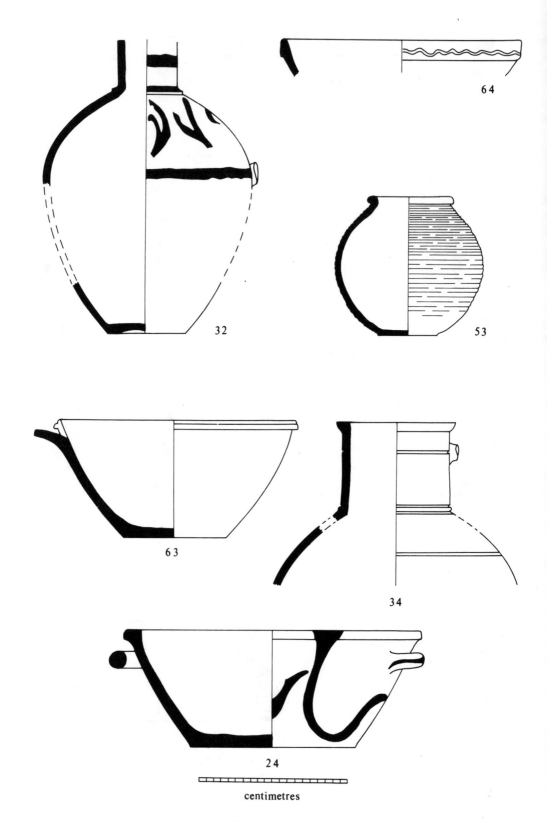

64

32

53

63

34

24

centimetres

FIGURE 9. – Pottery

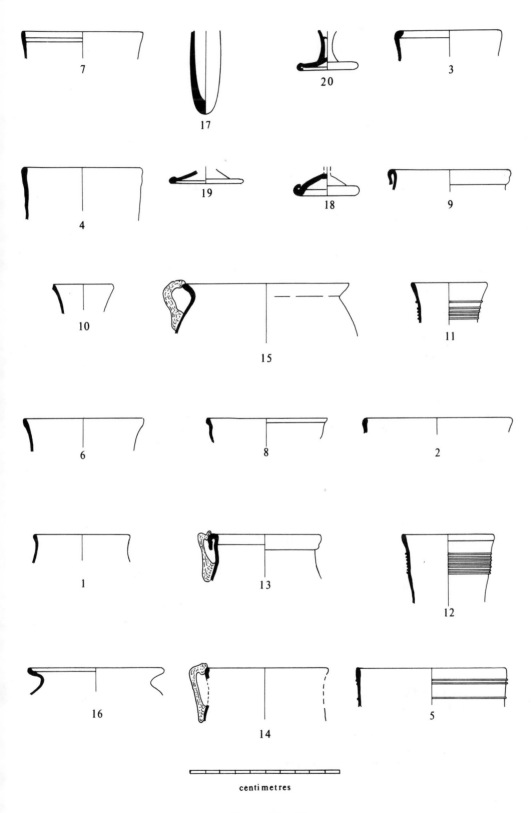

centimetres

FIGURE 10. – Glass

4

The Coins and Small Finds at Alahan

Jonathan Coulston and Mary Gough

A. The Coins

a. *Abbreviations*

LR   late Roman (fourth and fifth centuries)

References:

DOC 1   A. R. Bellinger, *Catalogue of the Byzantine Coins in the Dumbarton Oaks Collection ...*, 1: *Anastasius I to Maurice, 491-602* (Washington, D.C., 1966).

DOC 2   P. Grierson, *Catalogue of the Byzantine Coins in the Dumbarton Oaks Collection ...*, 2: *Phocas to Theodosius III, 602-717*, 2 parts (Washington, D.C., 1968).

DOC 3   P. Grierson, *Catalogue of the Byzantine Coins in the Dumbarton Oaks Collection ...*, 3: *Leo III to Nicephorus III, 717-1081*, 2 parts (Washington, D.C., 1973).

LRBC   P. V. Hill, J. P. C. Kent, and R. A. G. Carson, *Late Roman Bronze Coinage, AD 324-498* (London, 1960).

RIC   H. Mattingly, E. A. Sydenham, and Percy H. Webb, eds., *The Roman Imperial Coinage*, vol. 5.1 (London, 1927).

The Coin List was compiled by Jonathan Coulston, M. Phil, of the Department of Archaeology at the University of Newcastle upon Tyne, using site records and inventory identifications made by Michael Gough and plaster casts of many of the coins as indicated. The editor is most grateful to him for undertaking and fulfilling what must have been a difficult assignment.

The Small Finds List was compiled by Mary Gough.

Findspots:

B	Basilica	NA	Necropolis area
Bapt	Baptistery	SC	Spring Complex
EC	East Church	TSB	Two-Storey Building
LT	Lower Terrace	WB	area west of the Basilica
MT	Middle Terrace		

Information:

C	Plaster Cast	G	Michael Gough's notes

b. *Summary*

SUMMARY BY REIGN/PERIOD

1	Hadrian
1	Florianus
3	House of Constantine
1	Julian?
1	Jovian?
1	Theodosius I
2	Honorius
5	Arcadius
1	Honorius or Arcadius
3	Theodosius II
1	Marcian
2	Æ 3 (illegible)
1	Possible Æ 3
26	Æ 4 (illegible)
16	Possible Æ 4
9	Æ indeterminate
6	Anastasius I
3	Justin I
10	Justinian I
8	Justin II
1	Tiberius II
1	Maurice
1	Constans II
1	Anon. follis
2	Half folles (illegible)
1	Pentanummion (illegible)
5	Turkish
——	
113	

SUMMARY BY DENOMINATION

1	As
1	Antoninianus
7	Æ 3
39	Æ 4
27	uncertain
21	Folles
11	Half folles
1	Pentanummion
2	Turkish AR
3	Turkish Æ
——	
113	

c. *The Coin List*

		EMPEROR	DATE	DENOMINATION	REFERENCE	FINDSPOT[1]	INFORMATION
1.	(21)	Hadrian? (117-138)		As		MT 1965	C, G
2.	(1)	Florianus (276)	276	Antoninianus	*RIC* 5.1: 116	EC 1963	G
3.	(101)	Constantine I (307-337)	335-337	Æ 3	*LRBC* 1: 1024-5	Bapt 1965	C
4.	(37)	Constantine II (317-340)	335-337	Æ 4		TSB 1963	G
5.	(38)	Constantius II (337-361)	341-346	Æ 4	*LRBC* 1: 1398	TSB 1963	G
6.	(19)	Julian? (360-363)	361-363	Æ 4	*LRBC* 2: 2642?	MT 1965	G
7.	(90)	Jovian? (363-364)		Æ 3		B 1967	C, G
8.	(34)	Theodosius I (379-395)	383	Æ 4	*LRBC* 2: 2382 or 2734	SC 1970	C
9.	(6)	Honorius? (393-423)	402-408	Æ 4	*LRBC* 2: 1997?	EC 1963	G
10.	(10)	"	395-408	Æ 4	*LRBC* 2: 2215?	EC 1963	C, G
11.	(24)	Arcadius (383-408)	395-408	Æ 3		MT 1967	C
12.	(48)	"	395-408	Æ 3		TSB 1968	C
13.	(59)	"	388-392	Æ 4	*LRBC* 2: 1107	LT 1972	C
14.	(135)	"		Æ 4		LT 1972	G
15.	(67)	" ?		Æ 4		LT 1972	C, G
16.	(25)	Arcadius or Honorius (383-423)	395-408	Æ 3	*LRBC* 2: 2791-94	MT 1967	C
17.	(2)	Theodosius II (408-450)		Æ 4		EC 1963	C, G
18.	(11)	"	425-450	Æ 4	*LRBC* 2: 2243	EC 1968	C
19.	(92)	"	425-450	Æ 4	*LRBC* 2: 2236-40	WB 1967	C
20.	(91)	Marcian (450-457)		Æ 4		WB 1967	C
21.	(30)	Illegible	LR	Æ 3		MT 1960	C

[1] Owing to the stoney nature of the site and the continuous wash of winter rains over it, findspot and stratification evidence for small and light objects must be regarded with considerable reserve.

		Emperor	Date	Denomination	Reference	Findspot	Information
22.	(136)	Illegible	LR	Æ 3		LT 1972	G
23.	(64)	''	LR ?	Æ 3 ?		LT 1972	G
24.	(4)	''	LR	Æ 4		EC 1963	G
25.	(7)	''	LR	Æ 4		EC 1963	G
26.	(8)	''	LR	Æ 4		EC 1963	G
27.	(9)	''	LR	Æ 4		EC 1963	G
28.	(13)	''	LR	Æ 4		EC 1968	G
29.	(15)	''	LR	Æ 4		EC 1967	C
30.	(26)	''	LR	Æ 4		MT 1967	C
31.	(29)	''	LR	Æ 4		EC 1967	C
32.	(31)	''	LR	Æ 4		MT 1970	G
33.	(32)	''	LR	Æ 4		MT 1970	G
34.	(33)	''	LR	Æ 4		SC 1970	G
35.	(40)	''	LR	Æ 4		TSB 1963	G
36.	(41)	''	LR	Æ 4		Bapt 1965	G
37.	(45)	''	LR	Æ 4		TSB 1965	C, G
38.	(51)	''	LR	Æ 4		TSB 1965	C
39.	(56)	''	LR	Æ 4		B 1961	G
40	(63)	''	LR	Æ 4		LT 1972	G
41.	(95)	''	LR	Æ 4		B 1967	C
42.	(96)	''	LR	Æ 4		NA 1965	C, G
43.	(97)	''	LR	Æ 4		NA 1965	C, G
44.	(98)	''	LR	Æ 4		NA 1965	C, G
45.	(120)	''	LR	Æ 4		MT 1967	G
46.	(121)	''	LR	Æ 4		MT 1967	G
47.	(130)	''	LR	Æ 4		Bapt 1970	G

		EMPEROR	DATE	DENOMINATION	REFERENCE	FINDSPOT	INFORMATION
48.	(133)	Illegible	LR	Æ 4		Bapt 1965	C
49.	(134)	"	LR	Æ 4		TSB 1965	G
50.	(18)	"	LR ?	Æ 4 ?		MT 1965	G
51	(27)	"	LR ?	Æ 4 ?		MT 1967	G
52.	(42)	"	LR ?	Æ 4 ?		TSB 1965	C, G
53.	(43)	"	LR ?	Æ 4 ?		TSB 1965	C, G
54.	(44)	"	LR ?	Æ 4 ?		TSB 1965	C, G
55.	(49)	"	LR ?	Æ 4 ?		TSB 1965	C, G
56.	(53)	"	LR ?	Æ 4 ?		TSB 1965	C, G
57.	(77)	"	LR ?	Æ 4 ?		LT 1972	G
58.	(78)	"	LR ?	Æ 4 ?		LT 1972	G
59.	(79)	"	LR ?	Æ 4 ?		LT 1972	G
60.	(80)	"	LR ?	Æ 4 ?		LT 1972	G
61.	(87)	"	LR ?	Æ 4 ?		MT 1965	C
62.	(93)	"	LR ?	Æ 4 ?		MT 1967	C
63.	(94)	"	LR ?	Æ 4 ?		Bapt 1972	C
64.	(129)	"	LR ?	Æ 4 ?		EC 1967	G
65.	(132)	"	LR ?	Æ 4 ?		Bapt 1965	C
66.	(65)	"	LR	Æ		LT 1972	G
67.	(88)	"		Æ		B 1962	G
68.	(112)	"		Æ		MT 1970	C
69.	(123)	"		Æ		MT 1967	G
70.	(124)	"		Æ		B 1967	G
71.	(125)	"		Æ		B 1967	G
72.	(126)	"		Æ		MT 1967	G
73.	(127)	"		Æ		B 1967	G

		Emperor	Date	Denomination	Reference	Findspot	Information
74.	(128)	Illegible		Æ		NA 1967	G
75.	(50)	Anastasius I (491-518)	491-518	Æ 4	*LRBC* 2: 2288?	TSB 1965	C, G
76.	(68)	"	498-518	Follis	*DOC* 1: 23i	LT 1972	C
77.	(69)	"	498-518	Follis	*DOC* 1: 23j	LT 1972	C
78.	(70)	"	498-518	Follis	*DOC* 1: 23b, 2-10	LT 1972	C
79.	(71)	"	498-518	Follis	*DOC* 1: 23i	LT 1972	C
80.	(50)	"	498-518	Half follis (small)	*DOC* 1: 18	TSB 1965	C
81.	(3)	Justin I (518-527)	518-527	Follis	*DOC* 1: 8d	EC 1963	G
82.	(76)	"	518-527	Follis	*DOC* 1: 10	LT 1972	C, G
83.	(16)	"	518-527	Half follis	*DOC* 1: 34b	MT 1963	G
84.	(72)	Justinian I (527-565)	527-538	Follis	*DOC* 1: 28d, 1-3	LT 1972	C, G
85.	(73)	"	527-538	Follis	*DOC* 1: 28	LT 1972	C, G
86.	(74)	"	527-538	Follis	*DOC* 1: 30	LT 1972	C, G
87.	(75)	"	527-538	Follis	*DOC* 1: 28	LT 1972	C, G
88.	(76)	"	527-538	Follis	*DOC* 1: 28a	LT 1965	C
89.	(36)	"	546/547	Follis	*DOC* 1: 217a	TSB 1963	G
90.	(46)	"	547/548	Follis	*DOC* 1: 46b	TSB 1965	C
91.	(66)	"	541/542	Follis	*DOC* 1: 120a	LT 1967	C
92.	(54)	"	537/539	Half follis	*DOC* 1: 214	TSB 1970	C
93.	(14)	"?		Half follis		EC 1967	C, G
94.	(12)	Justin II (565-578)	568/569	Follis	*DOC* 1: 25e	EC 1968	C
95.	(35)	"	574/575	Follis	*DOC* 1: 157	TSB 1963	G
96.	(57)	"	574/575	Follis	*DOC* 1: 38	B 1962	G
97.	(62)	"	569/570	Follis	*DOC* 1: 26d	LT 1972	G
98.	(5)	"	570-574	Half follis	*DOC* 1: 49d or 51c or 55	EC 1963	G

		EMPEROR	DATE	DENOMINATION	REFERENCE	FINDSPOT	INFORMATION
99.	(20)	Justin II (565-578)	572/573	Half follis	DOC 1: 110.I	MT 1965	C
100.	(22)		573/574	Half follis	DOC 1: 111	MT 1967	C
101.	(39)	"	565-577	Half follis	DOC 1: 44-58	TSB 1963	G
102.	(47)	Tiberius II (578-582)	579/580	Follis	DOC 1: 12c	TSB 1965	C
103.	(58)	Maurice (582-602)	586/587	Half follis	DOC 1: 178	B 1970	C
104.	(86)	Constans II (641-668)	655/656	Follis	DOC 2.2: 75d	WB 1965	C, G
105.	(61)		ca. 1030/ 1035-1042	Anonymous follis	DOC 3.2: Class B	LT 1972	C
106.	(23)	Illegible		Half follis		MT 1967	C
107.	(28)	"		Half follis		MT 1967	C
108.	(117)	"		Pentanummion		MT 1970	C
109.	(60)	(Islamic)	1410	AR		LT 1972	C, G
110.	(85)	(Ottoman)	1730-1754	AR		MT 1968	C, G
111.	(55)	(Islamic)		Æ		B 1961	G
112.	(99)	(Islamic)		Æ		NA 1965	C
113.	(100)	(Islamic)		Æ		NA 1965	C

B. THE SMALL FINDS

This list comprises most of the small objects found at Alahan that can be said to have any intrinsic value or an identifiable use.[2]

D	diameter	L	length
FS	findspot	W	width
H	height		

1 Bronze pectoral cross with incised and moulded decoration. H: 9.5 cm; W: 5.6 cm. FS: Basilica, north aisle immediately west of door into pastophory, level 4 (1962). Figure 11.1.

2 Steatite pectoral cross with incised decoration. H: 2.9 cm; W: 2 cm. FS: Immediately northeast of Baptistery apse in connection with a burial (1962). Figure 11.2.

---

[2] See above, (The Coin List), p. 64, n. 1.

3   Bronze pectoral cross with impressed decoration of circles. H: 5.2 cm; W: 3.5 cm. FS: immediately east of Baptistery narthex in connection with a burial (1963). Figure 11.3.

4   Bronze button. D: 1 cm; shank to top surface H: 0.9 cm. FS: Collonaded Walk about 5 m west of Shrine, level 1 (1965). Figure 11.4.

5   Bronze buckle. H: 2 cm; W: 3.4 cm. FS: Lower Terrace south of south pastophory of Basilica, topsoil (1972). Figure 11.5.

6   Silver object, possibly part of a buckle. W: 2.7 cm. FS: Two-Storey Building, northwest of corner of room h, level 2 (1965). Figure 11.6.

7   Copper pendant ear-ring in three sections: wire ring to pierce the ear suspending a tapering cylindrical tube ending in a dark brown glass bead. Total H: 6 cm. FS: Lower Terrace south of south pastophory of Basilica, level 1 (1972). Figure 11.7.

8   Oval amethyst ring stone with Pegasus in intaglio. H 1.1 cm; W: 0.9 cm. FS: floor of Baptistry west of font (1963). Figure 11.8.

9   Bronze decorated ring, possibly lower member of an ear-ring. H: 3.7 cm; W: 4 cm. FS Two-Storey Building, east end of room h, topsoil (1965). Figure 11.9.

10 Copper wick holders for glass lamps of the type used in a polykandelon. These were found, whole and in fragments, in some quantity at various places on the site. FS: (a) Lower Terrace south of Basilica, level 1 (1972); (b) Colonnaded Walk adjacent to Shrine, topsoil (1967); (c) Spring Complex, chamber G, level 1 (1967). Figure 12.10.

11 Nails and tacks found in quantity in all areas of the site. The nails vary between 7 cm and 13 cm in length, the tacks between 3 cm and 4 cm in length. FS: All areas and periods of excavation. Figure 12.11.

12 Iron object, possible a "steel" (as in flint and steel) used for striking a light. H: 3 cm; L: 7.4 cm. FS: Two-Storey Building, room b, topsoil (1965). Figure 12.12.

13 Bronze spade-shaped object, use unknown. L (without "handle"): 5.8 cm; greatest W: 4 cm. FS: Lower Terrace, drainage channel south of south pastophory of Basilica (1972). Figure 12.13.

14 Bronze spatula with four ringed grooves at base of "spoon." L: 15 cm; W of "spoon": 1.5 cm. FS: Lower Terrace south of Two-Storey Building, room h, on the north side of the east-west wall, level 3 (1972). Figure 12.14.

15 Iron knife blade. L: 16 cm; greatest W: 1.3 cm. FS: Spring Complex, passage B, level 2 (1967). Figure 12.15.

16   Iron knife blade. L: 8 cm; greatest W: 1.4 cm. FS: Two-Storey Building, room d, level 4 (1965). Figure 12.16.

17   Part of a bronze lampstand with fluted and balustraded stem. H of fragment: 30.5 cm. FS: Spring Complex, passage B, level 2 (1970). Figure 12.17.
Cf. Marvin C. Ross, *Catalogue of Byzantine and Early Mediaeval Antiquities in the Dumbarton Oaks Collection* (Washington, D.C., 1962), vol. 1, n° 33, Pl. 27.

18   Assemblage of fragments of iron objects. Their use is unknown but **18a** and **18b** in particular bear a resemblance to the star or asterisk which, in the Byzantine rite, was placed on the paten to protect the Host from the veil that covers it. A complete example is shown in Ross, *Byzantine and Early Mediaeval Antiquities*, vol. 1, n° 89, Pl. 49. The Dumbarton Oaks asterisk is made of copper, however, and dated to the eleventh century. It is not known whether such an object would have been in use as early as the fifth or sixth century and it is doubtful whether iron would ever have been used in such a sacred context.

18a   Iron object. L between extremities of bar: approx. 7 cm. FS: Lower Terrace, drainage channel south of south pastophory of Basilica, topsoil 1 (1972). Figure 13.18a.

18b   Iron object. L between extremities of bar: approx. 10 cm. FS: Lower Terrace, drainage channel south of south pastophory of Basilica, level 1 (1972). Figure 13.18b.

18c   Iron object. L of fragment: 3 cm. FS: Two-Storey Building, room h, east end (1965). Figure 13.18c.

18d   Iron object. L of fragment: 2.5 cm. FS: Colonnaded Walk about 10 m west of Shrine, level 1 (1965). Figure 13.18d.

18e   Iron object. L of fragment: 5 cm. FS: Lower Terrace, south of southeast corner of Basilica, level 1 (1972). Figure 13.18e.

18f   Iron object. L between extremities of bar: approx. 10 cm. FS: Lower Terrace, east of Shrine, topsoil (1967). Figure 13.18f.

19   Bronze hook and link assembly, upper member broken. H: approx. 12.5 cm. FS: immediately east of east facade of Baptistery, level 1 (1965). Figure 13.19.

20   Bronze hinge. L: 9 cm. FS: Two-Storey Building, room c, topsoil (1963). Figure 13.20.

21   Iron buckle. H: 2.4 cm; W: 2.5 cm. FS: Forecourt of Cave Complex and Basilica, topsoil (1967). Figure 13.21.

22   Twisted bronze bar with two small medial and terminal blocks etched with lozenge pattern on four sides; other end terminating in a ring. Possibly a spindle. L: 15 cm. FS: Lower Terrace south of southeast corner of Basilica, level 1 (1972). Figure 13.22.

23 Bronze tweezers. L: 6 cm. FS: Colonnaded Walk about 5 m west of Shrine, level 2 (1965). Figure 13.23.

24 Assemblage of small crosses:

24a Fragment of small pottery cross with impressed and painted circle decoration. W of fragment: 42 cm. FS: south of East Church, topsoil (1967). Figure 13.24a.

24b Fragment of limestone cross. W of fragment: 23 cm. FS: south of East Church, topsoil (1967). Figure 13.24b.

24c Small calcite cross, carved and pierced for suspension. H: 2.3 cm. FS: northwest of Baptistery in connection with a burial, topsoil (1965). Figure 13.24c.

24d Fragment of limestone cross. H of fragment: 5 cm; W: 4 cm. FS: south of East Church, topsoil (1967). Figure 13.24d.

25 Assemblage of finger rings:

25a Ring of thin copper with exterior grooving. D: 1.9 cm. FS: Lower Terrace, south of south pastophory of Basilica, level 1 (1972). Figure 13.25a.

25b Plain bronze ring. D: 1.7 cm. FS: Lower Terrace, drainage channel below Two-Storey Building, topsoil (1965). Figure 13.25b.

25c Small bronze ring made of copper wire with elaborately knotted ends forming a decoration. D: 1.45 cm. FS: Lower Terrace south of south pastophory of Basilica, level 1 (1972). Figure 13.25c.

25d Bronze ring with green glass ringstone contained in cylindrical bronze casing. D: 2 cm. FS: Lower Terrace south of East Church, topsoil (1967). Figure 13.25d.

25e Plain bronze ring. D: 1.9 cm. FS: Two-Storey Building, room h, level 1 (1965). Figure 13.25e.

25f Plain bronze ring. D: 1.7 cm. FS: Lower Terrace, drainage channel south of Basilica, topsoil (1972). Figure 13.25f.

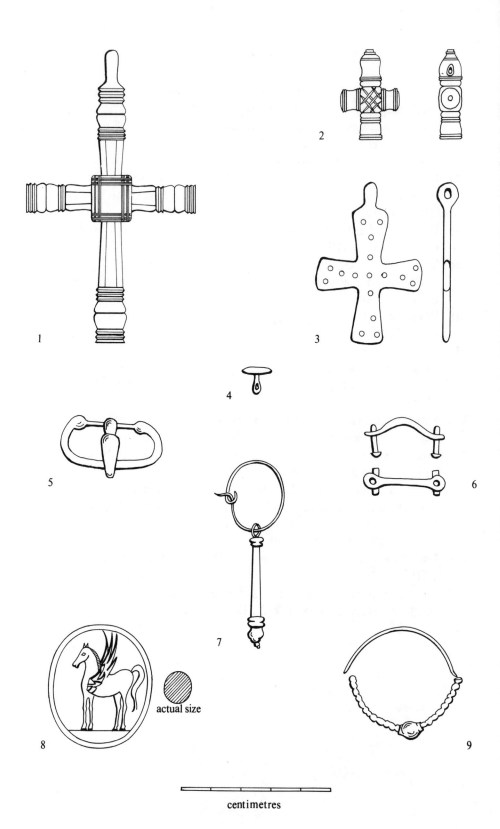

actual size

centimetres

FIGURE 11. – Small Finds

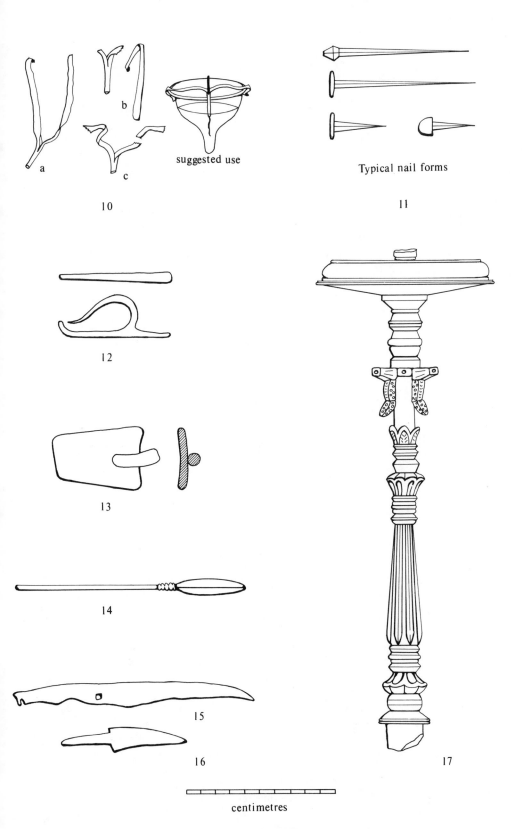

suggested use

10

Typical nail forms

11

12

13

14

15

16

17

centimetres

FIGURE 12. – Small Finds

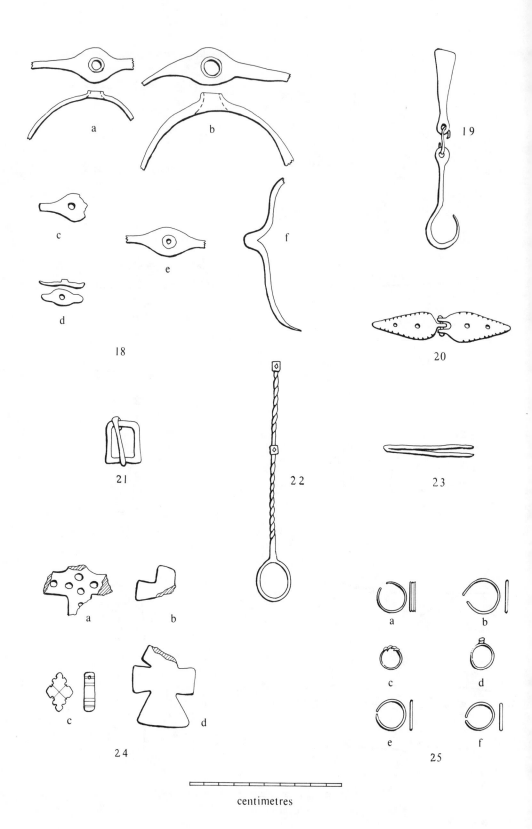

centimetres

FIGURE 13. – Small Finds

5

The Buildings at Alahan

Gerard Bakker

This chapter is devoted to the record of the monastery and the history of its development in so far as it can be ascertained from the architectural evidence. Michael Gough had invited me to contribute a technical account of the buildings, their layout and fabric, whilst he had intended to describe and discuss their embellishment. I have now extended the scope of this chapter to include an account of their decoration in a purely factual manner, relying on photographs and drawings to portray the aesthetic qualities. I have purposely neither attempted any comparative analysis of the architecture, nor have I made any iconographic and stylistic comment as these would be outside my province. Nevertheless, I have where appropriate turned to the excavator's publications for descriptions and comments to make good this deficiency.

The monastery is not contained within one distinct building, but is a complex which evolved from a group of rock cut cells. The buildings each have their own individual merits giving each a special importance, also the site has a geographical progression. There are thus a number of choices for the order in which to describe the buildings. I have decided on the general order in which I believe the monastery evolved. In this way I hope much of the evidence of the history will be made plain as each building is described. During the excavation of the Basilica (the first building to be excavated) it became clear that there had been two distinctly separate periods of occupation and that it was during the primary period that the quality of life reached its zenith. This account is therefore focussed on the primary period. The buildings as they were inhabited during the secondary period are described separately at the end of this chapter.

A. The Cave Complex

At the western end of the site there is a large limestone outcrop. The main feature is a large, possibly naturally formed, cave some 10 m high, 16 m wide and 9 m deep. To the west of the main cave the rock outcrop extends to the southwest and narrows into a spur into which has been cut a group of smaller interconnecting chambers. It is believed that the monastic settlement of Alahan was founded within this rock outcrop.

The main cave was enclosed by a 0.6 m thick masonry wall. Part of this wall remains at the east end where it joins the Basilica narthex and at its west end its location is suggested by the shaping of the bedrock. The line of the enclosing wall can also be seen by the abrupt and consistent termination of the paving of the forecourt. Although the rock face at the outer edge of the cave roof has decayed there are still signs of a cut water channel and below this a row of beam sockets shows that the gap between the enclosing wall and the bedrock was roofed. Inside, the cave soffit was slightly arched and was tooled to a moderately smooth surface. Although the main cave now appears as a large void, it clearly contained a number of rooms arranged on three floors. At ground level the bedrock appears to have been cut away with only some parts in the centre being retained and incorporated into dividing walls (Fig. 15, Pl. 6). Two tiers of beam holes in the walls show that the cave had three storeys each just over 2 m high. A central corridor leads in from the outer wall of the cave to divide the ground floor into two parts. Only the southern end of the corridor has been exposed, but its alignment is suggested by a recess cut into the rear wall. Access to the upper storeys would have been needed and, although not found, it was probably situated towards the back of the cave. The most important rooms are two churches built against the outer wall, one at ground level rising through two floors and the other, much smaller, above it on the top storey.

At ground level at the south end of the corridor a narrow doorway opens on to two shallow steps leading down into a west room (5 m long by 3.5 m wide) built against the outer wall of the cave. Its western extremity can be seen by the shaping of the rock where it forms a junction with the outer masonry wall, and its inner wall can be seen where its lower part was cut from the bedrock floor. A large opening in this wall gives access to a room beyond which may originally have been part of the same space, daylight thus being able to penetrate deep into the cave. The floor is bedrock and does not appear to have been covered. The complete absence of evidence makes it impossible to suggest a use, but by its size and location near the entrance, and with the possibility of windows, it was likely to have been a room of some importance. Deeper into the cave a recess cut into the west wall directly opposite the north wall of the north aisle of the church suggests that there was a third inner wall across the cave.

To the east of the passage excavation revealed a twin-aisled church, of which only the lower level of the walls, the rock floor and a stylobate survive. The church is 7.5 m wide and 7.7 m long and is divided into two aisles. Although the aisles have differently shaped apses, it is clear that they were intended to form part of the one church, as between the aisles there is a stylobate which once supported an arcade. The stylobate is laid on a bedrock plinth and is shaped on both sides to a plain undecorated ogee profile. The east wall of the cave has been cut to form a seating for an arch 2.2 m above the top of the stylobate. The curvature of the seating and the presence of three plain double arch springs, voussoirs and a single column base (all recovered from a wall built during the secondary period of occupation), suggests a colonnade of four spans. No traces remain of the respond at the west end of the arcade, but it is likely to have taken the form of a pier built into the wall of the central corridor.

The two aisles are each entered separately from the central corridor. The south aisle is entered through a narrow door to the north of its axis. The aisle is 3.8 m wide and 4.7 m long. At the east end there is a raised bema with an apsidal end. The floor is generally flat and has a series of grooves cut into the rock, possibly for drainage or to hold joists for a raised floor. At the east end, the stylobate, separating the aisles, is turned southwards across the front of the bema and has a groove to locate a cancellus screen. The bema is reached by two steps in the centre of the stylobate. To either side of the stair the ogee moulding of the stylobate block is turned outwards to make a vertical corner at its junction to the lower step. The apse is partly cut from the cave wall and partly built of masonry. The triumphal arch was constructed to spring from the cave wall on the south. Its position is shown by the change in alignment of the cave wall and the thickening of the south masonry wall at the transition from the aisle to the apse. Traces of painted plaster on the apse wall at floor level show a single red band on a white background following the line of the floor. The floor of the bema is paved with flagstones set slightly below the level of the top step. In the centre there is a rectangular altar base recessed at each corner for the posts to support the altar. The base is flat and its front face is decorated with a shallow moulding surrounding a cross. The top surface is similarly decorated with a large cross enclosed in a roundel at the centre of which is a circular recess possibly intended to house a reliquary.

The north aisle, again entered from the central corridor, is 3 m wide and 4.8 m long. The floor is bedrock and a low plinth has been cut across its eastern end indicating a bema beyond. The north wall of the aisle is built of masonry on which traces of plaster can still be seen. The block was found to have traces of a painted cross and part of an inscription (see Inscription 7, p. 26). As in the south aisle, the east end of the stylobate is moulded with the intention of crossing the aisle but here no blocks were found *in situ*. However, stylobate blocks were found in the secondary period walling and they may have been used here. The aisle terminates in a rectangular recess with an arched soffit cut into the cave wall. In the northeast corner of the recess there is a round cistern formed in the floor and above, in the side wall, there is a small rectangular niche cut with slots for shelving. The cistern was found partially covered by a triangular slab. It is uncertain from what period this originates and whether it is in the correct place. A shallow grave had been cut into the floor. The grave is precisely cut and has a recess around its top edges to locate a lid that would have been set flush with the floor. The skill with which it was cut compared with a rudimentary wall burial found in the secondary walling nearby suggests that it dates from the primary period.

The ground floor of the cave (Fig. 14, 15) thus contained a central corridor with the principal rooms being the twin-aisled church to the east and large rooms to the west. Between the church and the rear of the cave is space for a further small room. The support for the upper floors would have been provided by the cross walls of the west rooms and the church. Beam holes in the back wall of the cave show that joists spanned in a north-south direction over the large rooms, and it is reasonable to assume that the corridor was spanned across its width. It is also likely that the main walls continued up at least to the second storey (Fig. 16) and, on this assumption, the second storey may have comprised a series of rooms on the western side with most of the east part being taken up by the upper part of the two-storeyed twin-aisled church.

The arrangement of the top storey is shown by the shaping of the rock soffit of the cave (Fig. 17). The fine tooling of the rock suggests that the soffit was moulded to suit individual rooms to a layout similar to that of the lower two storeys. Over the western part the soffit is cut in the form of a shallow vault presumably over a single room extending to the full depth of the cave. Above the south aisle of the twin-aisled church, the cave wall has been cut to form part of a second but smaller twin-aisled church. The northern aisle terminates in a small arched recess and the southern aisle in an apse, part of which can be seen cut out of the rock. Here the rock face still retains traces of painted plaster but although almost obliterated by smoke from fires lit in the cave, a cross can still be seen, and in another area flaking soot reveals a figurative painting of blue and white brush-strokes applied over a deep red background. Between the church and the rear wall of the cave is a further room, presumably entered from the large west room. At the back of the cave, there is a smaller, roughly hewn chamber which may have contained a spring as the rock still bears signs of solution holes and could have served as a water cistern and, being cool, a food store.

At the west side of the main room of the top storey an opening leads to the middle level of a complex of inter-connecting smaller cells. This group of cells is linked by narrow passages and stairways with the chambers arranged on three levels. Of these the largest has a narrow passage leading in the direction of the west outer wall where there is a vertical shaft dropping to a very rough low cave at the present ground level. The outside face of this cave has possibly fallen away. This part of the outcrop could have been waterbearing as the surface is perforated by solution holes, and the presence of the vertical shaft could suggest that this cave, once totally enclosed, may have served as a cistern. To the southwest there are more cells and the exposed south east face of the spur reveals stairways leading to upper chambers or the open air above. At ground level there appears to have been a large single room adjoining the west room of the main cave. Beam holes in the rock face show that the southern enclosing wall to the main cave continued almost to the extreme southwest end of the spur. The surfaces of the caves and passages have been eroded through weathering, but traces of a straw-reinforced plaster base-coat remaining in the passage to the cistern show that these interior surfaces were originally plastered.

To the east of the Cave Complex (Fig. 14, 18) is sited the Basilica built tight against the rock cliff with part of the structure of its narthex obstructed by the south enclosing wall of the twin-aisled church. The relationship between the Cave Complex and the Basilica is seen as the key to establishing the next stage in the growth of the community. Michael Gough observes in the Fourth Preliminary Report:

> This cave-church must have existed before the Basilica, had it not, the latter's architects need have had no compunction in cutting away the rock to allow the western wall of the narthex to stretch its full extent northwards, instead of stopping short, as they did, at the southern apse of the smaller building. There is nothing at all to suggest either that an interval of time elapsed between the completion of the Basilica and the addition of the narthex, during which hypothetical period the cave-church would have been built. All evidence points to the fact that the Basilica was planned with

a narthex from the first. This being the case, the newly excavated building
in its primary phase probably represents the earliest place of worship on the
site, a likelihood that is enhanced by the existence of the complex of cells
that honeycombs the cliff immediately to the west of the cave. Here, close
to their church, would have settled the first monks of Alahan. There is little
doubt that the southern aisle was used for the celebration of Mass; the
northern could well have been intended for the withdrawal of Catechumens at the beginning of the Canon, and the presence of a water tank (?) in
its eastern recess suggests that baptisms might have been performed there.[1]

B. The Addition of the Basilica

In front of the Cave Complex a Forecourt extends southwards for
approximately 5 m before the ground falls steeply away. The original
boundary of the Forecourt and the approach to the monastery at this point
is no longer recognisable. Excavations took place to the south of the
Basilica in the hope of finding an approach from the east by way of a
gradually sloping ramp or steps along the line of the retaining wall.
Instead, they revealed a Lower Terrace containing abutment walls and
quarrying. The approach must therefore have been by a direct ascent of
the steep slope from the south or west. Nevertheless, what was probably
originally merely a levelling of the hillside became a Forecourt of some
importance, as it was paved. The addition of the Basilica to the east of the
Forecourt marks the transition from a small community centred on the
Cave Complex to a more established and better endowed one requiring
more splendid and sophisticated surroundings (Fig. 19).

The Basilica is 36 m long and 16 m wide and has three aisles. In order
to accommodate the building on the ledge, it was necessary to cut back the
cliff to form a sheer face for its north wall and to build retaining walls to
support its south wall (Fig. 71). The orientation of the rock cliff has caused
the main axis of the church to be well north of east. There is also a
tapering of the south aisle from 3.8 m at its western end to 3 m at the
east end, and a slight inclination of 3° to the cross-walls to the apse
and pastophories. These inconsistencies with a plan that is normally
orthogonal are probably due to faults or weak seams in the bedrock which
prevented its true orientation.

The entry to the narthex of the Basilica was through an arched portal
with trabeated openings to either side. From the narthex three doorways
lead to the nave and aisles which were separated by arcades of ten

[1] M. Gough, "Alahan Monastery, Fourth Preliminary Report," *Anatolian Studies,* 17
(1967), p. 45.

Corinthian columns with similar arcades above supporting the solid wall of the clerestory. The north aisle is built against the cliff and the south aisle, facing outwards, had large rectangular windows in its south wall to light the interior. To either side of the bema are pastophories. There was an upper floor over the narthex, aisles and pastophories, with access from a rock chamber at the western end of the north aisle. Today, the apse and pastophories remain to a height of about 3.5 m with the south wall of the southern pastophory rising even higher to 6.7 m (Fig. 20). Elsewhere, except for the doors from the narthex, only the lower parts of the south wall and stylobate to the nave arcading remain standing above floor level. However, sufficient masonry was found, mostly incorporated in secondary period interior walling and also on the surrounding terrace, to permit a reconstruction of the Basilica to be attempted.

Only sufficient rock was cut from the cliff to make way for the north wall and north aisle, and only a small amount of quarrying took place below the south wall to provide building stone. There are quarries to the west of the site but the rugged terrain would have made the movement of large blocks difficult and therefore they were used sparingly, only where necessary for underbuilding, architraves, lintels, columns and other main elements requiring decoration. Thus the outside walls are built of large ashlar blocks up to floor level (Fig. 20) with the large areas of blank walling above being built with smaller stones (0.20 m × 0.30 m), set two deep across the wall and embedded in mortar with the joints and outer faces of the blocks finished smooth.

The windows in the south and east walls are framed with large blocks decorated to the outside (Pl. 7) with a combination of raised flat and flush bead mouldings to outline the opening, sometimes using a single block for the entire jamb. The reveals are checked and have pivots for a door or window to open inwards. At ground floor level these windows are 2.1 m high by 1.3 m wide (Fig. 19, 20). Similar but smaller architrave blocks were found on the ground below the south aisle and were presumably used for windows to an upper gallery. These have flat slots cut into the outside edge of the reveal to hold a metal grille made of flat strips. On the inside there are pivots for inward opening shutters. From the number of architrave blocks found, it is likely that there were at least four of these large windows; two on each level. Much smaller, but similarly framed windows 0.80 m high by 0.55 m wide are used to light the south pastophories. The lintels are divided with the outer lintel set flush with the outside face of the wall, and relieved by semi-circular arches built of small voussoirs projecting slightly from the surface of the wall and infilled with small blocks.

Fallen masonry uncovered at the base of the south facade shows that the head of the south facade was crowned by a frieze and cornice with a combined height of 0.83 m (Fig. 28-30, Pl. 15-18). The frieze blocks are decorated with a continuous band of flowing acanthus enclosing rosettes and capped with a moulding of egg-and-dart. The cornice projects forward and has as its main feature acanthus decorated modillions framed with an ovolo moulding between which are motifs of crossed fish, partridges and, in one instance, a basket carved in full relief constructed of interlocking circles (Fig. 28, 30; Pl. 18). At intervals along its length are large rams' heads protruding into the cyma which is decorated with a progression of acanthus and anthemion motifs. The base of the cornice is defined by a convex moulding of oak leaves flowing from left to right. One cornice stone was found to have the base moulding of oak leaves running in a reverse direction. The cornice and its accompanying frieze may therefore also have capped the west facade; there being no apparent reason for such a change along the south facade.

The excavation of the interior of the Basilica revealed a layer of burnt wood, plaster and roof tiles beneath the covering of scree. In this were found some complete flat tiles together with fragments of ridge tiles. The flat tiles are 0.35 m wide by 0.43 m long and, on average, 0.035 m thick. They have a raised edge along the top and sides with a wedge-shaped thickening at the lower corners, presumably to shed water away from the joint between the tiles. The tiles may have been laid side by side with a slight overlap of the horizontal joint. The flat tiles have smooth undersides and, as there are no nail holes, they must have been fixed by nailing through the tile joints which were weathered by curved ridge tiles. The pitch of the roof is likely to have been 30°, similar to that of the East Church where a line of beam sockets can be seen on the east and west faces of the tower.

The structure and principle dimensions of the Basilica can be established from remains of the arcading and other parts of the building fabric. Its height can be assessed with a reasonable degree of accuracy by calculating the minimum height, arrived at by a summation of all the dimensions of the main components with assumptions of the size of the missing members. The method taken is to reassemble the two tiers of arcading and the clerestory of the nave (Fig. 21). The reconstruction of the south facade and south aisle roof establishes the likely height of the sill of the clerestory window from which the level of the narthex roof can be calculated. A final adjustment to this minimum height of the nave has then to be made to take account of a window located high up on the south wall of the south pastophory.

The column bases of the lower arcade are level with the floor. The arcade has a height of 3.53 m from the floor to the springing of the arches (base 0.47 m, shaft 2.60 m, capital 0.46 m) and the spacing between the columns is 1.40 m giving a radius for the arch of 0.70 m. The voussoir depth is 0.35 m. The upper arcade was based on a string course with a thickness of 0.31 m which in turn is likely to have been laid on a single course of masonry above the lower arcading keystone. If this course of masonry were 0.50 m deep, the distance from the floor to the top of the string course would have been 5.39 m.

The columns and capitals found for the upper arcade are slightly smaller than those of the lower; the bases are similar at 0.47 m, the shaft diameter is 0.43 m as compared with 0.52 m and the capitals are 0.43 m high. No complete shafts remain but an adjustment of the shaft height proportionally with the diameter results in a height of 2.15 m. The springing height of the upper arcade may therefore have been 3.05 m (base 0.47 m, shaft 2.15 m, capital 0.43 m). The intercolumnar spacing of the upper arcade probably coincided with the lower and the voussoirs probably had an identical thickness of 0.35 m. The height of the upper arcade from string course to the top of the arch keystone would thus be 4.10 m, with a total height above floor level for the top of the keystone of 9.49 m – say 9.50 m.

Above the upper arcade the clerestory is likely to have consisted of a solid wall pierced with either double or triple arched windows. As eleven dividers were found it is likely that the nave was lit from both the north and south clerestorys. A number of smaller string course blocks, 0.22 m thick, were found which may have served as sills to the clerestory windows and, as in the East Church, the windows may have been positioned directly above the apex of the aisle roof. The dimensions of the clerestory windows can be determined from the window dividers which have a base of 0.26 m, a shank of 0.90 m and a capital of 0.31 m high, together making the height of the arch spring above the still of 1.47 m. Similar clerestory windows in the East Church have an internal arch diameter of 1.20 m which, with an assumed voussoir depth of 0.30 m, give an overall height from sill to top of the keystone for the Basilica windows of 2.37 m. Above this there was probably at least one course of masonry of 0.50 m high below the roof eaves, producing a minimum dimension from clerestory window sill to eaves of 2.87 m.

To establish the level of the clerestory window sill above floor level the height of the south wall and the slope of the aisle roof have to be taken into consideration. It is certain that there was an upper gallery as the upper arcade bases are grooved to hold intercolumnar screens and there also appears to have been an upper floor over the south pastophories. The gallery probably had its floor level with the underside of the string course. From the number of window architraves found it is reasonable to assume that there were windows to both the ground and gallery levels and, using the smaller architrave type for the upper floor, a window height of 2.11 m is calculated (sill 0.51 m, jamb 1.09 m, lintel 0.51 m). The sills have no sockets for floor joists so they must have stood above floor level. The minimum height of the eaves can be calculated by positioning the frieze and cornice (total 0.83 m) directly above the window lintel. The height from the gallery floor to eaves is thus 2.94 m to which is then added the dimension from floor level to the underside of the string course to the upper arcade of 5.08 m making a total height from floor level to eaves of 8.02 m.

If this minimum height is used, the eaves of the south wall are thus seen to be lower than the upper tier of arcading. This apparent inconsistency can be explained by the fact that the south aisle roof, spanning 3.8 m, is likely to have been constructed using rafters sloping up to the clerestory wall, to a level above the arcading. By projecting the roof of the south aisle up at a slope of 30° its apex would have been 2.7 m higher than the eaves and therefore 10.72 m above the nave floor. The top of the keystone of the upper arcading is 9.50 m above floor level, and the space between the arcading and the aisle roof is likely to have been a solid wall. By adding the height of the clerestory (2.87 m) to the height of the apex of the south aisle roof (10.72 m) the minimum dimension from floor to nave eaves is seen to have been 13.59 m. The roof is likely to have risen at a slope of 30° thus adding a further 2.2 m to the height of the nave and giving a total height of around 15.8 m.

Adjustment now has to be made for the window high up on the south pastophory wall (Fig. 20). The south pastophory is wider than the south aisle and, in order to accommodate this extra width, the south facade turns southwards from the line of the triumphal arch for a distance of 2.0 m and then turns east again as far as its junction with the east face of the church. In the southeast corner the masonry rises to about 6.7 m above floor level. At the top there lies a single block moulded with an ogee profile and similar to the string course, but here instead of being a continuous band it is surrounded by a single course of masonry. This suggests that the plain external wall of the pastophory continued up and that the block may have been the sill for a window lighting the upper floor. Certainly the presence of plain masonry alongside the moulded block cannot be ignored. If this is a sill to an upper level window then the height of the south facade of the pastophory is in doubt and so also is the height of the nave. The sill of the window is about 1.5 m above the gallery floor and the use of the moulded block suggests a small arched opening. The sill is approximately 1 m long, so the height of the window may have been in the region of 1.5 m, allowing 0.20 m for the thickness of the arch voussoirs. Remembering that the level of the gallery floor was assessed at 5.08 m above the nave floor level, and by adding the minimum height of the wall of the upper floor of 3.0 m, the minimum height of the south pastophory could have been 8.08 m, say 8.1 m, almost the same height as that calculated for the south facade to the south aisle. If the roof had sloped up over the south pastophory to meet the aisle roof then the effect of the height of the south facade to the pastophory on the south facade of the south aisle would be to raise it by approximately one metre to 9.02 m, which in turn would raise the height of the apex of the south aisle roof to 11.72 m, and the apex of the nave roof to 16.8 m.

There is an alternative form of structure over the south pastophory that would reconcile the high sill of the window with the first assessment of the height of the building, and that is to raise the walls of the pastophory to meet a roof line projected down from the nave. In this reconstruction the upper storey would have been very high, it would have had an unnecessarily large volume and the resultant shape of the Basilica would also have been very ungainly. This arrangement would have been certainly less attractive in appearance.

Another key dimension needed in order to develop a picture of the building is the height of the apse and the triumphal arch (see Fig. 22). The lead here is given by the apse window which is still *in situ* with its sill 4 m above the level of the nave floor. The window consists of an opening with a central divider having a 1.2 m span on either side; it was presumably arched. It is not clear whether the divider stands to its full height, so the height of the spring of the window arches is assumed at 1.8 m, which results in an opening height of 2.4 m. If the semi-dome of the apse started directly above the window, as in the East Church, rather than at the spring point of the window arch, as in the Baptistery, then allowance must be made for the window voussoirs, say 0.35 m and an assumed string course, of which no curved blocks were found, of about 0.30 m. A height to the springing of the apse semi-dome could then have been about 7.05 m, say 7 m, above the nave floor. The width of the apse is 6.0 m, so the overall height of the apse could have been in the region of 10.0 m, leaving a wall above the triumphal arch rising 5.2 m to the eaves of the nave roof, and 7.01 m to its apex. The height of the arch so calculated is at the lower limit of its possible height.

The string course of the apse (7.0 m) would then lie between the level of the string course of the upper arcade (5.39 m) and the clerestory (11.72 m).

The narthex and west facade now need to be described to complete the reconstruction of the main components of the building. The Basilica was entered from the forecourt through the narthex (Pl. 1). Only part of the narthex structure, the bases of the pilaster complexes and one column remains *in situ*. Nevertheless a reconstruction is still possible on account of evidence from fallen masonry found nearby and from photographs of the south west corner of the south aisle that was standing until 1955. The narthex covered the west face of the Basilica, and was joined to the outer wall of the Cave Complex Church.

The substructure of the narthex was, like the south facade of the Basilica, built of large ashlar blocks, at least up to floor level as the lower courses remain exposed above ground at the south west corner. Intermediate support was given to the west facade of the narthex by the two piers aligned with the arcading of the nave which were presumably connected to the main structure by arches. The south end of the narthex finished in a pier joined at high level to the south facade of the Basilica by an arch, the springing of which can be seen on photographs of the southwest corner of the south aisle.

The main entrance to the narthex (Fig. 24) was through its west facade and took the form of a central arched opening with a span of 2.5 m, supported on two free-standing columns. On either side were trabeated openings spanning on to the solid masonry of the facade. The voussoirs of the arch and the lintels of the side openings are decorated on both sides with motifs flowing from the arch to the lintels as one element (Fig. 27). The more ornate side is decorated with a line of bead and reel at the base, above which is a broad band of flowing vine leaves capped by a narrow band of ovolo. Motifs of lotus and anthemion are superimposed on the cyma and the outer vertical face is left plain. The reverse is more plainly carved with a line of bead and reel followed by a broad, shallowly carved band of semicircular egg and dart finished with a narrow line of ovolo. On this side both the cyma and outer edge are left plain. The undersides of the voussoirs are undecorated, but those of the lintels of the side entrances are each decorated with a panel of bay leave garland surrounding a rosette at their centre. The two lintel blocks which were found had fallen outwards, and from their positions and the position of the arch spring it can be seen that the more ornate side lying downwards faced the forecourt.

A second group of blocks, three voussoirs and two straight frieze blocks was found (Fig. 27, Pl. 12). The blocks were decorated on one side only with the reverse side left roughly hewn. Their decoration matches the plainer decoration of the central arched opening and side lintels. The voussoirs have a span approximating to that to be expected in the arches between the piers across the narthex between the west facade and the west wall of the church. The length of the frieze blocks coincides with the space between these arches and jambs of the main door of the Basilica. Although the arrangement is not known for certain, the continuation of the decoration from the inside of the west facade of the narthex over the two cross-arches to merge into the main door of the Basilica is a very attractive possibility and would have been suitable for the main entry leading to the "Evangelists" Door, which, by its iconographical features, must surely have been the focal point of the western end of the building.

The Evangelists' Door (Pl. 19-22) is 3.6 m high and 2.1 m wide. The lintel was crowned by a cornice supported on a pair of consoles, one either side of the lintel block. The jambs and lintel still stand and, although exposed above the ground for many hundreds of years, weathering has been relatively slight and damage to the sculpture is confined mainly to the heads of the human figures. As Michael Gough has described the carving and its iconographical significance in his two Preliminary Reports it would be appropriate here to extract from his descriptions.

> Only the eastern side of the door is left plain; every other surface is richly carved with relief sculpture of a high quality .... On the underside of the lintel block is a composition of which the centre piece is a tetramorph of the four beasts of Ezekiel's vision, while the inner side of each doorpost carries the full-length figure of an archangel, Gabriel to the north and Michael to the south. In the centre of the western face of the lintel block is a medallion, enclosing the head of Christ with supporting seraphim to either side. At each end of the lintel, where it rests on the jambs, is a human bust, repeated about 0.60 m lower down on each of the doorposts which are otherwise decorated with degenerate "Classical" mouldings treated in the coloristic manner of the East ....

> The composition of the underside of the lintel block [Pl. 20] is a masterpiece of religious art, in which the mystical quality of the Apocalyptic vision is admirably expressed; indeed it may be doubted whether this essentially Oriental subject has ever been treated in a way more completely acceptable to a Western mind. In the figure of the angel which centralizes the composition, of the watchful lion, of the ponderous ox, of the flying eagle which covers the junction of the other three, is a solid foundation which emphasizes to the full the fine sweep of the wings to which the viewer's attention is irresistibly drawn. The effect is of immense power sustained by a transcendental inner life. The rest of the composition, though necessarily subordinate, enhances the strength of the great central

theme by its very subordination. On either side of the tetramorph is a tree, perhaps those trees that stand on either side of "the pure river of the water of life," and outside each tree is a human figure dressed in a pallium.

This relief contains all the ingredients to be found in the developed Byzantine art of the age of Justinian. The Hellenistic tradition is apparent in the plastic treatment of the figures, at the same time Syrian inspiration stands behind the sculptor's greater emphasis on the underlying idea than on the forms through which that idea was expressed, while the formal element of the East proper is represented in the coloristic treatment of contrasting areas of light and dark, of the heavily shadowed wings as opposed to the lighter surfaces of the two larger beasts. It is precisely because all these elements are so distinct that an early date appears likely, a date before the fusion of the three traditions that, in Constantinople at least, was the hallmark of the First Golden Age of Byzantine art.

The four beasts were recognized as the symbols of the four Evangelists very early in the history of the Church, and are found frequently in the iconographical repertoire of the West. The first known examples occur in the apse mosaic of Santa Pudenziana in Rome (Fourth Century), and they are found again in the mosaic decorating the Mausoleum of Galla Placidia in Ravenna (ca. 440). The tetramorph arrangement is, however, unknown in the West and the beasts are represented as complete figures or as separate *protomai*. In the Christian East they appear later, and it is an interesting fact that in the miniature of the Ascension in the Rabula Gospels (dated precisely to the year 586) they are arranged as a tetramorph. There is no earlier example known in the Orient, and even later the symbols were never in common use. There is indeed a fresco of a tetramorph in the church of St. Barbara in a valley leading out of the Soğandere in Cappadocia, but it is dated comparatively late, between 976 and 1028.

The reliefs of ss. Michael and Gabriel on the inner surfaces of the doorposts are less spectacular than the tetramorph and, owing to their relatively exposed position, are more weathered. They are, however, noteworthy both technically and iconographically. The better preserved of the two is St. Michael who, like his companion, is represented frontally, standing at full length below a scalloped niche [Pl. 22]. He is dressed in a short military tunic of which only the lower part carries incised details. The upper part of the figure is (apart from what appears to be a semicircle of medallions on his chest), like the wings, devoid of detail. In his right hand he holds an orb, while his left grasps a rod held obliquely across the body. At first glance there is a superficial resemblance in pose and attributes to the ivory of St. Michael in the British Museum, now usually dated to the Sixth Century. The Alahan archangels, however, lack the finesse of the ivory and represent a school in which the Hellenistic tradition of naturalism was fast losing ground to impulses from Syria and lands farther to the east. Indeed, the sculptor in cutting the figures sharply from their backgrounds, so that they almost resemble silhouettes, displays far less interest in modelling than he did in the case of the tetramorph, and his conception of the form here seems confined to two dimensions. The details on the wings of St. Michael and on the upper part of his body may have been rendered in paint. It is also interesting, as denoting the sculptor's indifference to the correspondence of the figure with its architectural background, that while the archangel's head is directly below the niche, the feet appear to be nearer to the spectator and on a different plane.

It is the niche, with its utter disregard of spatial illusionism, which most suggests the influence of the East. The two acanthus capitals are suspended in space with no supporting columns below them. As capitals they are remarkably unsubstantial, and the acanthus leaves, of which they are composed, are treated solely as stylised ornament with barely a reminiscence of the vegetable forms from which they are ultimately derived. Above each shoulder of the niche is a small bird of the partridge type facing inwards.

The reliefs on the western side of the door are perhaps less striking than those so far described; they are no less interesting, for once again the three elements characteristic of developed Byzantine art are all present and readily distinguishable. The place of honour in the centre of the lintel block is taken by the head of a bearded Christ included in a circular frame and supported by two six-winged angels [Pl. 19]. It is an arrangement which, as Headlam noted, recalls the winged sun-disc, the symbol of kingship amongst the people of ancient Egypt, which was transmitted to the East and appeared in Syria during the Hellenistic period. It has survived to the present day in ecclesiastical use in a modified version of the form found at Alahan, though nowadays the disc will usually enclose a chi-rho monogram or the letters IHS.

The four human busts (one at each end of the lintel block and the two others on the doorposts) are in very high relief. Only one is fairly well preserved, the others having been deliberately damaged in the past. Each bust consisted originally of a head and the upper part of the shoulders. The one relatively sound example is of a bearded man whose long hair falls in symmetrical waves on either side of the face, and it is possible that the four busts represent the four Evangelists whose symbols are below the lintel block.

The ornamental mouldings of the door [Fig. 32, Pl. 14, 19] are treated in an essentially Eastern manner, in which deep under-cutting produces the maximum contrast of light and shade, and further evidence that the sculptor was concerned more with overall decorative effect than with emphasizing the head of Christ with its two supporting angels or the four human busts, may be gathered from the fact that the areas which they occupy are in no case clearly defined or set apart. The ornamental mouldings are continued to a point where they may be thought to have disappeared under the figures and then re-emerge.[2]

What sort of an impact would the Church of the Evangelists have made on a pilgrim of the fifth century? He would have certainly faced the same stiff climb as the modern visitor, would then have approached the church over a paved courtyard, and entered the *narthex* through its western arcade before reaching the central church door with its striking sculptured decoration. Even now, in its present weathered condition this door remains one of the most imposing entrances to an early Christian church in the east. On the lintel block, the head of Christ supported by two flying angels suggests, perhaps speciously, the sun-disc of ancient royalty. Certainly it is a motif which appears time and again in slightly differing forms in Christian art. Below is the magnificent tetramorph of the four beasts of Ezekiel's vision and the Apocalypse of St. John [Pl. 20]. On the outer faces of the door jambs are the four busts which I believe to represent the Four Evangelists, while on the inner surfaces the relief sculpture has long been known to represent the Archangels ss Michael and Gabriel. Most scholars who have examined these reliefs are agreed that each Archangel stands on an object or objects, but so far there is no agreement as to what they are. After very careful examination in the favourable light of early morning, we have finally arrived at an identification which I believe to be substantially correct. St. Michael, to the south, stands on the busts of two female figures, each with a Phrygian cap on her head. The busts face eastwards, and the first is easily identifiable; the other is more weathered, with the face almost wholly destroyed. On the northern jamb, St. Gabriel stands on the back of a bull, below which is a male bust with head uncovered. It is not surely to strain the possible interpretation of these reliefs overmuch to suggest that in both cases the Archangel is represented as trampling down the enemies of Christ, and thus symbolizes the triumph of the Church over paganism. If that is a reasonable conjecture, it is tempting to see in the female busts below St. Michael devotees of Cybele but the meaning of the objects below St. Gabriel is much harder to assess. Is the bull the animal of Jupiter Dolichenus, or does it symbolize the *taurobolium* of Anatolian Ma or of Mithraism? Is it possible that the bare-headed man represents a priest of Isis? Even had the reliefs been completed by the sculptor or been less weathered than in fact they are, it would still be hard to answer these questions. One thing is however clear – that paganism was not yet dead, for the symbols must, if they were to have any meaning at all, have been familiar to the sculptor and to those who first saw his work. In this

[2] M. Gough, "Some Recent Finds at Alahan (Koja Kalessi)," *Anatolian Studies*, 5 (1955), pp. 119-122. References to the plates in the original article have been replaced with references to plates in this volume.

connexion, it is worth recalling the contemporary, or near contemporary silver reliquary of Çirga, on which a female saint, very possibly the Virgin herself, is portrayed flanked by lions as a Christian *Potnia Therōn*. Paganism may well have died hard in the fastness of the Isaurian mountains.[3]

There has been much debate over the exact form of the figures below the reliefs of the archangels ss Michael and Gabriel. For many years Michael Gough believed that the shape between St. Gabriel and the female figure below was a very indistinct outline of a bull. However, at the end of the last season (1973) he and the writer saw the composition lit in a new way; the season was earlier than usual in May-June and the low evening sun accentuated the relief of the carving. It then became clear that the carving depicted a pair of figures wearing Phrygian caps similar to the figures beneath St. Michael.

The two corner blocks of the cornice above the lintel have been found (Fig. 34, Pl. 10); an example of the arrangement can be seen over the central door of the East Church. It had long been thought that the cornice was originally supported on the two magnificent dolphin corbels found nearby (Fig. 31, Pl. 13) but these are too large for use here and smaller scroll consoles have been found which are considered to be more in scale. The lower half of the cornice consists of a convex band of richly carved, flowing vine with clusters of grapes. Above this, crossed fishes and partridges fill the spaces between modillions decorated with near abstract acanthus motifs. Again the cornice is finished with a band of anthemion.

The two dolphin corbels have cut-outs on their top surfaces to hold a beam and therefore they may well have been placed high up on either side of the cornice, similar to the corinthian capital corbels over the doorways on the west face of the East Church. Here they may have supported a main beam of the narthex gallery floor. The corbels are carved on the one side with a dolphin, head downwards, holding a ball in its mouth and its tail is bent outwards at the top to follow the shape of the corbel. The reverse side is plain. The curved part of the outer face is decorated with stylised acanthus, whilst the upper part – the vertical surface – is plain. It appears therefore that the pair of dolphin corbels were intended to be seen

[3] M. Gough, "The Church of the Evangelists at Alahan, a Preliminary Report," *Anatolian Studies*, 12 (1962), pp. 180-181. References to the plates in the original article have been replaced with references to plates in this volume; the drawing in the original has not been reproduced here.

only from one side and from below, and their position above and to either side of the Evangelists' Door would be appropriate.

The lower parts of the doorways leading to the north and south aisles still remain *in situ*. The architrave of the door to the south aisle is decorated with the raised flush bead, similar to the openings in the south facade, but it differs in its construction in that the jambs are made of coursed blocks tying into the masonry wall to the side. Little remains of the north doorway, but it can be seen that it was decorated as the south door but with additional embellishment of the flat band which is carved with a shallow, finely cut pattern of diagonal bands interwoven with circles.

The form of the west facade of the narthex between the main openings opposite the Evangelists' Door and the southwest corner is uncertain (Fig. 24, Pl. 7). The lower courses, which have been partially exposed during excavation, give no indication of any opening; yet it is difficult to believe that the wall to the south of the trabeated openings would not have been relieved by the insertion of a window opposite the doorway to the south aisle, especially as the decoration of the arched and trabeated openings may have continued across the facade to complement the upper frieze and cornice.

The details of the upper part of the narthex are also difficult to determine but from the variety of differently decorated capitals and voussoirs found, it is likely that an arcade of possibly three spans was incorporated into the west facade to light the gallery. If this were so then the openings could have been similar to the clerestory windows, 2.07 m deep, resulting in an overall height of the windows from sill to top of the keystone of 2.97 m.

The two major constituent parts of the west facade of the narthex (Fig. 24) are thus seen to have been a central arched opening opposite the Evangelists' Door with narrow trabeated openings to either side and a group of windows at gallery level. The vertical arrangement might have been as follows: the threshold to the central arched opening is 0.15 m below the datum for the nave arcade. From the size of the column bases to either side of this opening it is judged that the height of the columns was of the same order as those of the nave colonnade, say 3.3 m to the springing of the arch. The radius of the arch is 1.25 m and the depth of the voussoirs is 0.45 m. This gives a height of 4.37 m and in relation to the nave datum, a dimension of 4.22 m. The reconstruction of the cross section of the nave and aisle, already described, calculated the gallery floor level of the Basilica to be 5.08 m, which, if assumed to be the same for the level of the narthex gallery, means that its floor would have cleared the

keystone of the central arched opening to the Evangelists' Door by
0.86 m. The overall height of the narthex gallery windows, including the
sill of 0.30 m is seen to have been 2.97 m and, if placed directly above the
gallery floor level of 5.08 m, would make a height of 8.05 m. Add to this a
depth of 0.83 m for the cornice and frieze, and this combination would
just fit beneath the calculated adjusted height of the south facade of the
Basilica of 9.02 m (Fig. 22-25). If, as already proposed, the frieze and
cornice of the south facade of the Basilica were continued around the
narthex, it would follow that the narthex roof would have sloped up from
the cornice and would have risen to a clerestory in line with the west wall
of the church. It is also likely that the west face of the clerestory may have
been pierced with similar windows to those on its north and south faces.
The form so reconstructed resembles that of the much larger Church of
the Acheiropoeitos at Salonika – a suggestion made by Michael Gough.[4] If
the reconstruction for the narthex is correct then its west facade, with its
rich embellishment, would have been a most impressive sight to confront
the visitor approaching across the Forecourt from the west.

Inside the Basilica, the nave extends eastwards for 22.5 m to the steps of
the bema (Fig. 19). It is flanked on both sides by two tiers of colonnading
of ten corinthian columns, each supporting an arcade of plain arches
(Pl. 1, 9, 25). Many of the voussoirs have retained their plaster and with it
traces of decoration. The arcading and the solid walls above are seen to
have been plastered and painted on a white background. The edges of the
voussoirs are outlined in red, with a thicker band of black to emphasize
the curve. There are also various types of geometric patterns using shades
of red, yellow, green, blue and black. The soffits of the voussoirs are
decorated in these colours with squares, diagonal band and chevron
patterns. The column bases appear to have been unpainted, but the
colonnade capitals still retain traces of deep red paint. The upper
colonnade was built on a string course projecting into the nave with a
deep ogee moulding. The upper colonnade was also decorated as the
lower colonnade. A smaller version of the ogee moulded string course
formed the base of the clerestory windows and this may have been
continued along the length of the nave, as no examples of a return
moulding have been found. The clerestory windows above the nave took
the form of double or triple arches divided by oval-shaped columns with
lotus leaf capitals facing both the inside and the outside. Other capitals
were found with both sides having the corinthian order, or a combination

⁴ M. Gough, "Alahan Monastery, a Masterpiece of Early Christian Architecture," *The
Metropolitan Museum of Art Bulletin*, 26 (June 1968), p. 461.

of corinthian and lotus leaf. The arch voussoirs were probably plain and sprang from the side walls from simply moulded imposts – as can be seen in the East Church.

The colonnade terminates in a pilaster complex supporting the triumphal arch at the entrance to the bema (Pl. 25). The triumphal arch, supported on engaged columns, springs at a greater height than the nave arcading. The lower parts of the walls flanking the triumphal arch have traces of plaster and, like the capitals of the colonnading, the pilaster capitals still retain traces of red paint.

On either side of the nave between the narthex and the transverse wall to the triumphal arch are the north and south aisles. The north aisle has its north wall faced with small regularly coursed blocks set tight against the cliff and was thus unlit. The south aisle was lit by three or four large windows. There were no traces of any plaster but a few fragments of wall mosaic were found at the east end of the north aisle which may suggest the presence of mosaic decoration in the area. The colours of the tesserae cover a wide range of brown, green, red, yellow, blue, and, in addition, gold. Flesh tints were achieved by the use of rosy-pink marble, and the fact that many of the tesserae are minute and irregular suggests their use in figurative scenes. Both the nave and aisles are paved from the narthex up to the last column of the colonnade before the triumphal arch with large masonry slabs coursed in one direction with random joints in the other. The nave is coursed from east to west, the aisles from north to south. The paving is missing in the area of the nave and aisles between the last column of the colonnade and the steps up to the bema. The presence of floor tesserae in this area suggests a mosaic floor. The few fragments found were stone, generally regular in size (about 1 cm square), and coloured white, black, grey, red, light brown and buff set out in geometric patterns.

Whilst the aisles were continuous throughout their length, (Fig. 19) the nave appears to have been divided into two parts, each separated and screened from the aisles for most, if not all, of the length of the colonnading. The colonnade to the north of the nave is built directly on the bedrock, the south colonnade on a stylobate the same width as the column bases. After the erection of the colonnade a raised stylobate was added surrounding the bases, and these bases, the column shafts and the top surface of the new stylobate were grooved to support low screens. Fortunately, many fragments of these screens (Fig. 37-39) were retrieved from the secondary period walls which were built on either side of the nave and which were dismantled during the excavations.

There appear to have been three entrances through the colonnade leading from the aisles to the nave. The first is between columns 2 and 3, indicated by the lowering of the stylobate of the south colonnade, and a gap in the raised stylobate in the north colonnade. This is in itself not concrete evidence of an entrance, but it seems unlikely to be merely a coincidence. To the east of the entrance in the north colonnade the raised stylobate continues until column 6 is reached; the raised stylobate is missing along the south colonnade for the first six columns. However, on both sides between columns 6 and 7 there must have been a major entrance as the columns are grooved to hold pairs of screens projecting out obliquely into both the aisles and the nave. These short screens were held at their ends by posts set into the floor, shallow recesses for which still remain. Fragments of the posts were found and have a vertical band of laurel leaf decoration. The posts were surmounted with a pine-cone finial. One fragment of a completely pierced screen with acanthus leaf edging surrounding a tracery of vine leaves and grapes enclosing a cross was found which could have formed part of one of these entrance screens.

From these entrances and east as far as column 10 the raised stylobate, which now exists on both sides, becomes wider and is built of larger blocks. At column 10 it turns across the nave to separate the nave from the bema. This wider stylobate is decorated on the nave side, (Fig. 36) its vertical face having a shallow ogee profile deeply curved in a continuous band of fine guilloche moulding with small flowers, fleur-de-lys, fish and crosses filling the interstices (Pl. 26). Above the guilloche moulding is a narrow band of oak leaf. Midway between the major entrances and the turn across the nave, the guilloche decoration reverses direction suggesting that the decorated stylobate was only intended for that part of the nave to the east of the major entrance. The change in the form of the raised stylobate coinciding with the elaborate major entrances could indicate, as has been said, the division of the nave into two parts. The third entry from the aisles to the nave is between the end of the raised stylobate and the transverse wall at the triumphal arch and would have allowed access from the side pastophories to the bema across the end of the nave.

Between the columns of both levels of the nave arcading were low stone screens (Pl. 27-30) which rested on the raised stylobate for the lower floor and on the string course of the upper arcading for the gallery. There are two types of screen (Fig. 35, 37), the first of which is solid and decorated either on one side or both and which is likely to have been used at ground floor level as the carving is more delicate. A second type is completely pierced (Fig. 38) and probably belonged to the gallery as the decoration is much bolder. Of the solid type of screens the single-sided type could have been placed facing into the nave. The double-sided screens may have been placed on the raised stylobate crossing the nave to face both towards the nave and the bema. The screens are approximately 1.45 m long by 0.75 m high and have a wide variety of decorations. The simplest type consists of a single panel on which is carved a wreathed cross, either a cross entwined in foliage, or a cross with rosettes set in the corners between the arms. These panels are carved in shallow relief with a simple border. In contrast the divided screens have two, four or six panels outlined with deeply cut and moulded frames surrounding almost three dimensional motifs of linked circles with inset crosses, rosettes, basket-work or intricate floral arrangements of vines and pomegranates. Other panels are carved with shoals of fish; a bird holding a fish in its beak; and in a further panel a bird is shown preening itself.

Grooves cut in the columns and in the raised stylobate of the north side of the nave show that at ground level the screens started at column 4 and continued to Column 10; they then crossed the nave on either side of the entrance to the bema and return back along the south side of the nave to column 6. Here the raised stylobate and columns were disturbed by the building of the secondary period wall, but from the evidence of the north side, it is likely that the screens continued at least as far as column 4.

From the nave, a single step followed by a further flight of three steps lead up to the bema which is 0.9 m above the nave floor. In the north and south walls of the bema are entrances to the side pastophories. The transition to the apse is marked by a slight narrowing of the space without further articulation by means of any architectural feature or decoration. The apse is lit from the east by a pair of arched windows separated by a rectangular window divide set directly on the sill without any moulded base (Pl. 1). The window surround is slotted to hold a thin grille made of flat metal slats.

At the base of the walls to the apse and the bema there are tiers of stone seating forming a synthronon. Their construction suggests that when the building of the Basilica was well advanced or even complete, the original population of the monastery increased. The original seating is seen to consist of the two lower tiers around the apse, widened in the centre, presumably as a dais for a throne. These are carefully set out and carved on their vertical face with an ogee profile which returns at the line of the junction of the apse to the bema. Before their coursing was completed, the door to the north pastophory was filled in and the two lower tiers of seating, distinguished by their ogee profile, were extended westwards as far as the engaged column of the triumphal arch. On the south side, however, the seating was only built up to the east jamb of the opening. The extended seating was built directly onto the finished floor, fragments of which can be seen protruding beneath the lower tier along the north wall. Before plaster was applied to the apse wall the synthronon appears to have again proved inadequate and a third tier and a new dais added. This tier is taller and more crudely carved as if it was intended to be plastered. It may be suggested that the third tier was added during the secondary period of occupation, but this is discounted on the evidence of the wall plaster being finished against the top surface and also that although crudely shaped, the blocks are well fitted and do not appear to have had a previous use; the secondary period alterations being usually of re-used fallen masonry.

The floor of the bema, and probably the apse also, were paved in *opus sectile* using pieces of pink and black marble in extended hexagon and triangle shapes, together with larger square slabs of red and black mottled or plain white marble. In the area of the bema and apse pieces of crumbling plaster holding glass tesserae were found. Their colours are gold, red, green, blue and turquoise; others, of stone, are white, grey, pink and black. No fragment is large enough to suggest any particular pattern or form, but again, as for the tesserae found in the north aisle, from the variety and variation in size it is likely that the decoration had featured figured scenes as well as geometric patterned borders.

At the top of the steps leading to the bema there is a small podium carved from a solid block of stone 1.05 m high, 0.75 m wide and 0.72 m deep. Each of its four sides has a conch-headed niche supported by miniature engaged columns and in its centre a three-stepped cross. In the centre of the apse there is a badly damaged base to an altar. The base is rectangular and has a recess for a colonette at each corner.

The north pastophory is now entered by a door from the north aisle. The side entry from the bema, as has been seen, was filled in for the extension of the synthronon. The west wall, facing the north aisle, was found to have been strengthened by timber ties which had decayed to such an extent that part of the wall had to be demolished. The north and east walls are cut into the cliff and no traces of their lining have survived, but at high level the rock is cut square, and from this evidence the probable dimensions of the room are 3.6 m wide by 3.9 m deep. The floor of the north pastophory is also missing. Unlit and without any finish, the north pastophory may have served only as a store as here were found fragments of glass lamps and other glass vessels, together with a bronze lamp chain with three hooks for its suspension.

The south pastophory is entered by two doorways, one from the south aisle and the other from the bema. There is a present day doorway, conveniently leading out through the south wall to the terrace outside, which may not have existed during the primary period of occupation as it is without a threshold and has no moulded jambs in the manner of the other openings in the south facade. The south pastophory is in two parts; an anteroom and a diaconicon. The western part opens off the south aisle and is positioned between the line of the junction of the nave to the bema and a cross wall on the line of the transition from the bema to the apse which has a low horseshoe arch spanning 3.5 m and springing 2.2 m above floor level. The diaconicon is irregular in plan, as its north wall is angled to follow the curve of the apse. Both rooms are lit by small windows and are roughly paved; the flagstones in the anteroom are still reasonably level but in the diaconicon they have been disturbed and the present floor may well date from the secondary period of occupation.

The walls of the diaconicon were originally plastered and decorated with wall-paintings simulating marble revetment, traces of which still remain on the lower parts of the east wall. The wall-painting shows panels divided by fluted pilasters. In the north corner there is a panel painted so as to resemble split yellow marble with streaks of yellow, red and green. This is framed by a border of a double band of red and green triangles. Dividing this panel from its neighbour is a vertical band of pink marble, a fluted pilaster coloured yellow with red outline, followed by a repeat of the bank of pink marble. From the height of the fragment it is likely that the panel of marble was quartered thereby making a dado come 2 m high. The pilaster, of which only the base can be seen, would then have a reasonable proportion. Extrapolating the dimensions of the panels along the east wall it seems likely that there would have been three painted panels of quartered marble. Writing of the decoration, Michael Gough comments:

> The effect is unusual, as if the painter was trying to suggest some rich interior only partly remembered or understood. This suggested reconstruction can only apply to the lower half of the wall, and it may well have acted as a dado to some different decorative scheme above. In any case, if our assumption that the surviving fragments are intended to evoke an interior with intricate decorative stonework of the type known at Sta. Sophia in Istanbul and elsewhere is correct, we may assume that it was also a feature of important churches is Southern Asia Minor where the evidence is at present scanty.[5]

[5] M. Gough, "Excavations at Alahan Monastery, Second Preliminary Report," *Anatolian Studies*, 13 (1968), p. 108.

It became clear that the Basilica had an upper storey as its architectural components were classified. As has been seen, members of an upper arcade were found which would have been seated on the deep string course blocks. Some of these blocks have beam holes 25 cm × 25 cm × 11 cm deep along their rear faces. In addition the string course and bases for the colonnading are grooved for intercolumnar screens acting there as a parapet. Also the transverse arch dividing the south pastophory, springing from a low level for such a span, was obviously intended to support an upper floor, and the windows that lit this upper floor can be seen high up on the south wall. A large rock-cut chamber at high level at the west end of the north aisle, and the cutting away of the cliff above the north pastophory for an upper chamber, all suggest the presence of a second storey as well.

The entrance to an upper floor, however, is not so easy to determine. The size and location of doors rule out any stair rising within the narthex. No steps are cut into the cliff face outside the east end of the Basilica and, as will be shown later, the space east of the Basilica does not have ready access from the Colonnaded Walk. Similarly there are no signs of an entrance from the Cave Complex as, at both levels, only the Cave Church apses have contact with the west facade. The only signs of a possible way up lie in another chamber adjoining the west end of the north aisle of the Basilica. Close examination of the rock face here reveals two features: at floor level there is a sloping ledge which may have been cut to allow the construction of a timber stair, and at a high level there is a seating for an arch spanning east-west in line with the north end of the narthex, which suggests that the narthex was open to the north. These features point to the possibility that this chamber contained a rudimentary stair, with a half landing, rising out of the north aisle and turning back on itself along the narthex.

The upper storey of the Basilica (Fig. 21, 22) is thus seen to have covered the aisles and pastophories with a link across the narthex. The seating for beams in the string course to the upper arcading show that the floor of the galleries spanned the short, north-south direction and the evidence of the low arch across the south pastophory indicates that here the joists spanned in an east-west direction. The structure of the gallery floor in relation to the narthex has already been discussed and it is proposed that the joists spanned from east to west, the short dimension, but instead of being recessed into the walls, they were supported on baulks of timber lying along the narthex walls, bearing on the cross arches and the dolphin corbels, a type of construction that can clearly be seen in the East Church.

Over the south aisle the gallery was lit by rectangular framed windows and the upper storey of the south pastophory is seen to have been lit by at least one pair of arched windows in the south wall (Fig. 20, Pl. 8). The narthex gallery may well have been open at the south end and was also lit by an arcade along the west facade, which, together with a similar arcade between the narthex and the nave (Fig. 23, 24), could have illuminated the interior of the Church. To the north the cliff obscures direct daylight from the north aisle, but, as the rock stops short of the north wall masonry facing, the upper part of the wall may have been pierced by openings in order to allow light reflected off the honey-coloured rock to enter from the north.

Here then was a church of considerable size – a magnificent addition to the monastery. The completion of the Basilica must surely have marked the end of the phase in the history of Alahan, as it was placed alongside the Cave Complex with little evidence of any provision for future eastward expansion. Compared in size with the small churches within the Cave Complex, the addition of the Basilica signals a growth in population which, as it does not appear to be reflected by a comparable increase in the domestic apartments, suggests the opening of the monastery to pilgrims. This hypothesis is further reinforced by the rich exterior embellishments of the west and south facades which are surmounted by a frieze and cornice obviously intended to be seen from the hillside below on the approach to the site. In addition, there is the striking entrance through the west facade to the narthex and the "Evangelists's Door" which was considered by Michael Gough to be "one of the most imposing entrances to an early Christian church in the east." [6]

Within the Basilica the sculptured masonry of the corinthian colonnades, the pierced screens, the *opus sectile* floor of the apse and bema, and the rich mosaic of the apse, bema and eastern ends of the nave and aisle, all point to the advent of a wealthy patronage. As Michael Gough says in "The Emperor Zeno and some Cicilian Churches," "It is my belief that the Isaurian Emperor Zeno made this grandiose scheme financially viable." [7]

The completion of the Basilica marks the end of the development of the monastery around the Cave Complex and at that time no further building may have been envisaged as the Basilica neatly enclosed the forecourt from the east. These beginnings are now seen to have been only the first

[6] M. Gough, "The Church of Evangelists," p. 180.
[7] M. Gough, "The Emperor Zeno and some Cilician Churches," *Anatolian Studies*, 22 (1972), p. 210.

stage of a progressive expansion. Circumstances possibly connected with the establishment of Alahan as a place of pilgrimage and a consequent increase in funds, may have obliged and enabled the monks to enlarge further the complex by adding a second church, a Baptistery and more domestic quarters. They appear to have had a confidence in the future which allowed them to plan on an even grander scale than before. The only direction in which the monastery could reasonably expand was eastwards (Fig. 71). In order to accommodate the new buildings the hillside was cut and filled to make three terraces by quarrying the rock cliff to the north for building stone, and by infilling behind a masonry retaining wall to the south.

The Upper Terrace is at the base of the rock cliff and is divided into two parts by an outcrop of rock approximately midway along its length. The Middle Terrace, the main level for building, is below and is bounded on its southern edge by the retaining wall (Pl. 4, 74, Fig. 71). Below the retaining wall is the Lower Terrace comprising a levelling of the bedrock as a foundation for the retaining wall and its abuttments, a row of stores or baths and the outfall for the dispersal of the rainwater drainage from the terrace above. Excavation of the Lower Terrace and along the base of the retaining wall showed that, except for the possible presence of a stair opposite the Baptistery, the principal approach to the monastery remained by way of the forecourt to the Cave Complex. Described by Michael Gough as a great fortification wall[8] (Pl. 4) the retaining wall served to contain the monastery, not so much as a defensible space, as it could easily be assailed from the hillside above, but by restricting entry it afforded privacy to the monks.[9]

Access to the new extension of the monastery was achieved by extending the Middle Terrace and the retaining wall westwards and building up the ground to the south of the Basilica to the level of the Cave Complex forecourt. Traces of the approach to the gate have been confused by rebuilding during the secondary period of occupation, but evidence from the south pilaster complex of the gate, which had a pilaster termination to arcading only on its east face, suggests that the approach was contained only by a low parapet above the retaining wall. The Middle Terrace extends some 130 m from the Basilica to the narthex of the East Church which terminates the development at the eastern end. The width from the cliff to the retaining wall averages 25 m. The ground rises 8.5 m from the Basilica to the East Church.

[8] Ibid., p. 201.
[9] This idea was proposed by Michael Sheehan.

The East Church is linked to the west gate by a Colonnaded Walk built along the retaining wall. As well as joining the two churches, the Colonnaded Walk gives access to the other buildings along the terrace. A third of the way between the Basilica and the East Church is the Baptistery which divides the space between the cliff and the Colonnaded Walk into two areas. To the west of the Baptistery is a group of two-storeyed domestic apartments. To the east the site is more open. Adjacent to the Baptistery is a necropolis, and in front of the entrance to the East Church is an open court. This court is bounded to the south by the north wall of the Colonnaded Walk, to the west by a row of rooms built across the upper terrace, and to the north by two-storeyed domestic appartments built against the cliff.

Photographic evidence of the west gate to the Colonnaded Walk (which has now fallen) (Pl. 53) shows that it was plain and unadorned, in contrast to the ornate exterior of the Basilica. East of the Basilica the style of architecture changes to become inward looking; the buildings either relate to the Colonnaded Walk itself, or as in the case of the East Church, to an inner court. Even the exterior of the East Church, the focal point of the new development, is plain – its outer walls articulated only by masonry piers. This simplicity suggests that the new buildings east of the Basilica were intended to serve principally the monastic community and, secondly, the domestic needs of the pilgrims.

The chronological sequence of the building of this stage of the development starts with the commencement of the East Church and the Baptistery. Which came first is not known but we shall see that the building of both the East Church and the Baptistery was under way before the alignment of the Colonnaded Walk was settled. This part of the monastery is best explained by describing first the East Church and the way in which its narthex connects to the Colonnaded Walk, then the Colonnaded Walk itself, followed by the Baptistery (Fig. 55, 56). The living quarters which also opened off the Colonnaded Walk are seen as an infill between the principal buildings and are thus described next, and then the buildings on the Lower Terrace at the base of the retaining wall. Finally the Spring Complex, outside the monastery proper, will be described.

C. The East Church

The East Church, the building that has attracted so much attention in the past, is in a remarkable state of structural preservation. Whereas the other buildings on the site are reduced to all but their lower levels, virtually the entire masonry fabric of the East Church remains. Masonry cleared from the nave and aisles consisted mainly of voussoirs from the apse and the squinch arches of the tower. The exterior wall to the upper level of the north aisle has fallen.

That so much of the East Church remains is certainly due to it having a cross wall cellular structure which, although very light and slender, has retained its integrity. The narthex, not bonded into the west wall of the Church, lacked this rigidity and has disintegrated.

The remaining part of the church is 22 m long and 15 m wide which excludes the area covered by the narthex (Fig. 44). The distance from the floor to the top of the tower is 15 m.

The rock strata on which the East Church is built have been cut back to accommodate the building. Extensive quarrying must have taken place as almost the whole structure is built on bedrock at the floor level, with foundations only needed to a limited extent in the southwest corner. The north wall is cut sheer from the cliff up to the level of the gallery, and the rock is of such good quality that no inner lining appears to have been necessary. The rock was in fact shaped to form the lower section of the apse walls and the synthronon and the plinths for the columns. Here and in the area surrounding the East Church, especially to the west, was a convenient quarry capable of bearing high quality large building stone, making it possible for such a sophisticated structure to be realised. Remains of a quarry still being worked at the time of the abandonement of the monastery found beyond the east end of the church show how blocks were cut. The outline of the block was carved out of the bedrock by chiselling a deep groove about 0.15 m wide around the three hidden sides of the block, then channels were cut underneath the block and wedges were forced into the channels until the block was split free. The faces of the blocks used in the East Church are more roughly finished than those of the Basilica with only fine finishing by bolster along the edges which are shaped with a cut v-joint; the bearing surfaces are so accurately cut that the blocks are laid with only the finest of mortar beds. Walls are generally 0.60 m thick in a single block width. The coursing is irregular on account of the variety of size of block. The structure is well engineered with the exception of the tower, where the quality of the coursing deteriorates considerably.

The exterior of the East Church is plain, without formal expression and is a direct result of the internal organisation of the structure and the spaces enclosed (Pl. 31). As it was approached only from within the monastery complex, there was no need for any external embellishment. Except for doorways and the smaller windows where lintels and keystone relieving courses are used, (Fig. 45-47) the major openings are arched with plain voussoirs springing from simply moulded impost blocks, in contrast to the moulded frames to the rectangular openings of the south facade of the Basilica.

The layout of the East Chuch is that of a basilica on to which has been superimposed a tower over the eastern section of the nave (Pl. 34). But whereas the orthodox structure of the Basilica utilises longitudinal colonnades and arcading between the nave and aisles detailed uniformly from narthex to bema, the arrangement here (Fig. 48, 49) has been adapted to support the tower and the principal direction of the structure has become transverse with the east-west arcading to the nave taking a secondary role in the completion of the cellular fabric. Thus, on entering through the west door, the focal point, the apse, is seen through a progression of horseshoe arches spaced 3.5 m apart with the wider base of the tower being infilled with an arcade of three spans to preserve the line of the nave. The transverse walls cross the aisles with arches bearing on the rock cliff to the north and on to the buttressed south facade. The arcading along the length of the nave is in two tiers, the upper belonging to the galleries which extend over both side aisles and pastophories and which are linked by the narthex.

The church can only be entered from within the monastery complex by way of the narthex and the main approach would most likely have been from the Colonnaded Walk. Almost the whole of the narthex of the East Church has fallen away on account of the complete absence of tying into the west facade. In the Basilica the narthex was plainly integrated into the structure of the building. The reason for this inconsistency may have been the need to press on with the building of the main fabric of the church, while delaying the construction of the narthex until the approach from the west, especially the alignment of the Colonnaded Walk, had been decided.

Excavations to the west of the East Church uncovered a number of voussoirs and other masonry from which a reconstruction of the narthex may be attempted. At ground level the entire width of the floor had been levelled from the bedrock and from traces of the base of its west facade (Fig. 44) and the remains of pilaster complexes P1 and P1N of the Colonnaded Walk (to be described later) the line of the west facade is established and a start can be made.

The width of the narthex varies from 3.9 m at the north end to 2.7 m at the south, making it a wedge shape on plan with the west facade at right angles to the axis of the Colonnaded Walk (Fig. 71). This alignment suggests that the building of the narthex and the setting out of the line of the Colonnaded Walk in its final form, although not necessarily its construction, were contemporary. The south arcaded wall of the Colonnaded Walk abuts the narthex at pilaster complex P1 which in turn projects southwards by 0.9 m to align with the pier belonging to the buttressing of the southwest corner of the church. Two upright jambs on the south wall of the narthex suggest a window between P1 and the west wall of the church. The north wall of the Colonnaded Walk, solid throughout most of its length, joins the narthex of the East Church with an opening, some 2.9 to 3.0 m wide, facing on to the court. The opening is shown by the presence of a pilaster base at the east end of the solid wall and the weathered remains of its corespond at pilaster complex P1N.

The elevation of the west facade of the narthex (Fig. 44, 50, 51) can be considered to have had three main features: the entry from the Colonnaded Walk, the openings on to the court, and, possibly, the windows to the gallery. The junction of the Colonnaded Walk to the narthex was achieved by a wide opening, presumably arched, which is indicated by the north-south pilasters of pilaster complexes P1 and P1N spaced 3.4 m apart. The pilaster bases are set 1.62 m above the level of the colonnaded walk, and 0.58 m below the paving of the narthex; this will be discussed later. Only three base courses of these pilaster complexes remain but the height of the arch must have been set to suit the Colonnaded Walk at the lower level. Various types of voussoir were uncovered, of which one may have been used for this entry. It is decorated on both sides with a scallop design matching that used in the arcading of the Colonnaded Walk. The keystone has a rosette on one side superimposed on the arch decoration, and a roundel of interlocking circles on its soffit. The third face has a roundel enclosing a cross again superimposed on the voussoir decoration, and this stone, with the cross facing westwards, could well have been used to crown the arch at the entry to the narthex.

The sizes of the narthex openings on to the court are not so clearly defined. The base of the facade between the north wall of the Colonnaded Walk and the cliff face (Fig. 44) has the remains of two openings separated by a column base seated on a bedrock plinth. The extent of the openings is suggested by the ends of solid block walls to either side, but the absence of pilaster bases prevents the location of the coresponds from being firmly established. The bedrock floor of the narthex beside the southernmost pier, part of the complex P1N, is not level with the foot of the pier, neither has it been cut to form a base for any masonry above, and has all the signs of a temporary, unfinished threshold to an opening. From the remains, the pier is seen to be some 1.7 m long with its northern edge 8.8 m south of the cliff face. At the north end of the northern opening there are three courses of a solid masonry wall which, if the single central column base is in its original position, would frame an opening 3.5 m wide, identical to that of the assumed southern opening. The raised section of the bedrock between the central column and the north pier could have been a rudimentary threshold to the opening. A large plain, double arch spring with a diameter of 3.5 m and other voussoirs of the same span were found which may have fitted this pair of openings. The height of the springing of these arches is not known, but, judging from the span, the keystone of the arch must have been very close to the gallery floor level in order to give the opening a reasonable proportion.

The west facade of the narthex gallery is likely to have had windows opposite the three-arched large openings between the gallery and the nave (Fig. 51) and the presence of a set of decorated voussoirs, single and double arch springs which were found in the rubble in the narthex area suggests that they may have been used here. These voussoirs have an arch diameter of 1.16 m and a thickness of 0.31 m; the decoration is a wide, plain raised band with below a narrow band of bead and chevron followed by egg-and-dart. Three double springs and a fragment of one terminal spring were found. In addition two palm-leaf window divider capitals were found, one joined to its shank, and which are similar to the window of the south facade of the church. By using the proportions of these latter windows, the springing height of the arcading to the gallery windows is calculated to be 1.5 m so the overall height of the arcading to the top of the keystone would probably have been 2.04 m. Allowing for the possibility that some of the double voussoir springs are missing, a row of six arches is suggested as being the appropriate length of east-west arcading to be placed across the gallery, and, if arranged symmetrically on the axis of the nave, they would have been asymetrical to the elevation of the west facade of the narthex on account of its projection southwards to meet the arcading of the Colonnaded Walk.

The west wall of the church (Fig. 47) has a rectangular roof line along which is a row of beam holes on the west face to support the beams of the narthex gallery roof. If a roof slope similar to that of the nave or aisles is projected down from this line of beam holes, the level of the eaves would appear to be one course of masonry above the keystone of the gallery window arcading.

At ground level the south wall of the narthex aligns with the rectangular pier projecting southwards at the southwest corner of the church to meet the south facade of the Colonnaded Walk (Pl. 32). The pier is bonded into the corner and rises to gallery level where it stops with the corner continuing up to roof level without any keying to show that an upper section of the pier had fallen away. This lack of bonding poses the problem of the nature and the alignment of the south wall of the narthex. The two door jambs resting against, but not integrated with, the lower part of the pier or the east face of pilaster complex P1 show that at ground level at least the south wall of the narthex aligned with the south face of the pier. The only clues to the structure at gallery level are an open beam socket at the south end of the row of beam holes for the narthex roof which aligns with the southwest corner of the church, and a shallow key, one block thick, which appears to have been cut into the masonry at the top of the southwest corner of the church. The beam socket is open to the south and an adjacent block would have been needed to contain the beam. The length of the shallow key is one block thick and these two facts together suggest that the pier could have stopped at its present level, continuing upwards as a thinner wall above to roof level, with its west face in line with the west face of the church. This wall would then have allowed the narthex roof to cover the southern end of the narthex.

At its north end, the narthex is enclosed at gallery level above the cliff by the westward extension of the north wall of the north aisle, where there is a doorway giving access from the higher level of ground to the north. A single north-south aligned block bonded into the west end of this wall locates the northwest corner of the narthex.

The west facade of the church shows how the floor of the narthex gallery was supported (Pl. 32). The absence of any cross arches or bracing has already been noted (Fig. 47), yet the sensible direction of support for the floor must still have been in an east-west orientation. A method was used without the need to cut numerous beam holes into the masonry and thereby possibly weakening the south wall of the church. The main support for the floor takes the form of corbels, decorated as corinthian capitals, made to support large beams spanning the width of the church from north to south, and fitting into sockets that can be seen cut into the cliff to the north. Smaller beams of the floor would then have spanned the shorter distance across the narthex.

At ground level the floor of the narthex, and its approach from the Colonnaded Walk appears never to have been completed. Only a small area of paving laid with coursing from east to west remains between the doors to the south aisle and the nave. The bedrock has only been roughly levelled and at the south end, at the entry from the Colonnaded Walk, there has been no attempt to form any steps. What appears to have been a temporary drain was built above the stylobate level of the arcading of the south facade of the Colonnaded Walk.

At the north end of the narthex there is a cell cut into the cliff. This cell is 4.5 m deep by 3.1 m wide and its floor is approximately 1.2 m above the level of the narthex. The cell is devoid of any features or decoration to suggest its use.

Doorways lead from the narthex to the nave and each aisle of the church (Pl. 32, Fig. 47). All have decorated frames and reveals and are surmounted by cornices supported by voluted consoles. The frame of the main door consists of decorated bands of flat mouldings stepping in from a cyma recta profile on which is cut alternating motifs of acanthus and anthemion (Pl. 35). The flat mouldings are punctuated by two bands of bay leaf garland followed by a narrow band of bead and reel at the inner edge. The centre of the lintel has a garland surrounding a cross superimposed on the running decoration. The reveals of both jambs and lintel have inset panels containing vines issuing from cornucopiae. The north door frame is plainer with shallow carved bands of bay leaf, ovolo, bay leaf and bead and reel between the stepped flat bands of moulding. The reveals of this door are undecorated. Both these doors, central and northern, have a restrained and stylised decoration. In contrast the south door frame (Fig. 52, Pl. 38-40) has deeper cut, more plastic carving and a vitality which is associated with the Basilica. The major theme of the south door frame is a vine with its stem curving from side to side. Amongst the leaves are bunches of grapes and small partridges. The vine is bordered on the outside by a narrow row of acanthus and to the inside a band of oak leaf garland. The most notable feature of this doorway is the reveals which are decorated on each jamb with single panels of writhing fish and dolphins – some being attacked by gulls – and enclosed by a border of bay leaf garland. Part of the panels are finished, finely carved with great care, while whole sections are only roughed out. The lintel block has a similar panel framed with bay leaf garland quartered by ties from which the leaves flow in opposite directions. The panel contains two dolphins facing inwards to a scallop-shaped central motif from which grows acanthus leaves.

Above each door the cornices are supported on consoles with figures superimposed on the front-vertical section of their scrolls. Unfortunately the figures are badly damaged. The consoles of the north and south doors appear to be faced with birds (Pl. 37) probably either the familiar partridge or the eagles which are also to be seen inside the church. Their wings are folded back to form the volutes of the scroll. The consoles of the main door have busts on the outer face; the northern one being only roughed out, whereas the south console is more finished showing a figure from the waist up, wearing a pleated robe with a fine circular pattern punctuated by drilling and having the right hand folded across the chest. On the undersides of the console scrolls there are acanthus leaf sprigs. The main and north door consoles are framed by bands of laurel leaf garlands and the consoles over the more ornate south door are bordered by flowing vines. Between the frames and the cornices of the three doors is a broad convex decorated moulding. On the north and south doors it is a band of laurel leaf garland with the south door having a small cross superimposed at the centre of the lintel. On the main door the moulding is decorated with flowing acanthus growing outwards from the centre. The cornices are similar in form to that over the Evangelists' Door in the Basilica – a cyma recta supported on modillions (Pl. 35, 36). Their carving however, is much shallower and less plastic and the spaces between the modillions are filled with more stylised motifs of florets, roundels and interwoven circles with no fish or partridges. The art of the mason was, however, acknowledged by a representation of his tools which is to be seen between the northernmost two modillions to the cornice over the main door.

At their base (Fig. 47), the door frames stop abruptly at the threshold leaving a plain block some 30 cm above the narthex floor. This break seems incongruous when related to the three small niches between the centre and the north and south doors which have the bases to their surrounds set at floor level. These niches are 1.2 m high. Their conches are decorated with a scallop framed in a raised rectangular moulding of laurel leaves supported on either plain, round or fluted flat corinthian pilasters with their capitals having a very much abstracted acanthus leaf foliage. The inner surface of the niches is plain and no clue is given to their function. These niches do not occur in the original Basilica, but it is interesting to note that two were found in the same position by the main door to the rebuilt Basilica of the secondary period of occupation.

Inside the church the organisation is that of a basilica (Fig. 44) and, although the presence of the tower might indicate some special significance to the space below, no signs remain to show that the subdivisions of the nave differed in any way from those of the Basilica (Pl. 49). The nave extends from the narthex to the bema with aisles to either side, each terminating at its eastern end in an apsidal entrance leading to the pastophories which flank the bema and apse. The longitudinal arcading of the nave of the basilican form is retained (Fig. 49) but is subsidiary to the transverse arches and acts structurally as a diaphragm wall (Fig. 51). The sides of the nave are tiered with the upper (gallery) level repeating the arcading below. Within the tower there is a third level which is in effect, a clerestory (Pl. 43, 49). The tiers are defined vertically by an ogee profiled string course at gallery level which continues around the bema and apse. The nave is 13.7 m long by 6.5 m wide. The string course to the gallery is 6.4 m above floor level. The height to the ridge of the nave roof is 7.5 m and above this the tower rises to a height of 14.5 m from the floor.

Progressing eastwards from the west end of the nave, the first arch of the longitudinal arcade between the nave and aisles springs from free-standing columns supported on engaged plinths. The capitals are corinthian, their volutes consisting of birds facing outwards with outstretched wings (Pl. 46) (a form also used for the capitals of the columns supporting the transverse arches). Although abutting a solid wall these capitals are carved symmetrically in the round and rather than deface the bird volutes they have been allowed to project into recesses cut into the masonry of the west wall. The corespond to the first arch is a demicolumn built into the pilaster complex formed by the crossing of the first transverse wall and the longitudinal arcading of the nave.

The first transverse wall rises within the roof to support beams spanning east-west from the west wall of the church to the tower. Its supporting arch springs from free-standing corinthian columns projecting into the nave. Between the first and second transverse walls there is a repeat of the first longitudinal arch, this time springing from corinthian demicolumns.

The second and third transverse walls from the west and east sides of the tower and between these the longitudinal arcading takes the form of three equal spans springing from square pilasters at the corners of the tower on to two intermediate corinthian columns. Like the first, the second and the third transverse arches spring from free-standing corinthian columns. The capitals of the third arch have bird volutes similar to those of the first arch. The column below the southwest corner of the tower has fallen away, yet the tower remains, demonstrating how the forces acting on the arch have been transferred to the arches over the south aisle. The third transverse arch (the east wall of the tower) crosses the nave at its junction to the bema and its supporting columns stand on deep plinths bringing their bases well above the raised floor of the bema to contain the end of the synthronon around the base of the walls to the apse and bema.

The fourth transverse wall comes at the transition from the bema to the apse and its arch, the triumphal arch, is supported on flat pilasters formed by the narrowing of the bema (Pl. 45). The pilasters rise directly from the synthronon to corinthian capitals supporting the string course of the gallery arcading as it continues around the bema and apse. The two broad faces of each pilaster are decorated with a tall, slightly recessed convex panel with intruding semi-circular ends on which is carved a mat of laurel leaves. The west face of the triumphal arch is moulded with a series of flat planes projecting forward, each edged with bands of ovolo, small leaves, and bead-and-reel and framed on its outer curve with a plain cyma recta profile. At the springing from the string course, the moulding turns in a horizontal direction to merge into the side walls. The soffit of the triumphal arch has a panel similar to those of the pilasters, but it is decorated with upward pointing simple palmate leaves. At approximately a third of the way up the arch the panel was intended to be punctuated by a motif of interlocking roundels of which the setting out incisions can be seen. Above those the decoration is unfinished. The keystone of the arch is thicker than the voussoirs with its west face flush with the outer edge of the cyma recta moulding. It was presumably intended to have been carved into a feature to crown the apse. The rear of the keystone is semi-circular in plan to complete the masonry coursing of the apsidal semi-dome. Analogous with the second transverse wall, the wall above the triumphal arch would have continued up to the roof level to support roof beams spanning from the east face of the tower to the east end of the church.

The side walls of the bema are plain, and are pierced only for doorways leading to the side pastophories. Beyond the fourth transverse wall is the semicircle of the apse with solid masonry infilling the space between it and the rectangular pastophories to either side. The apse is lit from the east by two arched windows centred on the axis of the church. Their sill is 2.6 m above the apse floor and the total height of the openings is 2.3 m. The arches spring from splayed impost blocks on to an oval corinthian window divider (Pl. 45). There are no signs of slots for grilles or recesses for shutters, but the sides of the divider project out to be flush with the arch curve and the impost is cut away at its centre as if to hold a thick window insert.

The second tier of the nave arcading is supported on the string course to the gallery and repeats the form of the lower level. In the bema the blank walls to either side have a pair of small arched openings giving views down into the bema and apse from the upper rooms above the pastophories. These openings have very pronounced horseshoe outlines and spring from splayed impost blocks onto central dividers.

In the aisles, the side arches of the transverse walls transmit the thrust of the main arches to the cliff to the north and to the piers built into the south facade. These arches are supported on rectangular piers and spring from cyma recta profiled imposts. At gallery level the side arches are narrower than those of the lower level. Their springs are set below those of the longitudinal arcading to the nave. Above the arches the solid masonry walls support the roof and brace the corners of the tower.

Between the second and third transverse arches and above the second tier of the longitudinal arcading to the nave, the tower rises as a clerestory with windows facing southwards and also to the east into the upper level of the bema. The sills of the windows are placed one stone course above the arches of the longitudinal arcading and are just above the level of the apex of the aisle roof. The tower is almost square in plan (7.6 m by 8.0 m) and across its corners squinch arches once supported the roof. The top of the tower stops abruptly with a level course which is almost complete (Fig. 48, 49) except for the southwest corner which has fallen away and the northeast corner where a few blocks are missing. Although it was too dangerous to make a detailed inspection of the fabric of the tower, most of the features could easily be studied from the hillside above (Pl. 33, 34). There are no fragments of masonry above the level course at the top of the tower; and it has spread outwards at the top causing many of the perpend joints to open. The constant level of the masonry which coincides with the top of the squinch arches, together with the even spreading of the top course, point firmly to the possibility that the tower rose no higher than it does today yet no traces of any roof structure could be seen.

There has been much speculation on the form of the roof over the tower and in clearing the nave special attention was given to record any evidence of its fabric. "Fallen blocks below the central tower were carefully examined to ensure that evidence for a stone dome – a theory still cherished in some quarters – should not be overlooked. In fact there was none, though some stones from the squinches were recorded." [10] As already noted, most of the top course of masonry appears to be still *in situ* and there are no traces of a dome, which, had it existed and subsequently collapsed, might have been left as they would have been below the point of outward thrust. The tower is also braced only by the transverse and longitudinal walls of the nave and its corners rise only from light pilaster complexes. Compared with the massive substructure of the apse semi-dome the fabric of the tower would appear to be incapable of withstanding the thrusts of a dome. This evidence suggests that the roof must have been light and the most readily available and suitable material would be the timber and tiles used elsewhere on the site. The presence of the squinch arches indicates an octagonal form for its structure, and its pitch

[10] M. Gough, "Excavations at Alahan Monastery, Third Preliminary Report," *Anatolian Studies*, 14 (1964), p. 186. See also M. Gough, "Alahan Monastery, Fifth Preliminary Report," *Anatolian Studies*, 18 (1968), p. 165.

may have been similar to the roof of the nave. Small hipped additions will have been required to weather the corners of the tower which will have given the roof the shape of the Gothic broach spire but, of course, much squatter in its proportions.

The squinch arches are supported on corinthian colonettes framing semi-circular niches. The colonettes are seated on highly decorated console corbels (Pl. 41, 42, 43). The decorated moulding edging the corbels passes round the base of the niche. Above this the masonry is plain and at the springing of the squinch arch the niche flows smoothly into the conch with the outer face of the squinch arch left plain except for a cross in its centre as is seen on a keystone found in the rubble at the base of the tower. The console corbels (Pl. 41, 42) are designed to be viewed from below and the decoration consists of a scroll on the sides framing a main feature on the underside and outer vertical face. The edges of the corbels are outlined with a band of either ovolo or laurel leaf moulding and the spaces beside the scroll are infilled with fish, geometric or floral motifs. The most notable feature consists of rams' heads to the corbels of the northeast and southwest squinch arches. The corbels to the southeast corner combine the vertical face and the base into a single panel of vines flowing from a vase at the base to surround a latin cross on the vertical face, and the corbel in the northeast corner has a finely carved basket in full relief.

The south face of the tower (Fig. 45) has a pair of arched windows with a distinct horseshoe profile and springing from bead moulded impost blocks on to oval corinthian dividers. The arches are slotted to contain a window insert. The west window has its sill still *in situ*; it projects inwards and is moulded with an ogee profile. On the east wall (Fig. 46) is a single wider arched opening springing from a cyma recta moulded impost. Unlike the south windows it does not appear to have had a sill. Whilst the south windows let in daylight direct, the east window opens into the space above the bema, and its purpose may have been to allow reflected light to penetrate down on to the triumphal arch below, thus highlighting its decorative moulding.

The roof of the tower has already been discussed and the lack of evidence concerning it noted. Fortunately, however, there are sufficient signs of the roof over the remainder of the church to allow its reconstruction to be presumed with more certainty. The line of the nave, bema and apse roofs (Fig. 46) is shown by the sockets for beams spanning the length of the church in the east and west faces of the tower and the east face of the west wall of the church. If the line of the sockets on the east face of the tower is projected round to the south face of the tower it is seen that the roof line, when continued over the south aisle, would have obstructed the sill of the south windows of the tower. The line of the lower roof over the aisles can be seen from the beam holes in the east face of the west wall of the church and from a single block, with a beam hole in its upper north corner, which remains *in situ* in the wall projecting northwards from the northeast corner of the tower. The roof over the nave, bema and apse must therefore have had to step at its junction with the aisle and pastophory roofs. The span of the roof over the aisles changes direction along each side of the tower, with the support for the roof being given by two corbels projecting out from the tower walls. These would have held a main beam in turn supporting roof beams spanning the shorter dimension from the tower to the outer walls of the church. Beam sockets in the east face of the west wall of the church and on the wall projecting north from the northeast corner of the tower show that the roof beams spanned from east to west for the remainder of the roof over the aisles and pastophories, in a similar direction to that of the roof over the nave, bema and apse.

The east façade of the church probably followed the outline of its roof. At the west end, as already described (Fig. 47, 50, 51), the narthex roof sloped down from the west wall of the church and at its north and south ends the apse of the narthex roof is higher than the roofs over the aisles. The three courses of masonry above the centre of the west wall of the church do not give any evidence of this wall rising above the higher roof line of the nave for its entire length. It would either have followed the line of the narthex roof until it met the nave roof, where it could have formed a gable, or it could have taken the form of a raised parapet with its top level above the apex of the nave roof.

Returning to ground level in order to consider the interior of the church, we see that its layout is similar to that of the Basilica (Fig. 44) but with the tower adding height and light to give emphasis to the east end of the nave. The nave is separated from the aisles and bema by a raised stylobate built between the column bases of the arcading directly beneath the tower. The stylobate crosses the nave at the line of the eastern face of the tower and has at its centre a narrow opening to allow access to the bema.

The stylobate is simpler than that in the Basilica, carved only with a plain ogee profile facing into the nave. The top surface is grooved and the columns of the longitudinal arcading have shallow chases to hold stone screens. From the few fragments discovered, the screens appear to have been much plainer and more austere than those in the Basilica. The only significant fragment appears to be part of a screen formed of four solid undecorated convex panels set in a moulded frame; another fragment has a simple circle decoration. The shallow chases in the columns for the screens continue up to a height of 1.5 m above the floor and are terminated by recesses, probably to hold a horizontal rail. Similar recesses are cut to either side of the easternmost arch of the arcading. This part is open to the aisles showing that the screening, possibly timber, extended up to the line of the bema, perhaps with a door between the aisles and the nave.

Within the western section of the nave there are four pedestals. These were found lying on their sides and have now been re-erected in what is believed to have been their original locations. Two are positioned against the stylobate where it closes the nave west of the bema, and face west. The second two are placed on either side of the nave between the piers of the second and third transverse arches and face inwards. The pedestals are square in plan with chamfered edges making an octagonal shape. They are each carved from single blocks. The table tops (Fig. 53, Pl. 48) are defined by a moulded edge, the top part of which is flat and below this is a recessed concave moulding. The fronts of the pedestals are given prominance by adding decoration to these table edges. The corners of the pedestals are supported by corinthian colonettes aligned with the shorter chamfered faces, whilst the long faces are infilled with either conch-headed niches, or by concave panels each framing a cross. The vertical faces of the bases of the pedestals are given shallow plain mouldings.

The northeast pedestal has the front edge of its top decorated with acanthus leaves. Below this is a niche with the cross decorated with sprigs of leaves in the four corners. The side panels are concave; the panel to the south face has a finely carved cross surrounded by a vine growing out of a small amphora at the base of the panel (Pl. 48).

The southeast pedestal (Fig. 53) has the concave moulding of the front edge of its top decorated with a band of stylised hanging acanthus. The front face has a niche and behind this the body of the pedestal is cut back to a vertical rectangular shaft leaving a deep space behind the colonnettes. The body was so much reduced by cutting away that it has broken across its shaft and has had to be re-assembled.

The body of the southwest pedestal has three concave panels each decorated with a large cross. The front face is given prominence by the addition of small leaves to the crossing and the top of the panel is also decorated by a band of leaves. The front face of the top of the pedestal has a band of hanging acanthus.

The northwest pedestal has the most decorative mouldings. The front edge of the top has a band of flowing vine leaves and on the vertical face and the concave moulding has a band of flowing acanthus. In the centre of the top band of moulding there can just be seen the traces of a cross set in a roundel. This pedestal has conch-headed niches on each of its three carved faces, and the arch to the niche of the front face is given additional decoration of a band of incised flowing acanthus.

Two shallow steps lead up from the nave to the bema and apse (Fig. 49). Around the curve of the apse the bedrock foundation has been cut to form the three tiers of seating of a synthronon. On the axis of the church, the synthronon projects outwards to form a plinth for a throne. Just short of the triumphal arch (Pl. 45) the three tiers of the synthronon stop short with only the top tier continuing past the arch into the bema. The bedrock below the walls to the south pastophory has also been cut to make a seating, and this appears to have been done after the original layout of the bema and pastophories had been established, as the doorway is now blocked by the extended synthronon. On the north side the bedrock is partly cut as a door threshold and partly as seating.

The north aisle is built against the cliff where the rock is of such good quality that it needed no lining of masonry and from the absence of any traces of plaster, it appears never to have received any further finish. At its east end (Fig. 44, 48) the north aisle terminates in an apsidal recess capped by a semi-dome springing from a concave moulded string course. Here the fourth transverse wall is thickened to accommodate the recess and its extra thickness is taken from the south pastophory beyond. The doorway to the north pastophory is on the axis of the recess, the masonry above being supported by a keystone lintel with a relieving course over it. The north jamb of the opening is cut directly from the rock.

For safety reasons the north pastophory has not been cleared but, on looking down on to it from the cliff above, the room is seen to be rectangular and extends as far as the east end of the church, alongside the bema and apse, and is divided by a transverse arch on the line of the triumphal arch to the apse. Its eastern part is slightly wider due to the narrowing of the apse. In the southwest corner there is a door leading to the bema and the room is lit by a small window in its east wall. The room would have been poorly lit and, like its counterpart in the Basilica, it may have been used as a store.

Whereas the north aisle, built against the cliff, was dark, the south aisle (Fig. 44, 45) was lit through the south facade. Between the west end of the church and the second transverse wall there are two small rectangular windows, and, opposite the tower, a more generous illumination is given by a pair of arched windows. These have corinthian imposts and the arches span on to an oval-sectioned corinthian window divider. All the windows to the south aisle are placed high on the wall; their sills are

2.9 m above the floor level and their reveals have sockets for slotted metal grilles.

At the east end of the south aisle (Fig. 44) there is, as in the north aisle, an apsidal entry to the south pastophory. Here the niche is entirely of masonry and the door structure is reversed with a single lintel over the door and above this a flat relieving arch. The door threshold forms a step up into the pastophory, and the opening is socketed to hold a pair of doors.

Like the north pastophory, the south pastophory is entered from the aisle and from the bema. The south pastophory may have been divided by a high timber screen (or perhaps a curtain) between the piers of the transverse arch spanning across the room, as there are sockets for a beam 2 m above floor level. The south pastophory is lit by three small windows, again high on the wall (Fig. 44, 45). On the south wall are two rectangular windows and a third window, on the east wall, is arched. Being the better lit of the two the south pastophory may have been the more important as a group of sockets had been cut into the floor to contain legs of a table (Pl. 47). To the left there is a small recess cut into the apse wall to serve as a cupboard. A second cupboard is recessed into the masonry to the south of the entrance from the south aisle. Clearance of the north pastophory might, of course, reveal similar features.

The gallery over the narthex, aisles and pastophories is entered from the hillside above the cliff through an opening in the north wall of the narthex. From the narthex other doorways lead to the side galleries over the aisles which in turn lead to the pastophories beyond. As in the aisles, the transverse walls of the church span across the gallery with arched openings springing from plain impost blocks. The west facade of the narthex with its outer gallery windows has already been described. Opening from the gallery to the nave below is an arcade of three corinthian arches (Fig. 47, 51, Pl. 49) with the centre span slightly wider than the outer spans. The column bases and string course sill are grooved and the columns have slots to receive a masonry screen.

The north wall of the north gallery was built of ashlar on the edge of the cliff continuing the line of the rock wall face up from the aisle below. Only the lower courses of this wall remain and there is no sign of any windows. As the tower is blank on its north face, the north wall of the gallery may also have had no openings in order to give security from the hill above or for protection from the wind. The north pastophory gallery has only one small window in its eastern wall, which is clear of the cliff edge.

The south gallery, like the south aisle, is lit through the south facade of the church (Fig. 45). Again two small rectangular windows light the gallery between the narthex and the tower. Alongside the tower more light is let in by an arcade or four equal openings with the arches spanning from plain moulded impost blocks on to lotus leaf capitals. The windows have grooved arches, capitals and bases in order to hold a solid infill. Over the south pastophory there is a single small window at the eastern end of the south facade. It is positioned to be well away from the pair of small arched windows opening on to the bema so that as little light as possible would percolate through to the bema.

The upper tier of arcading of the longitudinal walls of the nave forms the openings for the aisle galleries to overlook the nave. The arcading stands on a string course which is raised one course of masonry above the gallery floor. Neither the string course, the columns nor the pilasters of the arcading are slotted for screens, so the arcading would have to have been open to the nave for its full height. Intercolumnar screens were thus only used in the arcading of the west wall of the church.

Beam sockets show that the gallery floors were supported on rafters spanning the shortest direction in each space. As already described (Fig. 51), in the reconstruction of the narthex, the narthex gallery floor beams spanned from the west facade on to the west wall of the church and was supported on beams lying along these walls and resting on corbels. In the aisles the floor beams spanned from the west wall of the church to the first and second transverse walls as can be seen by the sockets cut into the masonry. Alongside the tower, where the distance between the transverse walls is greater, the direction of the rafters changed to span in a north-south direction across the aisles. In the south aisle the rafters rested in sockets cut into the walls, but in the north aisle they were supported by beams spanning along the aisle walls and resting on corbels in the same way as the gallery of the narthex. In the south pastophory the rafters were again changed in an east-west direction bearing on the transverse walls.

As the East Church stands today, the main evidence for its decoration remains that of the stone carving, the use of the corinthian order and the embellishment of the narthex doors and the squinch arches of the tower. During the excavation of the floor the earth fill was thoroughly sifted, but no traces of any floor or wall mosaic were found. However, some areas of plaster and the sketch outlines of painting still remain on the masonry fabric in the bema, apse and south aisle giving some indication of surface decoration. Plaster appears to have been applied to both walls and columns, but to what extent is not known. It is hard to believe, judging from the small areas that remain, that the whole interior was plastered, as was the case in the Basilica. The pilaster complex of the south respond to the first transverse arch over the nave has traces of plaster on its demi-column. This was applied in such a rough way that if this quality of work had been employed throughout the building, most of the mouldings, especially on the columns, would have been obliterated. Generally the plaster is burnished smooth and gives a light cream or pink background for over-painting in reds, blues and blacks. The apsidal end of the south aisle has traces of pink painted plaster and the string course below the semi-dome has a series of red lines painted directly on to the masonry, resembling a row of birds feet, with a horizontal band of pink below. Elsewhere in the south aisle, red and pink strokes can still be seen on the piers of the south wall of the church and below one impost block of a transverse arch is a band of black.

Compared with the Basilica, the stone carving of the East Church, except for the door to the south aisle, is much more rigid and drilling is used to a greater extent. Motifs such as the flowing acanthus are used in both churches, but they are more restrained in the East Church (Pl. 44, 46). The nave of the East Church would also have been much plainer with its simply moulded stylobate and screens: the main features of the building are the pedestals, and the structure of the tower above. The floors are paved in stone with none of the richness of the *opus sectile* of the Basilica. The painting appears to have been sketchy and may not have contributed much to the embellishment of the interior. Nevertheless, the restrained use of decoration is amply compensated for by the structural form of the building. With the innovation of superimposing the tower on to the nave and the departure from the traditional basilican construction, more emphasis seems to have been given to the dramatic use of the spaces and the lighting of the interior than to the decoration.

The nave of the Basilica was evenly lit by the large windows at aisle and gallery level and at clerestory level by groups of smaller windows. Windows situated in the west wall would also have lit the nave. The lighting would have been mainly from the south on account of the rock cliff to the north, but some north light would have been given by the north clerestory as it was above the cliff (Fig. 22). In the Basilica the triumphal arch was on the line of the junction of the nave to the bema and the wall above would have been lit from the nave. Beyond, the apse and bema were lit by reflected light from the nave and through the pair of windows at the east end of the apse. The East Church, in contrast, does not have the linear characteristics of the Basilica (Fig. 49). As the nave and bema are crossed by the transverse arches all at the same height the space of the nave continues right through to the semi-dome of the apse, with the triumphal arch positioned at the junction between the bema and the apse. Compared with the basilican form there is not the transition from the high space of the nave to the smaller volume of the apse. The arrangement of windows gives an insight into the quality of light of the interior. Some light would have entered the nave from the windows in the west wall and narthex, but, at floor level, doors have brackets for curtains so little light would have come through at low level. Between the west wall and the tower the nave was only lit through small windows in the south facade. Opposite the tower the pair of arched windows in the south aisle and the triple arcade above it at gallery level substantially increased the intensity of light in the nave. In addition the pair of windows high in the tower would have given direct light to the nave below. The bema and apse, however, were hardly lit at all and care appears to have been taken to prevent direct light from entering at gallery level by placing the small windows into the pastophories away from the openings from the pastophories into the bema. The pair of windows at the east end of the apse had thick inserts and may thus only have given a diffused glow. A hole drilled in the keystone of the triumphal arch over the apse may have been intended for the suspension of an oil lamp or polykandelon over the apse. Some light, though, was focussed on to the wall above the triumphal arch by the window in the east face of the tower which opens into the void above the bema.

The development from the basilican form by superimposing the tower on to the east end of the nave has had two effects upon the interior. The spaces of the nave, bema and apse have been united and a prominence has been given to the east end of the nave by the volume of the tower and an intentional increase in light. At floor level this coincides with the enclosing of the nave from the aisles and the bema, and the positions of the four pedestals. Although this subdivision is not new (it occurs in the Basilica as well) the prominence given by the tower may well be connected with a change in emphasis in the liturgy of the day.

D. THE COLONNADED WALK

Linking the Basilica to the East Church the Colonnaded Walk was built along the edge of the Middle Terrace. Its south wall was arcaded with a colonnade of corinthian columns supported on the high retaining wall of the terrace (Fig. 55). The north wall was solid, pierced only occasionally by doorways or arches. The Colonnaded Walk rises 8.5 m from west to east by means of gentle ramps between steps marked by pilaster

complexes[11] joining the two levels of arcading and supporting transverse
arches with gable walls above to enclose corresponding changes of level
in the roof. The pilaster complexes occur at the western entrance, P4, at
the Baptistery, and at the entrance to the East Church narthex, P1, with a
further two east of the Baptistery P3 36 m, and P2 19 m to the west of the
East Church. In addition to joining the two principal buildings of the
monastery, the Colonnaded Walk gave access to the intervening spaces
and buildings to the north. It also controlled entry to the monastery from
the hillside below on account of the high retaining wall to the south, and
at the same time it provided a shaded and sheltered ambulatory with the
arcading framing magnificent views over the valley of the Kalykadnos.

Today only the retaining wall, the lower courses of the north wall and
parts of the pilaster complexes remain. The approach along the south face
of the Basilica has been rebuilt along its original line, and between the
Basilica and the Baptistery the retaining wall, which had fallen away,
has been rebuilt to the pavement level using the fallen masonry, with
additional courses of smaller blocks added to make up the height. From
the Baptistery to the East Church the retaining wall is more complete,
with part of the stylobate (Pl. 57-59) together with some column plinths,
bases of the colonnade still *in situ*. A number of plinths, bases and
fragments of shafts and voussoirs were found on the hillside below and
they have been reinstated. Of the pilaster complexes, P4, the western
gateway, was standing at the commencement of the excavations up to two
courses above the springing of the transverse arch, but unfortunately it
collapsed during the winter of 1962. Photographic evidence does however
exist (Pl. 53). Only the foundations remain of the two pilaster complexes
in front of the Baptistery but pilaster complex P3 has sufficient masonry to
mark the change in level of the stylobate, whilst pilaster complexes P2 and
P1 stand to the height of the springing of the arcading. Between the
Basilica and the Baptistery the north wall of the Colonnaded Walk is
marked by only a single course of masonry above the pavement level, and
onwards to the East Church the wall stands in places up to a height of
approximately 2.5 m above the pavement.

It will be seen later that the Baptistery underwent a change of plan
during, or shortly after, its original construction and that there was an
earlier route. The new walk strikes a direct line from the east wall of the
Basilica to the narthex of the East Church, with the north wall of the

[11] To avoid confusion with the references used in the Preliminary Reports, I have
adopted those used by Michael Gough.

Colonnaded Walk passing clear of the south aisle of the Baptistery, thereby allowing a narthex to be added. The difference in orientation of the Basilica and the East Church to this line caused irregular alignments of the two pilaster complexes P4, the western entrance, and P1, the East Church narthex. The Pilaster Complex, P4, is aligned with the east facade of the Basilica and thus presents a facade to the west correctly aligned to the approach from the Forecourt of the nave complex. At the eastern end, P1 is built orthogonally to the line of the arcading and the plan of the narthex of the East Church is wedge-shaped (Fig. 44).[12] It is therefore likely that the construction of the Colonnaded Walk commenced after the start of the building of the East Church and the Baptistery and that its design, and probably most of its construction was under way by the time that these two buildings were finished.

There is sufficient evidence to reconstruct the main structural elements of the Colonnaded Walk (Fig. 59, Pl. 59). The retaining wall is built of large ashlar masonry. The top is capped by a course of masonry which projects outwards over the south face of the retaining wall to form a stylobate. In places the retaining wall is strengthened by piers projecting outwards as far as the outer vertical face of the stylobate. To drain the spaces enclosed by the Colonnaded Walk, culverts were built crossing below the pavement, the water issuing out of the wall through small u-shaped spouts, one of which is to be seen to the west of pilaster complex P2. Pilaster complexes P1 and P2 stand to the height of the springing of the arcading thus establishing its level. The pilasters are built off a pair of deep plinths 0.5 m and 0.25 m high above which the rectangular shafts rise to corinthian capitals set on decorated moulded impost blocks. The height from stylobate to the springing of the arcading is 3.85 m. Between pilaster complexes the arcading is supported off columns with a spacing of 1.85 m. The height to the underside of the keystone of the arcading would therefore have been 4.78 m. The voussoirs are 0.4 m thick. If a single course of masonry 0.3 m thick were placed above the arch, the eaves of the roof would have been approximately 5.48 m above the level of the stylobate.

There is no direct evidence of the shape of the roof. At pilaster complexes P1 and P2 the transverse arches are seen to spring from the same height as the arcading. At pilaster complex P1 the span of the transverse arch is 3.4 m which would have meant that the height of the transverse arch would have been 6.0 m. Whether the roof was hipped or a monopitch is difficult to determine for certain, but a study of the north

---

[12] See above, pp. 104-105.

wall gives some clues. An opening in the north wall just to the west of the East Church narthex has its threshold 6.0 m higher than the stylobate on the south wall. The width of the opening suggests an arch. The width of the opening indicates that the level of the arch would have been higher than the arcading of the south wall. Such a situation could well have been accommodated within a high north wall rising to the apex of the roof. To have sprung a pitched roof from the level suggested by the arched opening in the north wall will have meant an unnnecessary height of plain masonry above the arcade. The proposal for a monopitch also satisfies the roof profiles for the Baptistery where, as will be suggested later, the narthex roof is thought to have pitched northwards permitting a symmetrical roof from over the twin aisles. Moreover a monopitch roof to the Colonnaded Walk sloping down to the south would have shed rainwater downhill, thereby reducing the amount to be channelled away from within the monastery site.

Between the pilaster complexes the arcading is supported by corinthian columns standing on deep rectangular plinths which are in two parts. Some of the lower plinths have ogee mouldings on the top edge (Fig. 60) whilst others have a rounded edge incised with ovolo decoration. Three sides of the plinths, those between the columns and the side facing into the Colonnaded Walk, are decorated with horizontal panels with semicircular inset ends containing laurel leaf garlands. The upper plinths are smaller than the lower plinths and have square cut top edges with decorated side panels similar to those of the lower plinths. One upper plinth has also been found with a panel bearing two pairs of crossed fish with shells in the upper corners. The base of the shaft is formed out of the same block as the upper plinth. The corinthian capitals, as seen at the Shrine (Fig. 57), probably followed both the naturalistic style of the Basilica to the west and the more rigid style of the East Church to the east. The voussoirs of the arcading are decorated on one side like the plinths, to face inwards. The main feature of their decoration is a wide band of scallop below which is a thin band of bead and reel. Above the scallop there is a moulding of ovolo capped with a plain bold projecting cyma recta profile. At the arch spring the mouldings turn to the horizontal before following the curve of the next arch. The large transverse (north-south) arches have a similar decoration, but on both sides, with the keystones embellished on one side with a rosette.

The pilaster complexes that mark the entry to the Colonnaded Walk and its changes in level are cruciform in arrangement. On the south wall the coresponds to the arcading cross the piers supporting and buttressing the transverse arches which supported the gable wall of the higher level

roof. The pavement level and the means by which the change in level was
accomplished is difficult to ascertain because of the lack of evidence, and
because of the fact that the paving at the eastern end appears never to have
been completed. To supplement the general reconstruction the following
account of the Colonnaded Walk proceeds from west to east, from P4 to
P1 to give a description of the various parts.

The approach to the Colonnaded Walk from the west is along the
terrace below the south wall of the Basilica. It has already been mentioned
that the southernmost extent of the Forecourt is uncertain, and that some
form of retaining structure must have linked it to the Colonnaded Walk.
The present retaining wall was built, or possibly rebuilt during the
secondary period of occupation as a fallen frieze block from the south
facade of the Basilica protrudes at its base. The wall is built of large ashlar
blocks, but is uncoursed and has the appearance of re-using old masonry.

The retaining wall follows the line of the south wall of the Basilica up
to within 9.6 m of P4, where it then curves southwards to align with the
Colonnaded Walk. The pavement level at P4 is approximately level with
the Forecourt to the Basilica.

Pilaster Complex 4 was built from large ashlar blocks abutting, but not
integrated with, the corner of the Basilica. The transverse wall is 7.5 m
wide and P4N projects out from the southeast corner of the Basilica by
1.5 m to enclose the west end of the north wall of the Colonnaded Walk.
Until 1962, when it fell, P4 stood to the height of the spring of the arcade
and the transverse wall, the capital and first voussoir were still *in situ*.

The stylobate for the south wall arcading is missing between P4 and the
Baptistery, but the level of the pavement can be established from the
threshold in the north wall to a door just to the east of the Basilica, and at
the entrance to the living quarters further to the east. Adjacent to the
Baptistery, the door thresholds to the living quarters, the thresholds to the
Baptistery itself and the threshold to the opening to the necropolis area
indicate a change in level of some 0.6 m probably by means of two
stairways, one to either side of the Baptistery entrance.

Opposite the Baptistery are two large buttresses 2.2 m by 1.5 m wide.
One is in line with the southwest corner of the narthex and the second is
opposite the cross wall dividing the narthex. A carved pilaster base is built
into the southwest corner of the narthex. Although this base was probably
originally intended for an arch at the present line of the north wall of the
Colonnaded Walk, it may well later have formed part of the corespond for
a flush springing transverse arch across to the western buttress of the
south wall. The base of its other respond may have been the loose base
found in the area and now placed to the east of the narthex door.

However, there is no firm evidence of a transverse wall and gable end in this location, but on the analogy of the other pilaster complexes at changes in level, the change in level here will also have been accompanied by a change in level of the roof on the line of the west buttress. Between the two massive buttresses there is a space of 3 m the purpose of which is not clear. Both Headlam[13] and Verzone have suggested an entrance to the Baptistery at this point on account of a long masonry block that was seen lying diagonally across the opening giving the appearance of a stair curving westwards. However, excavation showed no evidence of a stairway or even a continuation of the south wall between the piers below pavement level. It was found that the buttresses were resting on bedrock and the space between was filled with a gravelly clay. Within this fill two parallel retaining walls had been built diagonally across the pavement to contain the fill. No permanent masonry infill between the buttresses appears to have existed. For continuity of the arcading there was probably a large single-span arch between the buttresses, with the roof continuing from the east as far as the west face of the west buttress (Fig. 55). As shall be seen later, the pavement was never completed and a stair between the buttresses may well have been intended but never built.

To the east of the Baptistery the north wall is solid to retain the upper terrace with only a small arched opening alongside the Baptistery narthex leading to the necropolis.

Directly opposite the tomb of Tarasis the Elder there is a Shrine (Fig. 57, Pl. 60) incorporated into the colonnading of the south wall. The form of the shrine follows the architectural order of the pilaster complexes: the double plinth with corinthian capitals supporting the arcading. The main decorative feature of the Shrine is a scalloped niche within which are three subordinate scalloped recesses each framed with corinthian colonnettes rising from an acanthus leaf plinth. Although badly damaged, the central recess appears to have possibly been a *hetoimasia* with standing figures to either side. The niche is framed by pairs of fluted pilasters each separated by a shallowly carved panel of intertwining vines rising from amphora. Above this is a pediment with, on either side, a partridge with an angel above to fill the triangle below the pilaster capitals for the arcading. These angels, floating free on the plain background, are similar in character to those on the jambs of the Evangelist Gateway in the Basilica. Placed midway along the length of the Colonnnaded Walk, the

---

[13] Site plan as found in Arthur C. Headlam, *Ecclesiastical Sites in Isauria (Cilicia Trachea)*, Society for the Promotion of Hellenistic Studies, Supplementary Papers 1 (London, 1893), Pl. 1, Fig. 1.

Shrine marks a stylistic watershed between the Basilica and the East Church. Michael Gough writes in his Fourth Preliminary Report:

> To integrate the shrine with the colonnade, it had to be fitted with two pilaster capitals, facing east and west respectively. A difference in style between these suggests that the sculptor was aware not only of the shrine's almost central position, but of its role as a connecting link between the two main churches. For while the westward facing capital more resembles those in the Basilica – lively, florid and naturalistic ... – that which faces eastwards is in the more restrained, formalised style of the Eastern Church. Coincidence cannot be ruled out, but the difference between the two capitals is marked.[14]

This can also be seen in the capitals of pilaster complexes P4 and P1, which again suggests that the intermediate column capitals showed this difference.

Progressing eastwards, pilaster complex P3 marks the next major change in level of 1.81 m, which is indicated by a step up in the levels of the stylobate either side of the pilaster complex. No traces of any permanent steps were found. Excavation here showed four main layers of fill. Layer 1 was of fine limestone chippings and is thought to be the level of the pavement during the secondary period of occupation as below this level was found the top remaining base block of the P3N pilaster. Layers 2 and 3 sloped down from north to south across the Colonnaded Walk and represent a washdown of scree from the slopes above that occurred following the first abandonment of the monastery. Layer 4, level with the top of the base block of P3N consists of a yellow mortar, earth and masonry fill which appears to have been a primary levelling of the terrace for a pavement. On the other side of the pavement the level of fill is seen to be above the top of the stylobate of the south wall so the earth pavement must surely have been a temporary ramp that was never removed.

Between pilaster complexes P3 and P2 the pavement is nearly level for a distance of 17 m, only rising 0.29 m. At P2 there is again a steep rise of 1.82 m. The surviving structure of P2 is more complete than that of P3, rising above the springing of the arcading and the transverse arch where the first voussoir of a horseshoe arch remains *in situ*. The pavement here consists of a layer of fine limestone chippings and its original level can be seen in the rise of the base course of the north wall. Unlike the paving to the west of P2, the level follows that of the stylobate. A flight of steps must have been built at this point because the change in levels of the

[14] M. Gough, "Fourth Preliminary Report," p. 38.

pavement to either side of P2 is abrupt; two steps were found but as they had no foundations they may not have been part of the original structure. The cross wall at pilaster complex P2N continues northwards into the upper terrace, and as will be seen later, probably formed a wall to a building across the court to the East Church. To the west of P2N there is a vertical joint in the masonry showing that an opening to the north may have been originally intended. This was abandoned and the north wall was built solid right up to P2N.

Between P2 and the East Church the pavement continues as a graded ramp until it meets the bedrock beneath the floor of the narthex. At pilaster complex P1, the south facade of the narthex, the bases of the transverse arch pilaster are 1.62 m above pavement level; the floor of the narthex is a further 0.58 m higher. Although there are the remains of paving in the narthex adjacent to P1, the change in level here seems never to have been completed since the floor is above the base of the transverse arch, and only sufficient bedrock was cut away to clear the lower plinth of P1 at the start of the colonnade. Furthermore, the opening in the north wall leading to the court was built without its threshold being completed. Also, to drain the forecourt, a shallow stone gutter was built across the pavement to issue over the top of the stylobate above the expected level of any pavement floor.

It is clear that the three main buildings of the monastery complex were structurally completed and had also reached differing stages of decoration before being abandoned. The Colonnaded Walk, however, shows obvious signs that it may never have been finished. These doubts were raised by Michael Gough in his Fifth Preliminary Report:

> It may be recalled that in 1965, for reasons of expediency, the surface of the walkway between P2 and P3 was left in the form of a ramp although it was quite clear that the true surface was much lower, at the level of the column plinths on the southern side. In 1967, this sector was excavated, and it was soon established that the walkway had been begun from the east end, had progressed a certain distance – probably as far as the shrine – and had been left only half finished. In the first place, while two steps were discovered at the change of level at P2/P2N, further west, at P3/P3N there were none at all; furthermore, the rock face west of P3N is only roughly chiselled and the lower courses of P3N itself are crude and unfinished in contrast to the lowest blocks of P3 where all the mouldings are complete to the smallest detail. Noteworthy also is the fact that while there are a number of column plinths and bases *in situ* to the east of the shrine, there are none at all to the west of it. There are other factors which contribute to the near certainty that the work on the colonnade was abandoned before completion. The first is the extraordinary dearth of even fragmentary material on the slope

south of the walkway; for example, only one capital has yet been discovered in the area east of the shrine. A second was the fact that in 1967 two column plinths of the dimensions used in the walkway were found built into the secondary walling of the Basilica. These plinths had not been completely finished.[15]

Since this report, excavation of the Lower Terrace below the Basilica has revealed more evidence. Two voussoirs and a double arch spring were found below P4 and a further single voussoir was found at the east end of the Colonnaded Walk. It thus appears that arcading was also built at the west end. The buttressing walls and workshops of the Lower Terrace can be seen to extend further east into an area unexcavated owing to Michael Gough's untimely death. Until this area is cleared for its entire length, possibly revealing more fragments of arcading, the extent of the arcading will not be settled. The finds might clear up some of the earlier doubts, but there are still some further questions of the state of completion which need explanation.

If completed, the north wall of the Colonnaded Walk would have contained a vast amount of plain building stone. Most of the north wall, however, is missing – to the west of the Baptistery its entire height, and to the east its upper part – yet little trace of fallen masonry from this wall has been found. To the east of the Baptistery the north wall only remains where it may have been built to retain the Upper Terrace, which may have protected the Colonnaded Walk from falling stone from above. Excavations below the lower retaining wall do not reveal any large masonry blocks, and furthermore the ground layers excavated at pilaster complexes P3 and P3N showed only a sloping scree fill in Levels 2 and 3 without signs of masonry. The masonry may, of course, have been cleared during the secondary period of occupation. However, had the north wall here been built to its full height and subsequently fallen, the shrine would surely have been vulnerable and would have fallen as well.

Another problem concerns the two large buttresses opposite the Baptistery. Their size suggests that they should have been foundations for a masonry wall and pilaster complexes more massive and more rigid than the others. The masonry should have been protected from falling scree by the Baptistery and surely considerable remains might have been expected. Yet the masonry of both these buttresses stop at an identical height just at the pavement level.

What is known with more certainty is that the groups of rooms to the west of the Baptistery were completed and were inhabited. On this

[15] M. Gough, "Fifth Preliminary Report," pp. 164-165.

account the north wall of the Colonnaded Walk must have existed to its full height between the Baptistery and the Basilica. This wall has now gone and may well have followed the retaining wall, which had fallen foreward, thereby releasing the earth fill below the pavement. From this evidence the minimum length of the Colonnaded Walk that was actually built could be reconstructed thus: the whole of the south retaining wall and a part of the arcading at either end, together with the western entrance and the pilaster complexes P1, P1N, P2, P2N and P3 and P3N, the bases of the pilaster complex opposite the Baptistery and the lower part of the north wall between the Baptistery and the East Church, and also the entire north wall between the Baptistery and the Basilica. The pavement was only an earth ramp.

It is clear that, from the outset, the Colonnaded Walk formed a major feature in the plan for the expansion of the monastery, yet may never have been finished. Perhaps a continuing growth of the population could have pressed the builders to concentrate more on the utilitarian structures, such as the Two-Storey Building, the Living Quarters and the Spring Complex, rather than the early completion of the cloister – the main use of which would merely have been the one of protection and delight.

E. THE BAPTISTERY

Approximately a third of the way between the Basilica and the East Church on the Middle Terrace there is a twin-apsed building. It is orientated east-west and has a narthex to the south which is entered through the north wall of the Colonnaded Walk. When excavated, the discovery of a fine cruciform-shaped font in the north aisle led to the conclusion that the building was a Baptistery. As Michael Gough writes in the Second Preliminary Report:

> When the floor level was reached, it was found that the building was not, as we had earlier supposed, a twin-apsed chapel, but a baptistery of the most unusual type. In the western half of the northern room was a font in the form of a Greek cross, so sunk into the floor that the top of it was slightly above the level of the paving. Three steps led down from each of the arms of the cross to a square central space 1.35 m below. This space, lined with plaster, was designed to accommodate a pair of medium sized feet. The font was fed with running water from a channel connected with one of the main aquaducts and drained away through a plug-hole at the bottom.[16]
> (Pl. 50)

[16] M. Gough, "Second Preliminary Report," p. 114.

The north aisle of the Cave Church, (Fig. 14) with its circular sinking in the floor that may have been a font, possibly served as the original baptistery. The expansion of the monastery necessitated a larger baptistery and the placing of it well to the east of the Basilica must have meant that it was part of the grand design of the two churches at either end of the terrace. During the construction of the Baptistery its fabric was altered enabling its exact position in the phasing of the expansion of the monastery to be postulated.

As has already been described, the main structure of the East Church was started before the final alignment of the Colonnaded Walk had been settled. Likewise, the Baptistery appears to have been originally designed as a twin-apsed building to open directly off the walk. The south wall of the south aisle of the Baptistery has all the appearance of being originally intended as an external wall; the door has a moulded frame, and the south face of the wall is tooled to a smooth surface. In the southwest corner of the south aisle there is an arch spring of an arch that would have spanned westwards onto a wall to the north of the present Colonnaded Walk (Fig. 63). Excavation of the area to the west of the Baptistery showed that this wall was never built (Fig. 66). This arch and presumably the wall to the west was abandoned almost immediately after the arch spring was erected, as the masonry course above is that of a normal external corner and the arch could never have been built. Also, opposite this corner, in the present south wall of the narthex (Fig. 63), there is a group of blocks coursed to suggest the east end of a solid wall which could have been part of a south wall of the original walk from the Basilica to the East Church. The completion of the structure of the Baptistery without the arch springing from its southwest corner must have taken place at the earliest after the line of the new and present Colonnaded Walk was decided. The new south facade of the Baptistery was then completed incorporating part of the south wall of the original walk into the new north wall of the present walk. The space between became the narthex to the Baptistery.

The structure of the Baptistery remains to a height of approximately 3.5 m with the apse walls and lower courses of the semi-dome still *in situ*. The Baptistery is 10.4 m long and 8.8 m across the two aisles with the narthex adding a further 3.1 m to its north-south dimension. During excavation some fallen blocks were uncovered and could be returned to their original positions, enabling the semi-domes to be partially restored and the apse windows to be entirely rebuilt. In addition the decaying bedrock at the base of the west wall was strengthened and a substantial part of the masonry wall above was replaced.

The narthex is entered through an undecorated door in the north wall of the Colonnaded Walk. The opening is rebated and has pivots cut into the threshold for a pair of doors. Small crosses have been scratched into the jambs. The interior is plain with the north wall tooled smooth from the period when it was intended to be an external wall. The other walls are rough, presumably as a base for plastering. The floor is of badly coursed flagstones within the narthex but to the east of the entrance to the south aisle there is a doorway leading to a small room. The north jamb of this door is cut from a pier that is integrated with the south wall of the south aisle. The south jamb, however, is cut from an upright block against which are coursed the blocks of the dividing wall. The opening is rebated and has a socket for a single door. Beyond the door, built into the north wall there is a second pier with a spring for a transverse arch in line with the apse arch of the south aisle. There is no co-respond for this arch in the south wall and this spring, seemingly without a function in the completed narthex, may originate from the earlier plans for the Baptistery. Likewise, the masonry of the north jamb of the door, also tied into the wall, may originate from this period.

The doorway leading to the south aisle has its frame decorated with a raised linear moulding similar to that used for the windows on the south wall of the Basilica (Fig. 63). The lintel is relieved by an arch. This doorway is rebated and has sockets for a pair of doors. The sockets here are interesting as they differ from the type used elsewhere. The top sockets are round and penetrate fairly deep into the lintel and the threshold has square sockets with a lead-in groove to the inside. Rust stains suggests that some form of ferrous sleeve had been inserted. The lintel and threshold are also slotted to receive a bolt to lock the doors. This suggests the Baptistery probably stood by itself until the completion of the Colonnaded Walk, and would have needed to be kept secure.

The interior of the Baptistery (Fig. 62) consists of two similarly sized aisles with apsidal east ends, each slightly narrower than their aisles. The two apses are separated by a demi-column with a lotus leaf capital from which spring the triumphal arches and also the first arch of an arcade that divided the aisles. From the curve of the arch spring it is reasonable to assume that the arcade had three spans requiring two columns. No trace remains of the western corespond of the arcade. The height of the springing of the arcade as seen by the position of the capital at its eastern end is 2.75 m above the north aisle floor (Fig. 61, Pl. 52). If the arcade were of three spans the arches would have been around 1.5 m in diameter resulting in a dimension from the north aisle floor to keystone of 3.50 m. The apse semi-domes spring from a cyma recta string course which returns at the north and south walls of the Baptistery to form imposts for the responds to their triumphal arches. In addition, the string courses frame the upper part of small arched windows which are set in the axis of the apses. The span of the apses is 3.10 m and their semi-domes are horseshoe in profile with their centres of curvature approximately 0.30 m above the level of the spring. A total height of the apsidal semi-domes must then have been in the region of 4.60 m – 1.10 m higher than the arcading.

The south aisle is empty and no traces of its floor remain. In the west wall is a large rectangular opening facing a small yard. The opening is 1.13 m wide and 1.70 m high and has splayed rebates and pivots for inward opening shutters. There is a relieving arch near the lintel. The traces of wall plaster which remain are too encrusted to reveal an indication of any decoration but fragments of plaster at low level do, however, show that there was a floor as they stop to a definite line, which is slightly lower than the floor of the north aisle so there may have been a step along the arcading dividing the two aisles.

The north aisle has a small arched window in the west wall in addition to the window (Fig. 63) in the apse. The aisle is paved in random coursed stone slabs arranged in a north-south direction. The paving stops at the line of arcading between the two aisles. A small altar base was found *in situ* set into the floor of the north apse. Michael Gough again writes:

> Most unusually it had only three sockets, instead of the canonical four, for the legs and the centrally placed reliquary recess, its stone lid still in position, raised hopes of a most interesting discovery. Most unfortunately it had been robbed.[17]

Nearby was found the altar top. Although broken, all its fragments remained and have been reassembled. The top is rectangular with a shallow recess cut into the top surface. Within the north apse there is a low single-tiered synthronon with a raised section of three roughly carved blocks in the centre, presumably added during the secondary period of occupation. In front of the apse, between the altar and the font, were found two large column bases and plinths. These were obviously too large for this location and on account of the design of the plinths they probably originate from the arcading of the Colonnaded Walk. Fragments of smaller column shafts and bases were found built into the secondary period lining of the north wall, which may well have been originally used

[17] Ibid.

here, as they are too small for use in the arcading of the building and too large to have been part of any furniture.

Fragments of wall plaster in various stages of decay and encrustation were found throughout the interior of the Baptistery. The only plaster that could be successfully cleaned is in the north aisle and apse and from these fragments their decoration can be reconstructed. Within the apse, painting covered the wall from the synthronon up to the string course. On the axis of the apse are remains of a single central panel with a wide border to either side. This panel has a dark red background with white, grey and black diagonal stripes, which suggest a panel of split marble. There are three parts to the borders; in the centre there is a wide red vertical band on which is painted white grain and bead shapes outlined in dark red and arranged in a diagonal cross pattern. This pattern may represent a debased form of the classical motif of crossed and twisted ribbons. To either side of this panel, again framed in deep red, there is a narrow vertical yellow stripe which is in turn followed by a wider band of yellow forming a background to a miniature painted arcade facing inwards to the centre of the border in deep red with white dots over the abutments. To either side of the central panel and its borders there are traces of painting depicting split panels of *verde antico*. These panels appear to extend as far as the demi-column of the dividing arcade and on the north wall of the apse and aisle as far as the west wall.

The style of painting resembles closely that of the Basilica, especially the south pastophory. The style, carried over from the Basilica but absent in the East Church, suggests that, although completed after the re-alignment of the Colonnaded Walk, the Baptistery may have been finished and decorated before the East Church was sufficiently far advanced for the painters to need to move on. The change in style of the decoration between the Baptistery and the East Church may also indicate a considerable lapse in time and that the painters of the Basilica and Baptistery were no longer resident at the monastery at the time that the East Church was ready for painting.

Above the north wall of the Baptistery (Fig. 61, 62) there is a chamber 8.5 m long by 3 m wide cut into the cliff for three of its walls and using the masonry upper courses of the north wall of the north aisle to complete the enclosure. The chamber is entered through a doorway in its east wall. The southern jamb is built of masonry, and the north jamb is cut out of the rock. The jambs are rebated to accommodate a door. To the east there is an arch cut into the wall containing a stone sarcophagus and a second sarcophagus is placed diagonally across the entrance to the chamber.

Unfortunately, the walls of the Baptistery do not rise high enough to give any indication of the roof line. However, by studying the cross section of the building from the rock cliff to the Colonnaded Walk, a reasoned proposition can be attempted (Fig. 58, 61). The cross section consists of five elements. The Colonnaded Walk is thought to have had a monopitch roof rising to the north wall which formed the south wall of the Baptistery narthex. This is followed by the narthex and the two aisles built against the rock cliff. To the north of the north aisle, 3.0 m above its floor level is the upper chamber which has its north wall some 4.5 m high also cut into the cliff. The Baptistery is thus contained between two high walls, the north wall of the Colonnaded Walk and the face of the cliff. If these walls were ridges of the roof then it would have sloped downwards to the north wall of the narthex and the north wall of the north aisle. The roof over the aisles could then have been either a single pitched roof with its ridge over the arcade dividing the two aisles, or a pair of smaller pitched roofs (as illustrated) with a third valley on the line of the arcade. The former suggestion has a very high roof with its ridge some 8.5 m above floor level resulting in an excessively high wall above the arcading between the aisles. This roof form would not have followed the spatial intention to divide the Baptistery into two parts, each aisle being architecturally independant and with its own apse. The second proposal with two separate pitched roofs is therefore preferred.

F. Living Quarters

As the community grew so it needed more living quarters. The Cave Complex had limited opportunity for expansion, so new domestic buildings were added on the terrace between the principal buildings (Fig. 71). The space between the Basilica and the Baptistery is almost entirely filled with building. Beyond the Baptistery the terrace contains the necropolis, an open space. Further to the east buildings were arranged around the forecourt of the East Church. Below the Basilica the western end of the Lower Terrace was excavated revealing retaining and abutment walls and possibly more domestic buildings which may have included another bath house. Although some of the buildings and spaces listed are not strictly of domestic use, they are dealt with here for the sake of convenience.

Between the Basilica and the Baptistery there are four separate groups of rooms (Fig. 66, Pl. 61). The space is 37 m long and approximately 11 m deep from north to south. The bedrock slopes up from approximately 1 m below the Colonnaded Walk to approximately 2 m above it at the base of the rock cliff at the east end, and to approximately 3 m at the west end. Part of the building had two storeys, with the lower rooms cut into the bedrock, and the upper rooms resting on the rock at the higher level at the base of the rock cliff.

Only the north wall of the Colonnaded Walk is built of large ashlar masonry; the remainder of the masonry walls is built of small blocks. Part of the way along the Colonnaded Walk, at the west corner of the central group of rooms, there is a decorated plinth without evidence of any accompanying feature. The plinth may remain from the early alignment of the Colonnaded Walk which had been built over and incorporated into the blank new north wall of the Colonnaded Walk. The entrance to the living quarters have their thresholds cut into the coursed ashlar as it stood, sometimes straddling two blocks. The plan to build living quarters here may thus have been conceived after the commencement of the Colonnaded Walk along its present alignment.

The main group of rooms is the centre of the three groups abutting the Colonnaded Walk. It is arranged round an entrance hall (a in Fig. 66) entered by a doorway with sockets for a single leaf door, which as there are bolt sockets in the threshold, could be made secure. The hall is 3.0 m wide and 3.7 m deep. Opposite the entrance is a stair leading to an upper storey and to both sides are openings to rooms to the east (b), and to the west (c and d). Room (b) to the east of the stair (Pl. 61, 64) is 2.5 m wide and 6.0 m deep and is at the same level as the entrance hall (a). It was separated from the hall by a single leaf door. The lower part of the walls and most of the floor is cut out of the rock and had been tooled to a smooth surface curving up at the walls (Pl. 62). A fault lying diagonally across the floor had been carefully filled with small chips of stone. Uphill, outside the north wall of this room, there is a channel cut into the rock to divert ground water. The channel turns southwards at the northwest corner to pass along the west wall of this room and disappears below the entrance hall stair. The carefully smoothed floor, the channel around the outside and the door all suggest that this room may have been a store; and as it was possibly dry, it may have been a granary. To the west of the entrance hall (a) (Pl. 61) there is an opening (with a step down of 0.41 m) to two interconnecting rooms (c and d). The first room (c) is 3.6 m wide and 5.2 m deep. The lower parts of the east and north walls are cut into the rock. The west wall which divides it from the adjoining room is built of masonry for its full height. As in the store (b), the floor is partly smoothed bedrock, but here it has not been tooled to such a fine surface. The remainder of the floor is compacted earth. The second room (d) has its floor slightly higher (0.13 m) than room (c) and again the floor is cut from the rock in the northern part and compacted earth in the southern part. The north wall is, as in the adjoining room (c), cut from the bedrock to a height of approximately 2 m with the west wall again built entirely of masonry. Across the room is a line of two monolith piers and base for a third arranged in a north-south axis. The piers and the north wall have grooves cut to hold a shelf. A stone bee-hive oven was found in the southwest corner. The rubble fill from these two rooms (c and d) contained a considerable amount of plaster which suggests that they were possibly a store opening off the entrance hall with a kitchen beyond.

From the entrance hall (a) a masonry stair (Pl. 62) rises to a height of 0.71 m above the floor to stop level with the remaining courses of the north wall. Beyond is an intermediate level of rock leading to a higher rock shelf on which was built the base course of the building's north wall. As there are no beam slots for a suspended upper floor, it must have been solid and retained by the top of the north wall of the lower rooms (a, b, c and d). If this were so, then the level of the floor would have been approximately 2.4 m above the level of the entrance hall. The intermediate level at the head of the stairs may have been infilled to the height of the upper floor with the steps rising along its east side. The entrance hall may have risen to the full height of the building. It is not certain how the upper storey was divided. The stair rises towards its eastern end and the wall between the entrance hall (a) and the western rooms (c and d) continues past the north wall of the lower rooms which suggests that this wall rose to roof level. There is a short length of wall between the north wall of the lower room (c) on the line of the stone piers which links the north wall of the lower level to the north wall of the upper level. However, the north wall of the upper level continues westwards and the roof may have extended over this area covering a space only accessible from outside. The entrance hall (a) is likely to have extended to the full height of the building to give headroom to the stair thus separating the room above the east store (b) from those above the west rooms (c and d). The suspended floor over the lower level rooms could have been supported on beams spanning the shorter distance between the north-south walls with additional support being given in the kitchen (d), by the line of piers.

If a man's height of 1.8 m is taken at the line of the north wall of the upper storey (Fig. 58) and a tiled roof sloping between 20° and 25° is projected upwards to the south, the apex of the roof would coincide with the calculated level of the roof of the Colonnaded Walk.[18] The high rear

[18] See above, pp. 122-123.

wall of the Colonnaded Walk may have been pierced with windows to light the upper storey making the upper rooms most attractive – shaded but lit by reflected light from the Colonnaded Walk. The roof would then have drained to the north into the narrow space between the building and the face of the cliff which is drained by a shallow channel cut into the rock to flow westwards. At the line of the dividing wall between rooms (c) and (d) the channel branches, with one part following the dividing wall southwards, perhaps to serve a cistern in the kitchen. The other continues westwards to the end of the building, where it turns south along the west wall, passing below the Colonnaded Walk, and reappears below in the lower terrace. This group of rooms forms one unit of two storeys (Pl. 61), and as it possibly contained stores, a sizeable kitchen and comfortable dry rooms above, it could have been a domestic building of some quality and importance.

Between this Two-Storey Building and the Baptistery there is an open yard (f) (Fig. 66, Pl. 61) entered from the Colonnaded Walk through an opening close to the west facade of the Baptistery. As the doors and windows of the west facade of the Baptistery open on to this space, it is most likely to have been open. The floor is very rough with the rock cut to various levels and the short lengths of block walls that remain are in such disarray that any interpretation is virtually impossible. At the north end of the space there is a cistern (e) partly hollowed out of the rock cliff. The cistern was supplied from a water course cut into a rock ledge above the cliff and also from the overflow of the water channel which leads to the Baptistery font. The cistern was partially a cave with a roof added to bridge onto a south enclosing wall, of which all but the lower courses has now disappeared. The enclosing wall is built of rough masonry and in the centre, at ground level, there is a narrow opening blocked by a single stone into which had been cut two holes. The lower hole is thought to have been a drain and the upper an overflow. The cistern must have been emptied by hand as, apart from a drain, there are no water courses leading from it to serve any of the apartments. The overflow drain is cut into the rock floor of the yard (f) and flows south to the Colonnaded Walk where it disappears. On the west side of the yard (f) and adjoining room (b) is a small wedge shaped room (g) which is reached through its north wall by means of two shallow steps. The earth floor in the centre is sunken leaving two stone ledges 0.6 m wide on either side on which were found fragments of large earthenware storage jars. The floor was kept damp by a water channel leading from the cistern overflow and, being thus cooled, the room may have been an ideal store for wine and oil (Pl. 63).

Between the Two-Storey Building and the Basilica, is a third group of rooms (h) 14 m long and 3 m deep. It is entered from the Colonnaded Walk through a door adjacent to the pilaster complex P4N at the southeast corner of the Basilica. The room is empty and the floor is missing. Excavation revealed the continuation of the drainage system from the area behind the Two-Storey Building. The drain channel that skirts the northern walls of the Two-Storey Building flows along the west wall of the room (d) and passes beneath room (h) in a stone culvert. A branch of the drain also passes westwards along the north wall of room (h), again branching twice along its length to flow south. This length of drain is again culverted and a retaining wall was built uphill to protect it further from falling scree from the slopes above. A wall was built across this room to the east of the door but this may have been a later addition, as it is not bonded into the side walls. No clues as to the use of this room were found, and all that is known is that it was kept secure by a pivotted door and kept dry by the extensive drainage along the base of its north wall.

The bedrock immediately below the east facade of the Basilica was also exposed and more drains were found along its base flowing south and disappearing below the floor of the long room (h). Considerable care seems to have been taken to ensure the disposal of surface water from the rock face and roofs to keep the area from becoming saturated. The blocking of these drains after the first abandonment of the monastery may have caused an accumulation of water which resulted in the collapse of the south wall of the Colonnaded Walk at this point.[19]

Perched high on the rock cliff above the northeast corner of the Basilica and reached by steps cut from the rock is the fourth group of rooms. This area was first a quarry (Pl. 65) as is seen by the sheer cut walls and the varying levels of the floor which still retains the grooves cut during the process of quarrying the stone (Fig. 67, 71). The first chamber (i) measures 11 m by 5 m and, from the arrangement of beam holes in its walls, it appears to have been a single storeyed, lean-to cell. The tiled roof, of which both pantiles and ridge tiles were found, was supported on beams bearing on pockets cut into the rear wall and on timber posts set into recesses cut into the outer edge of the rock floor. At the northeast corner of the cell there is an archesoleum containing a sarcophagus. "On the rock floor we found tiles, obviously used for roofing and finds of pottery and glass fragments also suggest that the cave was more than a simple

---

[19] This is suggested by a similar collapse of the rebuilt section of the wall that occurred in 1966.

dormitory." [20] Below room (i) there is a smaller room (j) (Fig. 71) 5.5 m wide by 2.7 m deep, also built into a quarried area. Like the upper room it was roofed with rafters bearing on pockets cut into the rock wall. Being at a lower level than room (i) it could be entered directly from the sloping rock shelf below. If the quarrying dates from the building of the Basilica, then these rooms may also have belonged to the period when the monastery was centred around the Cave Complex and Basilica. Set aside from the body of the monastery, these rooms may have been built for use by guests. The addition of the later buildings along the Colonnaded Walk would have blocked access to these rooms except by way of the narrow passage between the Two-Storey Building and the rock cliff, which in turn, could only have been entered from the upper storey of the Two-Storey Building. This difficult access might indicate that with the completion of the rooms along the Colonnaded Walk, these rooms (i) and (j) may have lost their importance, their role being taken over by the new building, possibly the "hospice" referred to in the inscription on the tomb of Tarasis.

Directly to the east of the Baptistery the ground was open. Quarrying continued eastward along the edge of the Upper Terrace forming the cliff face which extends as far as the East Church. The base of the cliff would have had flat shelves left from the quarrying which provided sites for lean-to structures similar to the apartment above the Basilica already described. In the area of the necropolis the cliff was also a surface into which arcosolia were cut. Above the Baptistery there is a large ledge (l in Fig. 71) 7.0 m deep, on which are traces of the rock cut base of a north-south oriented wall. Beam holes in the rock face to the rear indicate that there was a roofed lean-to cell. In the west corner of the cell there is a sarcophagus framed by the outline of an arch cut into the plain rock face behind. Further east there is a second tomb (m) set in an arcosolium cut into the cliff. Here the arch is outlined with a deep groove, and by fine tooling of its edge in contrast to the surrounding rough-hewn rock. Close inspection of the quarried faces of the cliff reveals a number of small eyelets cut out of the rock in the open area above the Two-Storey Building and above the main group of tombs in the necropolis. The eyelets in this last area are especially notable as crosses had been carved into the rock face around them. The presence of these crosses suggests that the eyelets

[20] M. Gough, "Domestic Appointments at Alahan Monastery," unpublished address given under the auspices of the American Institute of Archaeology at various centres, notably at the Institute for Advance Study, Princeton.

were possibly intended to hold ties for tents erected during large influxes
of pilgrims at the time of festivals.

The main group of tombs in the necropolis is located away from the
cliff in a lower outcrop of rock (n). At the west end of this outcrop there
are four arcosolia hewn out of the south face. Below the level of the scree,
protected from damage, the outer face of the arcosolia can be seen to be
cut and finished to a definite outline. Above, the rock is so weathered that
its original form is now indistinguishable. As the other tombs, especially
those cut into the cliff, are surrounded by a fine cut surface of rock with
the arch accentuated by tooling, it is likely that this outcrop was also once
finished in a similar manner. The three western tombs are located close
together and each hold one sarcophagus cut out of the rock, whilst the
fourth contains three sarcophagi. The second tomb from the east is more
elaborate than the others as it has its front face cut to resemble a free
standing sarcophagus, with an ogee moulding defining its edges, within
which are two circles enclosing crosses to either side of a central *tabula
ansata* bearing an inscription showing that the tomb belonged to Tarasis
the Elder.[21] At the foot of this tomb there is a further sarcophagus cut into
the bedrock in front of its entrance. Some 20 metres east of this group of
tombs, at the end of the outcrop of rock there is a further single arcosolium (o) with the inscription referring to Tarasis the Younger on the
wall behind the sarcophagus.[22]

Except for the cell (l) at the west end above the Baptistery, the
necropolis was free of building. It was cut off by the north wall
Colonnaded Walk and was only entered through a narrow arched
opening to the east of the Baptistery. Although visually separated from the
tomb of Tarasis the Elder, the Shrine, incorporated into the arcading of
the Colonnaded Walk, is, in fact, placed directly opposite to it. This may
be a coincidence but it is tempting to suppose that it was not, and that the
Shrine was deliberately placed there as a tribute to the founder of the
hospice.

The last complex of apartments within the confines of the Monastery
faces on to the open court in front of the East Church (Fig. 71, Pl. 66)
where large quantities of building stone had been quarried, leaving a large
area (p) 9 m wide and 4.5 m deep. In front of this recess there is an open
space (q) with the bedrock cut to a level well below the floor of the East
Church. The recessed area (p) has its north, east and west walls formed by

[21] M. Gough, "Some Recent Finds," p. 116, inscription Z and above, p. 22, inscription **1**.

[22] Ibid., inscription Y, and above, p. 23, inscription **2**.

the cliff. Beam holes cut into the rock show that it contained another two-storey building divided into two rooms on each storey by a north-south cross wall. To the west, sockets cut into the rock indicate a roof and floor structure spanning from front to rear, whereas in the eastern part sockets in the east wall show a structure spanning across to a dividing wall which may have been keyed into large recesses cut into the rear wall at the change in direction of the beam holes. Around the top of the cliff is a water channel to divert ground water away from the walls in order to keep the building dry. A seating for a masonry wall was cut in the floor of the quarry across the recess so the building may have had a masonry south facade, making it a substantial structure. Inside, the bedrock had been left with ledges of rock remaining from the quarrying. One ledge in the northeast part has a shallow basin with a runaway cut into it. Three knife blades were found here suggesting that this part may have been a store or kitchen with a refectory or living quarter above (Pl. 67). To the east of this building the face of the cliff has been carefully shaped with a water catchment groove designed to collect water into a groin probably to discharge into a basin which has now disappeared.

The lowered area (q) in front of the refectory building (p) left by quarrying was raised to form the forecourt to the East Church by building masonry cross walls in an east-west direction, and by infilling with masonry chippings. Four metres further west, in the north wall of the Colonnaded Walk, is the pilaster complex P2N, which has the buttress to the transverse arch extending northwards into the rubble fill. Opposite, to the north, just outside the refectory building, (p) at the base of the cliff, an arched oven was found with one arch complete and the lower part of a second arch remaining *in situ*. These arches were covered with soot. The presence of the oven between the west end of the refectory building and the northwards extension of the transverse pier of the pilaster complex P2N suggests that there was a building (k) here completing the fourth side of the forecourt and enclosing it from the necropolis to the west.

Below the Basilica is the Lower Terrace (Fig. 68, Pl. 73, 74) which was uncovered during excavations aimed at finding an entrance to the fore-court to the Cave Complex, and the Basilica. As has been seen, such an entrance was not found but more domestic structures were uncovered. The Basilica is built on a steeply shelving bed of rock and the functions of the structures built on the Lower Terrace appear primarily to have been that of buttressing the retaining wall of the terrace leading to the Colonnaded Walk.

The first area excavated, that opposite the west end of the Basilica (s), revealed only a north-south buttress wall. Further excavation opposite the south pastophory (t and u) uncovered a masonry grid structure of two rows of cells built off the sloping rock face. Shallow drainage channels had been cut at the base of these walls to divert ground water through the structure and out over the hillside below. The lower row of cells (v and w) have a series of breakwaters cut parallel to the slope with channels cut between; the southern wall is breached with openings. No traces of any flooring which would suggest that the cells were rooms were found.

The two easternmost cells (x) and (y) have a number of important features, and appear to have had a definite use. The first cell (x) has a tiled, arched opening 0.60 m high by 0.40 m wide built into its south wall. The wall between this cell (x) and the second one (y) is abnormally thick and is lined on its west face with small blocks of stone and on its east face with brick tiles. The tiles are 0.28 m square and 0.04 m thick and are bedded in a similar thickness of mortar. The second room (y) was made watertight by having its floor partially tiled and rendered. In its south wall there is an overflow which suggests that it may have been a cistern. The room is divided by two massive brick piers each 2.0 m square. In the eastern part of the room there is a large burnt area. An open drain flows across this part of the room and passes in front of the south face of the northern pier into the western part, where it is covered with slabs. If the space between the piers were blocked, as is suggested by the enclosure of the drain at this point, the west part could have been filled with water, discharging through the overflow in the south wall. The two rooms with the fire in the eastern part and the plunge in the western part may have served as a bath house. The line of the masonry of the south wall continues eastwards and traces of the wall can be seen further east below the Colonnaded Walk.

This part of the excavations, while lacking any impressive domestic or architectural feature, did, however, reveal greater quantities of broken pottery, coins and small objects than were found elsewhere on the site. In addition, this excavation brought to light voussoirs from the Colonnaded Walk arcading, thereby helping further to reconstruct the likely state of its completion.

G. The Spring Complex

Excavation of the living quarters showed that the dispersal of ground water had been a serious problem at Alahan, and that the first builders had given much attention to diverting the water around and below the buildings in an attempt to keep them dry. At the same time they also went to considerable lengths to provide for the supply of fresh water, both to the cisterns and the main cells.

The strata on which the monastery is built are not in themselves water bearing, and until 1967, although the presence of the western end of aqueducts cut into the rock face at the top of the cliff along the north edge of the monastery was known and had been surveyed, the only active spring was about 100 m to the north of the Basilica, and no link between this spring and the channels could be seen. However, some 150 m east of the East Church, there is an area where the vegetation is richer than the usual coarse scrub and it was rumoured by local villagers that here was a spring that occasionally active. On closer inspection an outcrop of rock that had once been water bearing could be seen, but it appeared to have been inactive for a long time, as the line of solution holes had become completely lime encrusted. A trial area was excavated at the foot of this outcrop in the hope of finding the spring, the excavation was taken down for approximately 2 m where the roof of a cave was exposed. The floor was found a further 2 m below and from the rear of the cave there flowed a spring, partially blocked by incrustation, but when cleared, capable of delivering some 1500 litres of water a day in summer.

The cave was originally a natural formation and had been enlarged by lowering the floor (Fig. 69). It had then been divided to form a cistern and store. Access to the cave was gained through two vaulted cuttings leading in from the southwest. The complex was completed by the addition of a masonry building across the south ends of the two passages. The western passage leads directly to the spring, and the eastern, or cistern complex, comprises a series of store rooms, leading to the internal cistern. Across the front, between the two passages, is a bath house. The entire site had filled with scree. The vaults over the passages had fallen in and only their lower courses remained *in situ* but the walls of the outer building still stand in places to a height of 1.8 metres.

The south external wall of the complex is solid except for two doors at the extreme east end (Pl. 68), one leads to the cistern complex and the other to the furnace room (e) that served the bath house (d). The entry to the spring (c) and the bath house (d) is from the west, at the west end of this wall. The opening is narrow and the absence of jambs suggests that it may not have had a door. Outside the main entrance is a small water trough possibly for washing feet before entering. The entrance leads to a vestibule (a). The floor is smooth rock and all traces of paving have disappeared. Opposite the entrance is a wall dividing the vestibule (a) from the bath house (d) and access to the bath house is made by turning east at the entrance to the passage (b) and back into a narrow corridor leading to a small, single person steam room. The corridor is paved with flagstones which are about 0.40 m higher than the rock floor of the vestibule (a), which may indicate that the vestibule was also paved.

The bath house is 1.1 m by 2.5 m and has a hot water tank built against the inner rock wall (Pl. 71). The room is paved with brick tiles and the hot water tank is built entirely of tiles and is plastered all around to make it water-tight. As a bronze base of a lamp was found here, the room probably had no window. The tank and the floor of the room were heated from below by a hypocaust which had two earthenware pipe flues rising up the north wall of the tank and a third embedded in the wall to the corridor. The hypocaust was fired from the adjacent furnace room (e). The remains of its fire were found still in place. The tiled floor of the bath house and tank is 0.53 m above the bedrock floor of the furnace room. The tank is supported on a central pillar of tiles and from the space below the tank a narrow gap opens into the space below the floor of the bathing room which is also likely to have been supported in the same way. Care was taken to keep the furnace room dry as a drain passing across the outer wall is made of interlocking earthenware pipes. The room was probably also used as a store for fuel.

At the north end of the vestibule (a) two steps rise 0.53 m to the passage (b). The passage is 2.4 m wide and has its rock walls cut sheer to a height of 1.4 m and 1.43 m above floor level. The lower courses of a vaulted roof were found at the north end of the passage. The height of the vault would have been about 2.5 m. The passage ends at the entrance to chamber (c) with a large rock threshold 0.58 m across its entire width. Access is made easier by the addition to a step below the threshold. The floor of the passage is rock and no traces of any paving were found. Along the eastern side is a drain flowing from the chamber (c) in the form of a channel cut into the floor with a check along its edges as a seating for flat stone covers some of which were found *in situ*. The care with which they are set in place suggest that the floor was no more than the rock exposed by the excavation.

The cave containing the spring and the cistern is 1.5 m wide and 5.5 m long with the spring now entering halfway up the rear wall in the northwest corner (Pl. 69, 70). It is uncertain how deep the original cave was as enlarging must have destroyed much of its shape. The cave is divided into three chambers. The spring issues into the northwest chamber (c) which is 1.5 m square, with the rock threshold at the end of the passage (b) forming a low barrier. The floor is paved with random places of flat stone and is level with the floor outside. At the base of the threshold is an outlet leading to the drain in the passage. The spring may also have flowed along the groove cut into the rear wall into the next chamber (j) which was made into a cistern. The cistern is enclosed by two masonry walls built across the cave. The floor of the cistern is 0.62 m below the floor of the spring chamber (c) and between these two spaces the dividing wall stands to a height of 0.98 m above the floor of the cistern. Encrustation on the cave sides above this wall shows that the wall may have continued up to the roof of the cave separating the cistern from the spring chamber (c). The wall between the cistern and the third chamber (h) stands 1.0 m above the cistern floor. The sides of the cave had been cut to a height of 2.2 m and above this two parallel lines of encrustation indicate that the upper part at one time may have been filled in. The roof over the cistern rises to a point where there is a solution hole of another spring. An opening in the cave roof had been filled in to prevent surface water and debris from polluting the cistern. The walls of the cave above the cistern have a smooth stalactitic encrustation on its upper levels and a more granular and rougher deposit on its lower levels; the rougher deposit possibly being left below the water level in the cistern. The water in the cistern may thus have stood to a depth of about 1 metre. The floor of the cistern is partially paved with the remainder covered with masonry blocks. A drain passes through the base of the wall to the next chamber (h), but, although no sign of any plug or overflow at a higher level was found, the outlet was presumably only used for draining and cleaning the cistern. The cistern is seen to have been totally separated from the spring chamber (c), water was drawn from the northeast chamber (h) and to facilitate this, three steps were built against the dividing wall.

The northwest chamber (h) is approached through a passage (f) and an eastern chamber (g). This part of the complex is distinct from the access to the spring and bath house, and logically, to describe the access to the cistern, it is necessary to progress, as was done for the spring, from the outside in. The passage (f) is entered through an opening at the east end of the south wall. The opening has a rebated threshold and jambs, but no trace of any sockets for a door. The floor is 0.10 m below the door threshold and there are no traces of any covering. The floor substructure consists of bedrock over the eastern half with a mixture of earth and block fill over the remainder. Embedded in this fill is an open drain flowing from the cistern. As the drain was not culverted the floor may have been made of large flagstones covering both the substructure and the drain. In the north wall of this passage is a door, again with a masonry jamb. There is no threshold, but the paving along the line of the opening is socketed for a door, so the space beyond could have been made secure. A beam hole in the west jamb indicates that the doorway had a timber lintel. The door leads to the eastern chamber (g) which for the most part is cut deep into the rock; only the south wall and the entry from the passage (f) being built of masonry. The floor is superbly paved with smooth finished flagstones laid with very fine joints. A shallow step 0.14 m high, leads into the last chamber (h) and the fine paving continues in as far as its back wall.

Water from northwest and northeast chambers (c) and (h) was led away by drains following the two passages. Drains also traversed the building along the line of the south wall. The drain from the cistern flows out through the south end of the steps in the northeast chamber (h) and then submerges below the paving to reappear in the sub-floor of the eastern passage (f). The drain curves to the west to pass clear of the south door connecting with the drain flowing across the furnace room (e) before passing through the outer wall to flow down the hill in a culvert just below ground level. The drain from the northwest chamber (c) follows a similar route below the floor of the western passage (b). The drain passes below the paving of the entrance to the bath house steam room (d) to discharge through a clay pipe built into the lower courses of the outer south wall. Adjacent to this outfall, but 0.40 m below and oriented in an east-west direction, is a further line of clay pipes protected by a cover of rough blocks at its western end. The drain penetrates the foundation of the south wall presumably to connect to the drain in the furnace room. The purpose of this drain is not known, but the absence of a culvert at the outfall to the drain to the western passage (b) may indicate that they were connected (Fig. 70).

The fabric of the Spring Complex has two forms of construction; the southern section comprising rooms (a), (d), (e) and (f) and probably the narrow entrance to chamber (g), is clearly a masonry structure. Iron nails were found here, the sole remnants of a timber roof structure. This suggests a tiled roof which probably sloped down to the south. The north walls of these four rooms are built against and incorporate the bedrock into their structure. The remainder of the complex is hewn out of the rock and enclosed by masonry vaulting. The eastern passage (f) is seen to have had a vaulted roof supported on the rock side walls leading up to the spring. The eastern chamber (g) is irregular in plan, but here a large proportion of the room has a rock roof. The south wall is built of masonry and the open area of the roof was probably enclosed by a part masonry vault resting on the rock east wall and the edge of the cave roof on the west. The heavy construction of the inner part of the complex with its entrances protected from the direct sunlight by the lighter structure across the south face must have been cool all year round. The eastern chamber (h) with its fine paved floor and access to the cistern was probably, therefore, a cool store for such commodities as wine, cheese, oil and game, as well as a source of water. The western passage (b) with the steam room (d) and the cold spring chamber (c) as a frigidarium could have been the centre of the bath house.

The outcrop of water bearing rock was able to provide the monastery with an ample water supply. Although now dry, the fissures in the rock above the Spring Complex must also have produced a considerable quantity of spring water which was able to be channelled the entire length of the site to serve the living quarters. At the base of the outcrop a channel had been cut to collect the spring water from a number of fissures and to lead it eastwards towards the Spring Complex. When the area to the west of the Spring Complex was being cleared the beginnings of a second channel was uncovered and was seen to lead away to the west towards the monastery. This channel was subsequently cleared throughout its length. The channel follows the contours almost due west in as straight a line as possible with a gradual fall for a distance of approx. 250 m to the rock ·outcrop above the Baptistery. About 100 m west of the Spring Complex a second spring was uncovered uphill from the channel adding water to the system. The water channel is 0.20 m wide with its sides made of small blocks of stone bedded in a gravel mortar and now covered with an encrustation of lime (Pl. 72). At its west end, where it encounters the exposed strata of rock, the water course is cut into the bedrock and falls steeply over the edge of the outcrop above the Baptistery, flowing over pans to check the flow and to deposit silt before discharging into the cistern beside the Baptistery, the cells to the east of the Baptistery and the Basilica. The water distribution system may have been far more extensive than is seen by the water courses along the monastery terrace, as an isolated part of a stone conduit was uncovered far below the monastery when the approach road to the site was being built in 1963.

H. Conclusion and Secondary Occupation

The description of the individual buildings within the monastery complex has revealed part of the history of its development and expansion. The sequence of events can be determined from the architectural features themselves, but the chronology is not as clear and must rely on other evidence discussed in a previous section. The buildings have been described in the final stage of primary period as it is considered that at this stage the community was at its zenith; but within the primary period there are a number of phases which can be identified.

It is seen that the monastery started in the Cave Complex (Fig. 71) where a nucleus of the future community was built. The Primary Phase 2 is signalled by the addition of the Basilica, this being the logical first expansion of a monastic community growing in numbers, wealth and importance. Although the choices of sites available for expansion were limited, there appears at that time to have been no vision beyond the building of this church. We have seen that it was fully completed and reached an advanced state of decoration – the whole nave was plastered and painted, and the apse and bema were decorated with mosaic. The floor of these areas was covered with *opus sectile* and the floor to the eastern end of the nave was covered with mosaic. Nearly all the stone carving was finished, the stylobate was added and the stone screens were installed between the columns at both ground level and gallery level. All this work is an intricate and painstakingly thorough accomplishment and does not show any sign of being hurried. It suggests that the Basilica reached its completion before the period of rapid expansion that was to follow. With the advent of Primary Phase 3 the whole pace of the work on the monastery changes.

The Primary Phase 3 sees the start on the East Church and the Baptistery more or less together, as these two buildings are linked in time as well as space by the addition of the Colonnaded Walk. We know that the final establishment of the Walk succeeded the building of the structure of both the Baptistery, as is shown by the addition of its narthex, and the East Church, by the construction and the alignment of its narthex. Possibly at the same time the domestic apartments were also under construction to serve the growing community. This burst of activity may have taken place over a relatively short period. Construction appears to have moved so fast that decoration is sporadic and unfinished in many places, as if the sculptor had to keep moving forward to work on new important features as they were built, leaving lesser decoration to be filled in later. At the same time the style of building changes from an extrovert, highly carved, formal Basilica construction to an inward looking, plain, but much more sophisticated structure designed to impress from within rather than from without. Similarly a change in feeling of decoration is seen from the realistic and flowing carving of the Basilica to the abstracted and more formally rigid interpretation of the East Church, the watershed taking place at the Shrine incorporated within the Colonnaded Walk. This break is not complete, as the doorways to the East Church, especially the south door, have the realistic qualities of the Basilica carving. This may indicate that although a new style had arrived, a mason from the old order was still at work at the time of the building of the East Church. The Primary Phase 3 may have thus followed shortly after the completion of the Basilica.

Both the Basilica and the East Church have the synthronon in the apses extended after an initial addition westwards into the bema, indicating either a continuing growth of the community or a change in its organization or purpose. In the Basilica, the extension obliterates the floor and wall finishes and blocks the door to the north pastophory. In the East Church it extends across the doorway to the south pastophory. The expansion in the Basilica would, if both churches were used for differing functions, be reflected in the East Church. Furthermore, if the expansion of the synthronon in the Basilica preceded the construction of the East Church, then surely the bema and apse of the later East Church would have been made larger from the outset during its construction. Thus this change would seem to have taken place in both churches during the Primary Phase 3 or possibly later in a fourth phase.

The duration of these last phases was long enough for the East Church and Baptistery to be structurally completed but only partially decorated. The wall painting of the Baptistery only covers the apse and north aisle, whilst the south aisle appears to have been left plain. In the East Church plastering was only attempted in a few areas. The living quarters were built and the Spring Complex and water courses were in use during this period, but at the same time a major element (but maybe not the most important functionally) appears to have been never finished. The state of completion reached in the Colonnaded Walk is uncertain except that it is known that the grading of the floor at its eastern end is far from finished (Fig. 55, 59). Thus, the buildings of the monastery in Primary Phases 2, 3, and 4 were all in use and the aims of the expansion must almost have been realised by the time that the monastery was evacuated.

What caused the desertion is not known; there are no signs of violence or fire. A local rock fall would not have caused the extensive damage shown by the amount of rebuilding that was done during the second occupation. However, if the structural forms of the buildings are compared, the East Church with its cross-wall cellular form is more rigid than the Basilica which has linear form. The Baptistery is compact with the solid apses forming a major part of the structure. The Colonnaded Walk was a long structure relying only on its north wall for strength. Of these only the East Church and the Baptistery have any appreciable structure remaining today, and we have seen that, except for the East Church, in most instances all arcading has collapsed. The consistent destruction of the weaker structures across the site could point to a minor earth tremor, and this could be further borne out by the spreading out of the upper courses of the tower of the East Church. This, of course, remains very conjectural and it may be that the community was made to uproot itself more by changes of circumstance or by political pressure, rather than as a result of some natural catastrophe.

After the abandonment, the site was reinhabited and again used as a monastery as the buildings appear to have been reinstated to their original uses. The Secondary Period is revealed by the rebuilding of a number of structures in the complex in a method totally lacking any masonry craft and without any intent to re-establish the high architectural order of the earlier occupation. Indeed the newcomers had lost all regard for the skills of their predecessors. From the amount of rebuilding that was done, the monastery must have been in an advanced state of dereliction with only the structure of the East Church and Baptistery remaining to any appreciable height. However, most of the buildings appear to have been re-used.

The outer wall of the Cave Complex had fallen away and was rebuilt further into the cave, thereby enabling it to rise up to the roof of the cave (Fig. 18). The cave, enclosed by the rebuilding of the outer wall must have been put to some use at ground level at least. The main features of the Primary Phases – the central passage, the rooms to the west within the Church to the east – were maintained, but altered to suit new requirements. The Cave Church was divided into two chambers by the introduction of a solid masonry wall along the line of the earlier arcading between the two aisles. The doorways from the central passage were blocked up and the entrance to the two rooms was now to be only from the outside. To achieve this the south aisle was only enclosed for two-thirds of its length using the parts of the south wall and apse remaining from the earlier period and leaving room for an entrance to the north aisle. Here there is a confusion of block walls and the structure may have needed to be strengthened during the construction. Only a narrow doorway was left leading to the north chamber with a second narrow entrance at right-angles giving access to the south chamber. The entry to the north chamber was given a threshold with pivots for a door and a socket for a lock. The main feature of this chamber is the presence of two tombs, one cut into the floor and the second recessed into the new north wall. The south chamber retained the apse form and an altar base was found *in situ*. A small niche was built into the new west wall and it is therefore likely that this part at least continued as a church. The central passage was retained with its west wall remaining intact but the entrance was restricted by the addition of a masonry pier built into its east side. Opposite this the new outer wall extended without any opening up to the west face of the cave, the former front room having been abandoned.

Outside the Cave Complex the Forecourt was raised by the addition of a new layer of paving on top of the original one; this can still be seen in front of the Basilica. In the Basilica most of the structure must have collapsed leaving only the lower parts of the outer walls intact. When the area was excavated the lintels and arch springs of the central arched opening of the west facade were found to have fallen forward on top of the earth fill above the forecourt paving, so this part of the narthex at least, must have been left standing. Also a group of columns from the extreme western end of the nave arcading was found where it had fallen. On the assumption that these would have been removed had they fallen prior to the Secondary Period, they must have been standing during the Secondary Period. There is also a lack of evidence of original structures being re-erected in their previous form by the builders of the secondary occupation. A substantial amount of the bema and apse may also have been standing, possibly to its full height as there was no secondary building or repair visible in this area, which, from the layout of the secondary church, must surely have been in use. Moreover, traces of mosaic decoration were found in the excavations having survived the Primary Period and subsequent clearing of the Basilica only to fall during the decay of the Secondary Period.

Within this shell a new church was built, smaller than the original, using only the nave, bema and apse for its interior (Fig. 41-43). Two-thirds of the nave was enclosed within a massive solid wall built from reclaimed masonry using bases, shafts, capitals, voussoirs and even fragments of the carved screens of the former church roughly cut to fit where necessary. The walls were given additional strength by incorporating four equally spaced piers which are thought to have supported arches as crudely cut voussoirs were found. At the west end there was a single opening off the narthex or atrium with a threshold and pivots for a pair of doors. The three remaining bays of the Primary Period nave may have been left without a roof to form an atrium with the north and south aisles alongside roofed over, for had the structure survived to support a roof over the nave, it is reasonable to suppose that it would have been incorporated into the new church. To either side of the new west door of the church two niches were built in the same place as can be seen in the East Church. Their use is not known.

The north and south walls of the original Basilica were also strengthened, the north wall by a new inner skin of masonry and the south wall by the addition of five piers coinciding with the piers within the nave. The north aisle thus was probably roofed across from the new wall to the nave and was divided into two chambers. At the west, a small room could be entered only from the atrium. The east room, the longer of the two, was reached through an opening between the first and second piers in the nave wall. The long room led to the original north pastophory through a now more narrow doorway. The pastophory was also now completely separated from the bema by a new block wall which is attributed to the Secondary Period as fragments of mosaic were found in the mortar. The south aisle was approached through the second and third columns of the original arcading of the nave, now part of the atrium. The south wall may not have been sufficiently sound to support a new roof and the five piers would have supported beams across the aisle to support the new roof. The openings between the first two columns of arcading were filled in, the south door in the west wall was blocked up, and an inner wall with a doorway was built across the south aisle to make a small room. At its east end the south aisle led into the original south pastophories which do not appear to have needed any rebuilding, at least of their lower structure. In front of the atrium, the original narthex was restricted in width by a cross wall between the centre and south doors. In front of the original north door there was a cistern feeding a small ablution bowl, so the water system must therefore have been re-instated.

It is reasonably clear that the nave, bema and apse were re-used as a church, because the altar table base was found nearly in its original position with the standing podium toppled over on its side at the head of the steps up from the nave. The use of the side rooms, however, is not known although the south pastophory may have continued in its original function as its relationship to the nave remained unaltered.

Progressing eastwards, the Two-Storey Building between the Basilica and the Baptistery was repaired during the Secondary Period. In one repair a minute stone column shaft was found which could have fitted the altar base in the Baptistery. The kitchen was sub-divided by a masonry wall between the west wall and the centre pier.

The Baptistery (Fig. 64, 65) is still standing today with its walls rising to a storey in height; it also bears the signs of rebuilding. The roof and central arcading must have fallen in as, in order to support the new roof, the north, west and south walls were lined with masonry and three massive piers were built between the aisles to replace the arcading. The font was not touched and the remains of the altar were found in the north aisle. A pair of re-used columns had been erected between the font and the apse. The Baptistery, thus appears to have been repaired so as to continue in its original role.

The last area to show any rebuilding is the refectory on the north side of the court in front of the East Church. The narthex of the East Church had fallen away and some of the material had been re-used to build piers to support a new upper floor in the refectory.

The East Church was standing in its original form except for its narthex. It is not known what state the roof was in, nor is it certain whether this building was used during the secondary occupation. There are no remains of secondary alterations and it is likely that re-roofing the structure was beyond the skill of the newcomers, bearing in mind that the repairs done elsewhere were rudimentary, using only salvaged materials. To re-roof the East Church would have required considerable skill as well as abundant supplies of timber and new tiles.

The monastery therefore returned somewhat to its former life with the Basilica and Baptistery continuing their previous roles, albeit in a much more humble manner, and most of the domestic apartments were reinhabited. The newcomers lacked the abilities of the original masons and maybe had neither the wealth nor the aesthetic understanding to give the monastery its former beauty. In fact they even went so far as to build the richly carved screens and capitals indiscriminately into the structure (Fig. 43) and there appears to have been no inclination to preserve the old order. Nevertheless, they did possess a certain drive to re-establish the community, however primitive it may appear by comparison, and it must not be denied that the act of clearing the rubble and re-building was no mean feat.

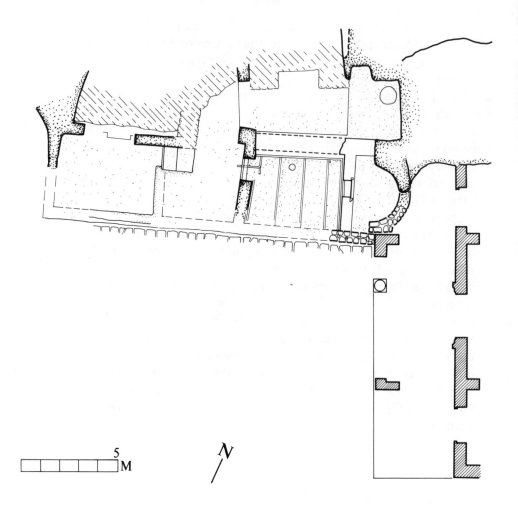

5
M

FIGURE 14. – Cave Complex: Period 1, Level 1

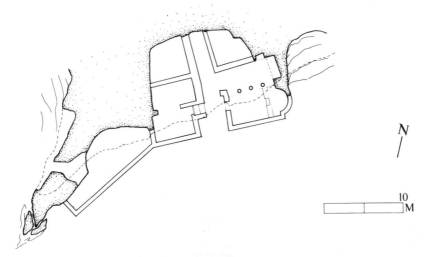

N

10
M

FIGURE 15. – Cave Complex: Reconstruction, Period 1, Level 1

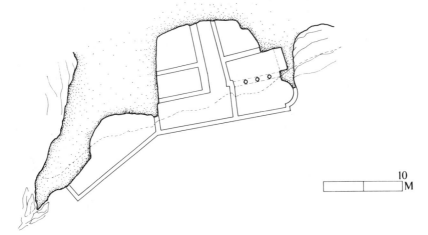

10
M

FIGURE 16. – Cave Complex: Reconstruction, Period 1, Level 2

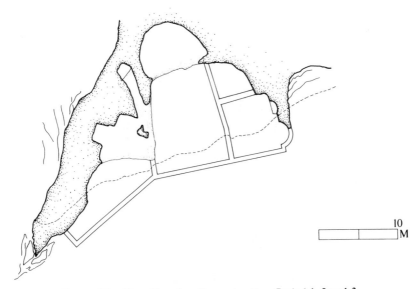

10
M

FIGURE 17. – Cave Complex: Reconstruction, Period 1, Level 3

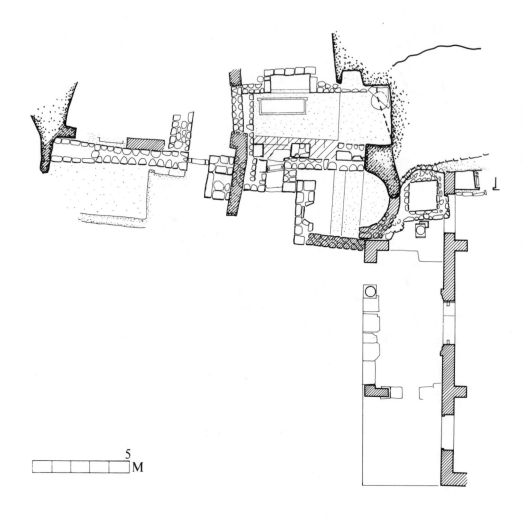

FIGURE 18. – Cave Complex: Period 2, Level 1

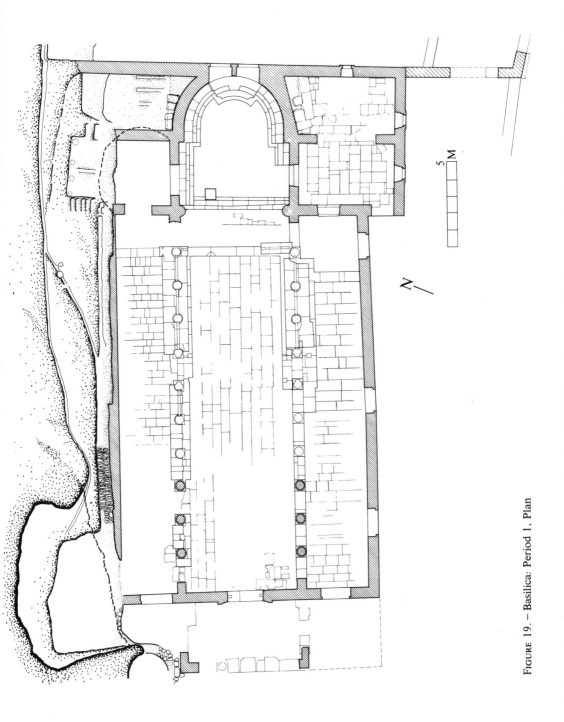

FIGURE 19. – Basilica: Period 1, Plan

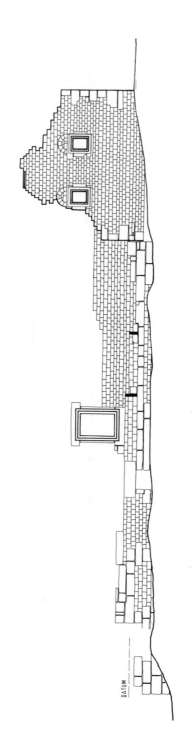

DATUM

5 M

FIGURE 20. – Basilica: South Elevation

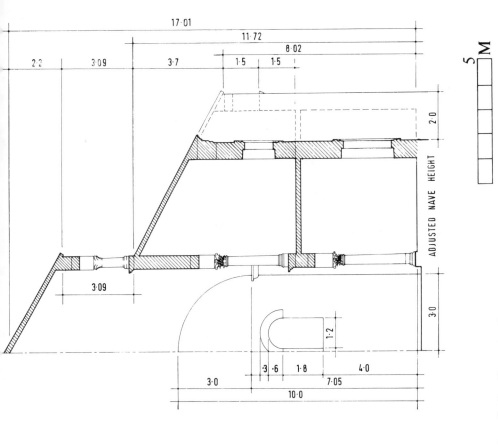

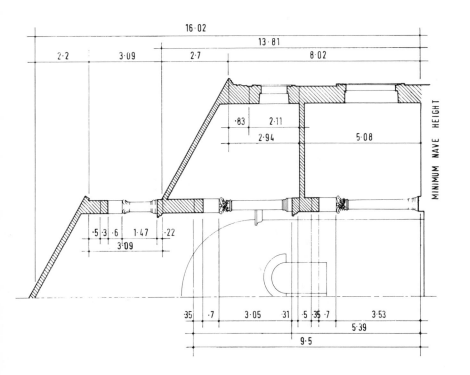

FIGURE 21. – Basilica: Cross Section Reconstruction

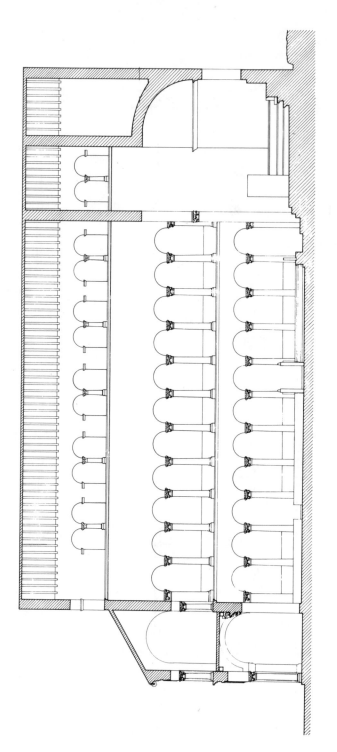

5
M

FIGURE 22. – Basilica: Long Section Reconstruction

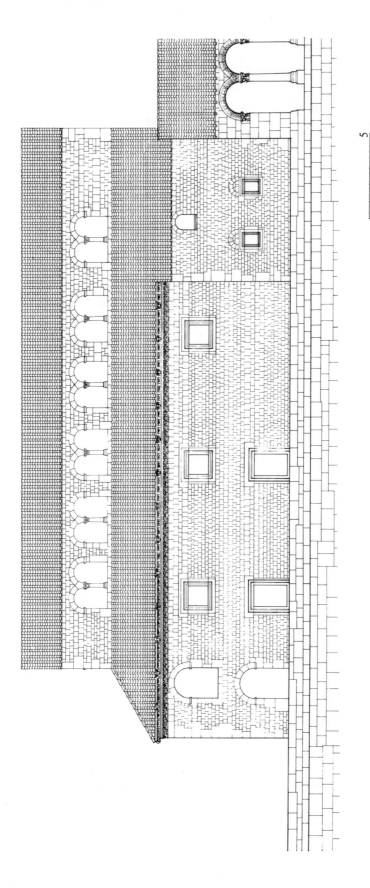

5

M

FIGURE 23. – Basilica: South Elevation Reconstruction

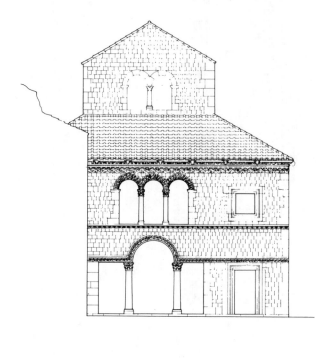

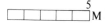
5
M

FIGURE 24. – Basilica: Reconstruction – Narthex (West Facade)

FIGURE 25. – Basilica: Reconstruction – View from Southwest

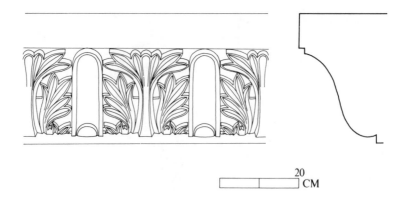

20
CM

FIGURE 26. – Basilica: Decoration – String Course

20
CM

FIGURE 27. – Basilica: Decoration – Voussoirs

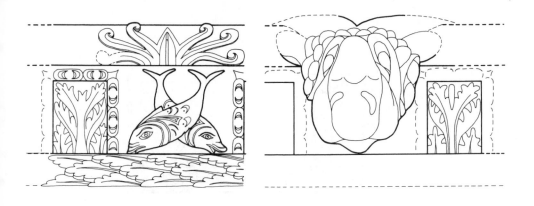

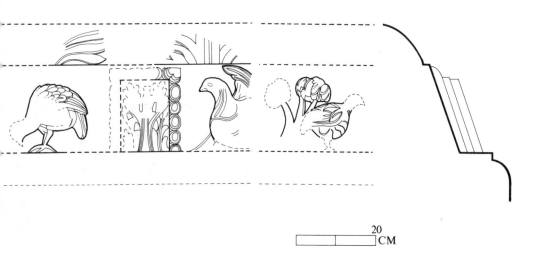

20
CM

FIGURE 28. – Basilica: Decoration – Cornice Details

20
CM

FIGURE 29. – Basilica: Decoration – Frieze Details

20
CM

FIGURE 30. – Basilica: Decoration – Cornice Details

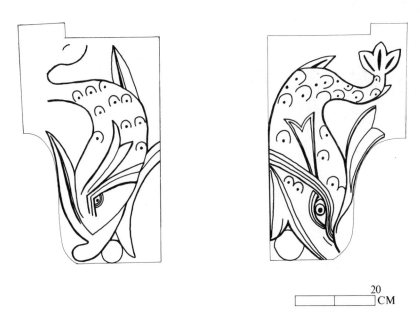

FIGURE 31. – Basilica: Decoration – Corbels

FIGURE 32. – Basilica, Evangelists' Door: External Mouldings

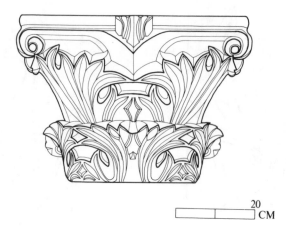

20 CM

FIGURE 33. – Basilica: Decoration – Main Arcade Capital

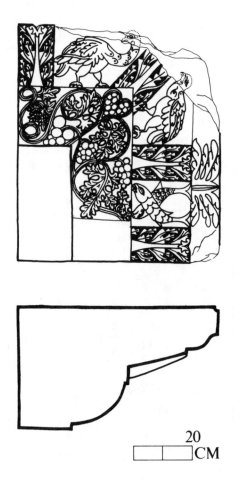

20 CM

FIGURE 34. – Basilica, Evangelists' Door: Cornice Detail

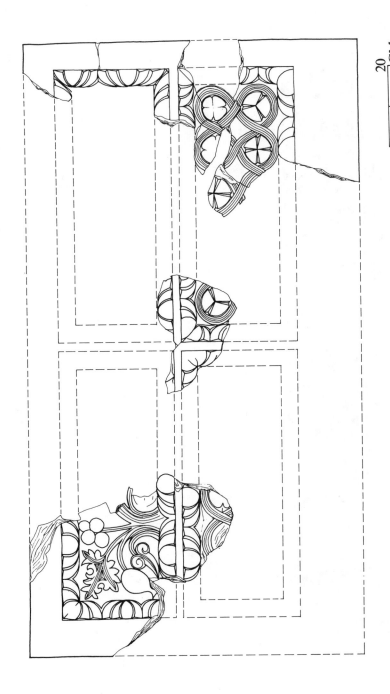

FIGURE 35. – Basilica: Screen Fragments

FIGURE 36. – Basilica: Decorated Stylobate

20
CM

20 CM

FIGURE 37. – Basilica: Screen Fragments

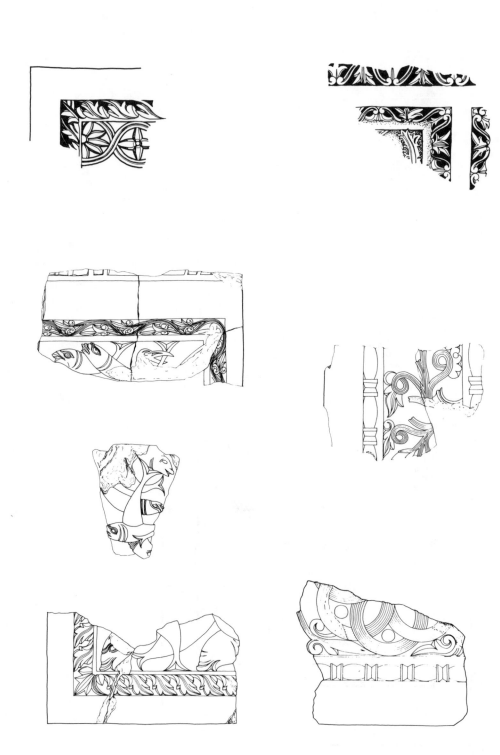

FIGURE 38. – Basilica: Screen Fragments

20
CM

FIGURE 39. – Basilica: Screen Fragments

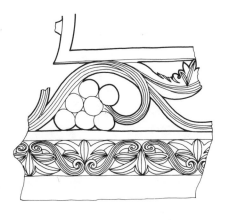

5
CM

FIGURE 40. – Basilica: Screen Fragments

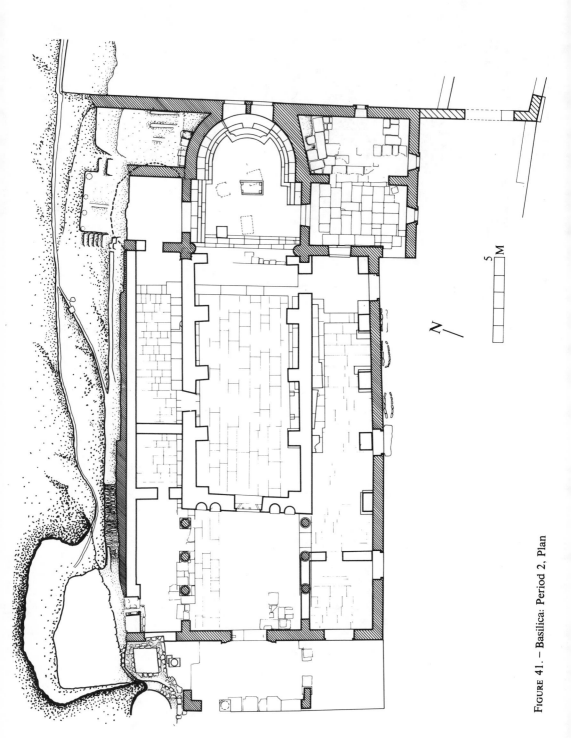

FIGURE 41. – Basilica: Period 2, Plan

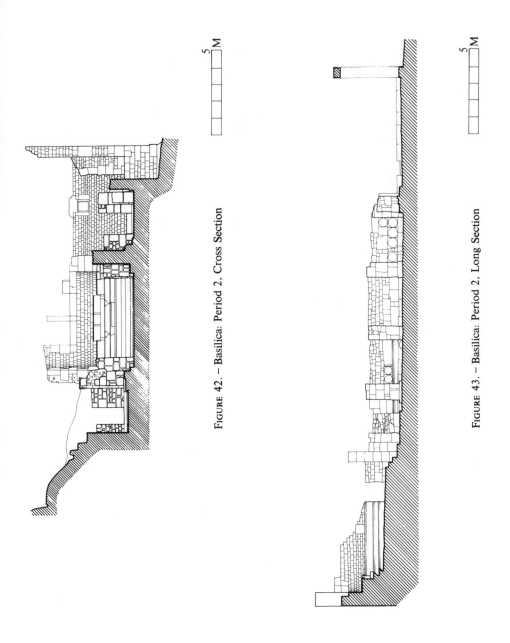

FIGURE 42. – Basilica: Period 2, Cross Section

FIGURE 43. – Basilica: Period 2, Long Section

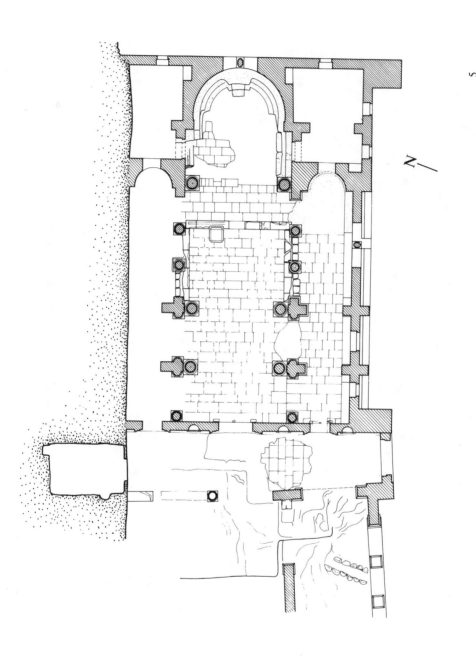

FIGURE 44. – East Church: Plan

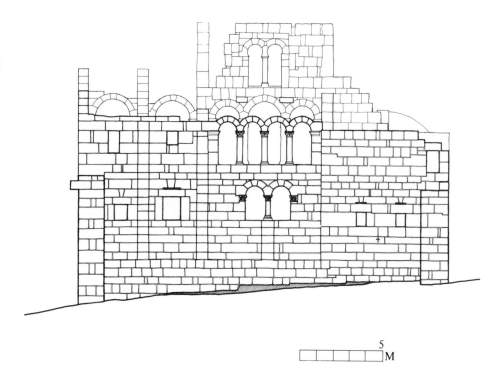

Figure 45. – East Church: South Elevation

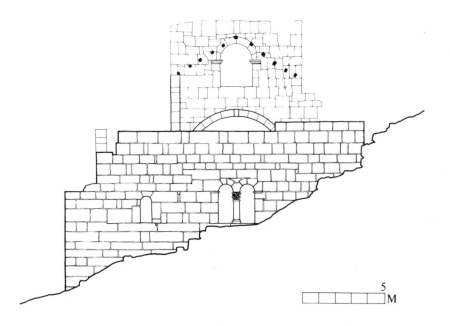

FIGURE 46. – East Church: East Elevation

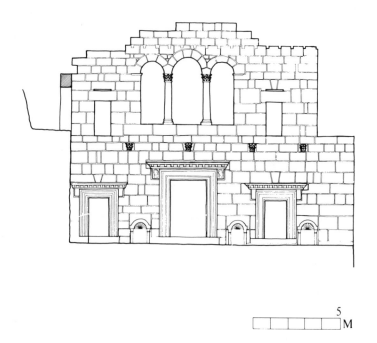

FIGURE 47. – East Church: West Elevation

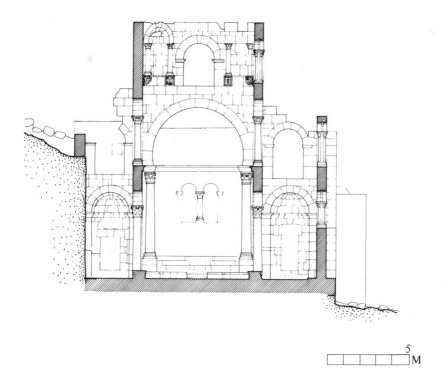

FIGURE 48. – East Church: Cross Section

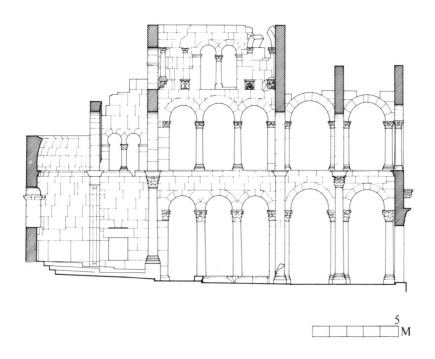

FIGURE 49. – East Church: Long Section

FIGURE 50. – East Church: Reconstruction – View from Southwest

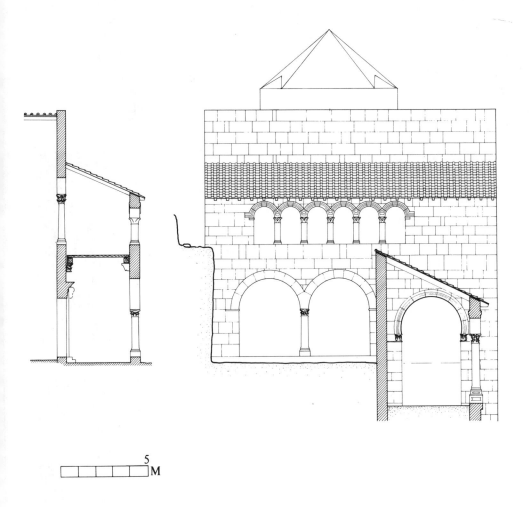

5
M

FIGURE 51. – East Church: Reconstruction – Narthex (West Facade)

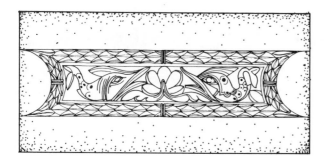

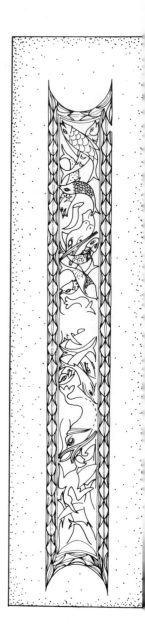

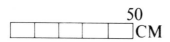

50
CM

FIGURE 52. – East Church: Decoration – Door Details
left Head; *right* Jamb

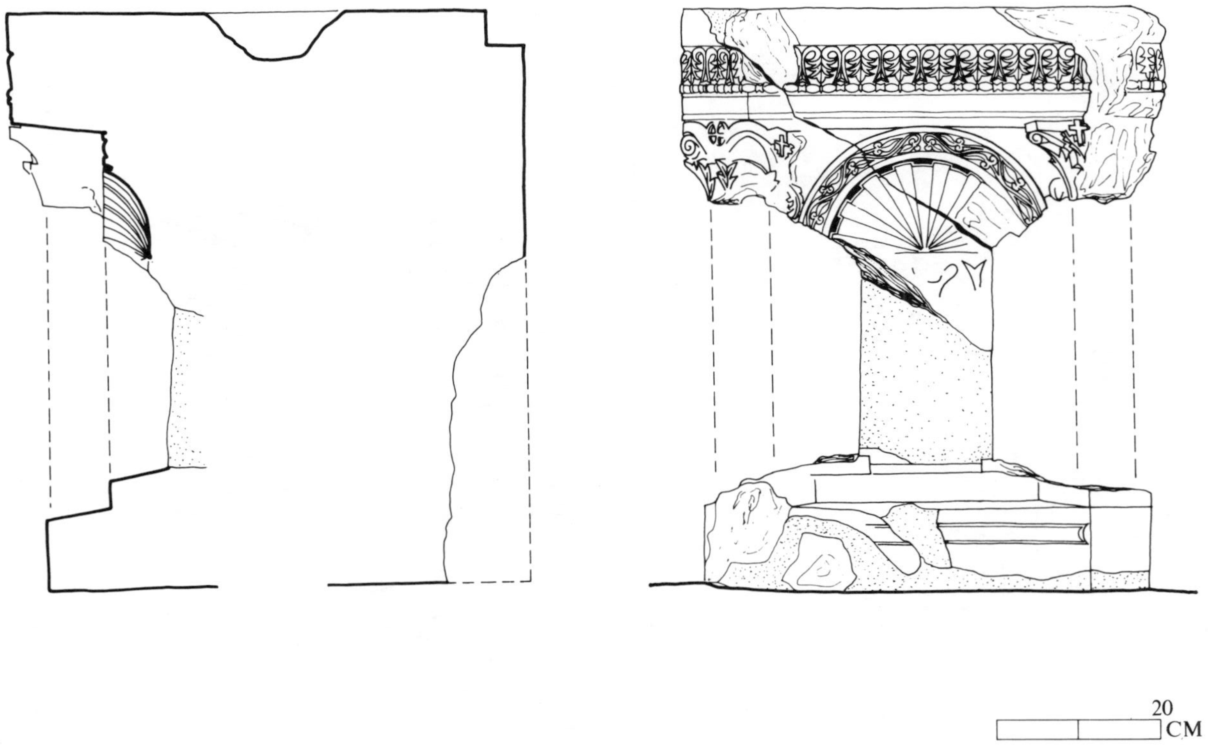

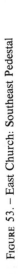

20 CM

FIGURE 53. – East Church: Southeast Pedestal

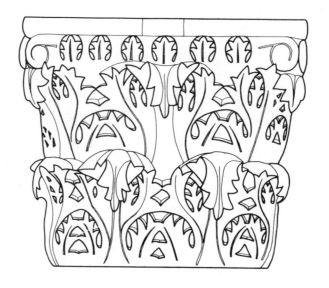

FIGURE 54. – East Church: Decoration – Capitals

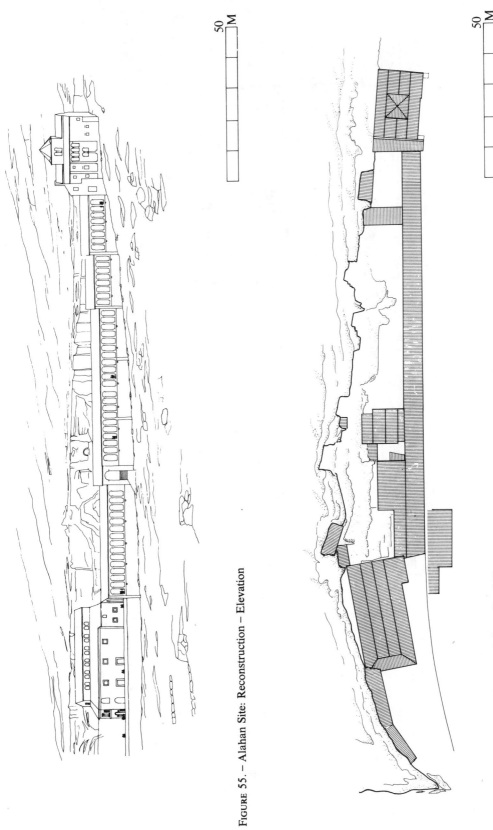

FIGURE 55. – Alahan Site: Reconstruction – Elevation

FIGURE 56. – Alahan Site: Reconstruction – Roof Plan

FIGURE 57. – Colonnaded Walk: Shrine

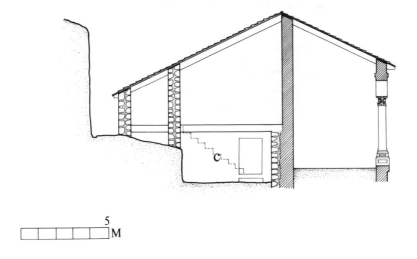

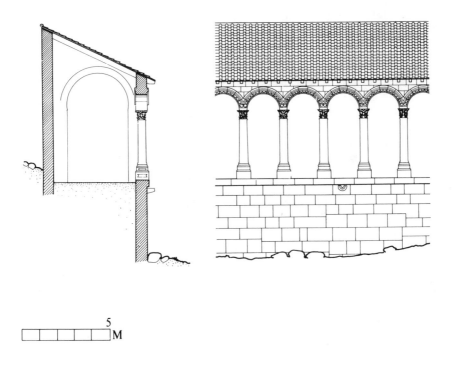

FIGURE 58. – Colonnaded Walk and Two-Storey Building: Reconstruction – Cross Section

FIGURE 59. – Colonnaded Walk: Reconstruction

20
CM

FIGURE 60. – Colonnaded Walk: Reconstruction – Plinths

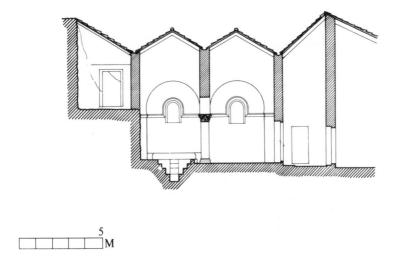

FIGURE 61. – Baptistery: Reconstruction – Cross Section

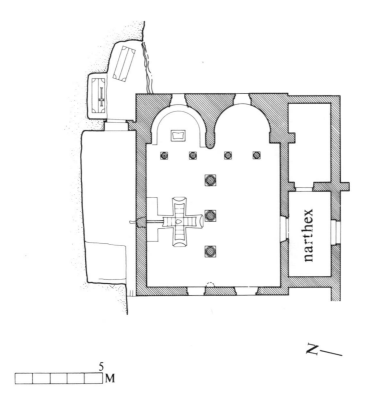

narthex

FIGURE 62. – Baptistery: Period 1, Plan

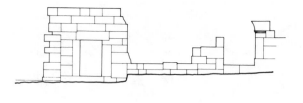

south

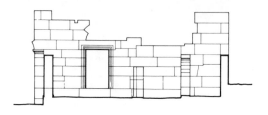

narthex

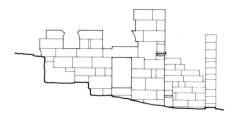

west

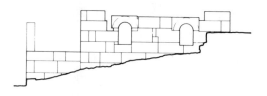

east

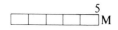

5
M

FIGURE 63. – Baptistery: Elevations

FIGURE 64. – Baptistery: Period 2, Cross Section

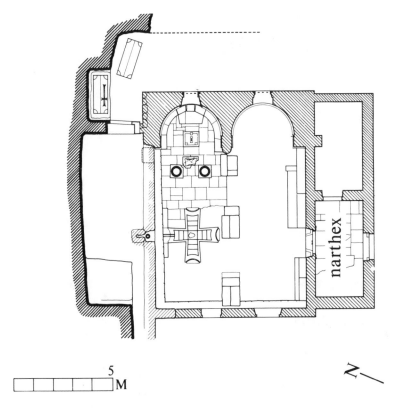

narthex

FIGURE 65. – Baptistery: Period 2, Plan

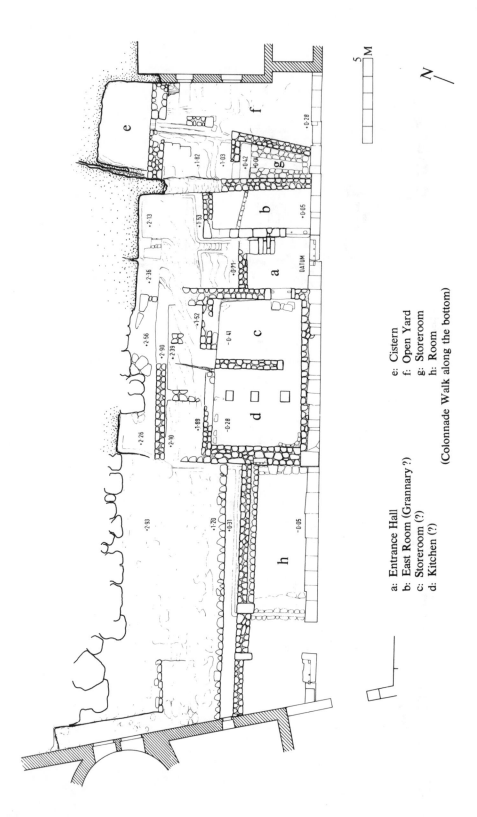

a: Entrance Hall
b: East Room (Grannary ?)
c: Storeroom (?)
d: Kitchen (?)

e: Cistern
f: Open Yard
g: Storeroom
h: Room

(Colonnade Walk along the bottom)

FIGURE 66. – Living Quarters: Two-Storey Building Area – Plan

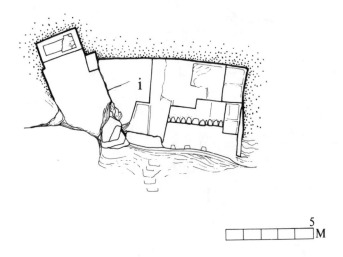

FIGURE 67. – Living Quarters: Ledge above the Basilica – Plan

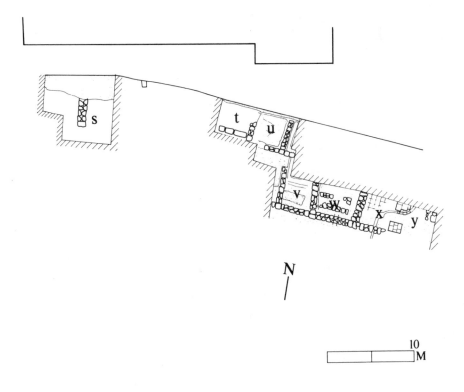

N

FIGURE 68. – Living Quarters: Lower Terrace – Plan

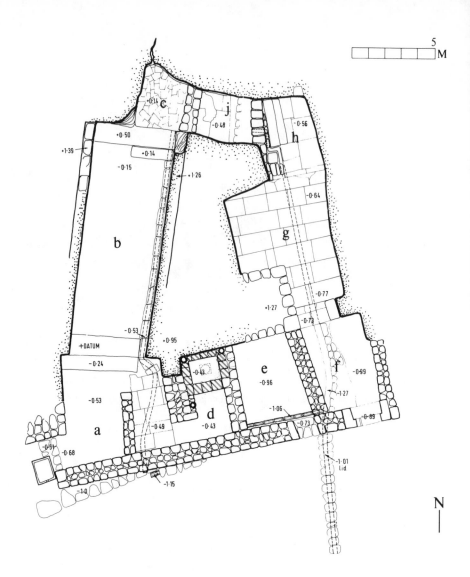

FIGURE 69. – Spring Complex: Plan

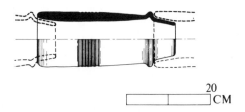

FIGURE 70. – Drain Pipe

Part Three

6

Religious Life
and Monastic Organization
at Alahan

Michael M. Sheehan, csb

Wind and water have weathered the porous limestone on the south flank
of the Taurus mountains to form many caves. In one group of them, cut
in a wedge-shaped outcrop high above the Göksu river, the monastery of
Alahan began (Pl. 4-6). The caves were shaped and improved by chisel
and trowel, but they soon became inadequate; beside them on a narrow
shelf a series of buildings was begun. Eventually an important complex
was constructed, one member of which still graces the slope on which it
was placed long ago.

Of the life of the religious community that resided at Alahan scarcely a
written word remains. Its numbers, the material conditions of life, forms
of public and private prayer, the relations of the community with the
population of the region – in short the shape and structure of monastic
organization – must remain virtually unknown so far as literary references to it are concerned. There is a considerable body of information
about the development of different forms of monasticism from the fourth
to the sixth centuries in other parts of the Mediterranean basin; there may
be analogues to Alahan in Cappadocia, in Syria or further afield. However, there is as yet no general information on monasticism in Cilicia so
relation of its forms to one or other of those in neighbouring regions is
problematical.

The author's obligation to other members of the Alahan expedition will be obvious to the
reader. In addition he wishes to express his gratitude for the information, advice and
criticism offered by Professor Elisabeth Alföldi, Dr. Sheila Campbell, Dr. Susan Keefe,
Dr. Giovanni Montanari and Professor James Russell.

On the one hand, the community at Alahan may well have been influenced by Syrian monasticism. Whether it belonged to the diocese of Coropissus (probably Dağ Pazarı which is some fifteen kilometres to the east and at about the same altitude) or, as is less likely, to the diocese of Claudiopolis (Mut), in the valley twenty one kilometres to the south (see maps, p. 18), Alahan was part of the ecclesiastical province of Isauria, with its archiepiscopal see at Seleucia (Silifke), and thus of the patriarchate of Antioch.[1] This fact, as well as several similarities between the main Alahan churches and some Syrian buildings, suggest that analogues may be found among the numerous and comparatively well-reported monasteries of Syria and Palestine. On the other hand, St. Basil's teaching and the model provided by his foundations are known to have been of wide influence: they may well have reached Cilicia by the fifth century. The problem is to discover some evidence that would suggest the monastic influences that were brought to bear on the community at Alahan. If an answer to the problem is to be found, it lies among the ruins on the mountain side.

The buildings to which the ruins are witness once sheltered and, to a certain extent, imposed their limitations on those who lived in them. Their design, sequence of construction and adaptation of form reveal something of the beginning, growth and organization of religious life. Even a preliminary examination indicates a development that was more than an enlargement, one that suggests an adjustment of purpose. In the beginning the monastery probably housed a few monks who went there to withdraw from the world. By the end, the world had come to it: religious life adjusted accordingly and buildings were erected to provide for visitors as well as for the resident community. Other monastic centres in the immediate neighbourhood, less accessible and certainly less splendid, were to outlive Alahan.[2] Perhaps the monks withdrew because in the political conditions of the early seventh century their admirable site was no longer viable – "a city set on a mountain cannot be hidden."

---

[1] See Paolo Verzone, *Alahan Monastir: Un Monumento dell'arte Tardo-Romano in Isauria* (Turin: Viglongo, 1956), p. 45.

[2] On the monastery at Al Oda, on the west side of the Mut – Karaman road in a deep water-course about 1500 metres northwest of Alahan monastery, see Michael Gough, "A Church of the Iconoclast (?) Period in Byzantine Isauria," *Anatolian Studies*, 7 (1957), pp. 153-161. Between Alahan and Al Oda an outcrop contains scores of caves. There is strong reason for thinking that this too was a monastic site; surface sherds suggests habitation after AD 600.

Though there is no surviving text to tell us of it, it is clear that the Alahan community began in the outcrop at the western extremity of the site (Fig. 71)[3]. The reasons for its choice are immediately evident to an observant visitor. Natural caves on the south face provide shelter from sun, wind and rain. These caves are a few metres below a series of water-bearing strata; one of the springs in the immediate vicinity is about 100 metres north of the outcrop. The site was difficult if not dangerous of access, so that it offered the privacy that favoured the life of the recluse.[4] Those who have stood at the entrance to the caves to look down at the Göksu valley know of its splendid view.[5] In a word, conditions of physical life and spiritual growth were nicely joined in the Alahan caves.

The motives for the foundation of the monastery remain unknown. The relentless triumphalism of the Basilica's west doorway (Pl. 7) – a majestic Christ supported by seraphim, with the figures and symbols of the Evangelists by whom his gospel was spread, carried on uprights decorated by archangels who tread the symbols of pagan religion under foot (Pl. 19-22) – had been seen to suggest that the site had housed a pre-Christian shrine.[6] To such places, holy men or communities of monks often came to win them for Christ and turn them to Christian usage.[7] However, excavation has yielded no sign of such prior occupation. The sculptured doorway can be explained in more general terms of the triumph of Christ, so evident to believers of the fifth century, and of the invocation of divine power against evil.[8] What is more likely is that some devout person, like many other men and women of his time, withdrew to a secluded place to

[3] See above, pp. 29, 75-79.

[4] In a letter to St. Gregory of Nazianzus, St. Basil points out that to grow in the spirit the soul must be free from its sympathy with the body and that solitude is most conducive to that end; see Ep. 2 in St. Basile, *Lettres*, ed. Yves Courtonne, vol. 1 (Paris, 1957), p. 7. Cf. *The Long Rules*, q. 6 "Concerning the necessity of living in retirement" in St. Basil, *Ascetical Works*, trans. M. M. Wagner, The Fathers of the Church (New York, 1950), pp. 245-247, and PG 31: 925-928.

[5] Remarked by Leon de Laborde in 1826 in his *Voyage de l'Asie Mineur* [Voyage en Orient 1] (Paris, 1838), p. 125. Cf. St. Basil's description of his mountain retreat, Ep. 14 in *Lettres*, ed. Courtonne, 1: 43-44.

[6] See Michael Gough, "Some Recent Finds at Alahan (Koja Kalessi)," *Anatolian Studies*, 5 (1955), pp. 119-123, and "The Church of the Evangelists at Alahan," ibid., 12 (1962), pp. 180-182. Cf. G. Forsyth, "Architectural Notes on a Trip through Cilicia," *Dumbarton Oaks Papers*, 11 (1957), p. 229.

[7] On a common notion that demons inhabited desert places see A.-J. Festugière, *Les moines d'Orient* vol. 1 (Paris, 1961), pp. 23-39.

[8] See N. Thierry, "Notes sur l'un des bas-reliefs d'Alahan Manastiri, en Isaurie," *Cahiers archéologiques*, 13 (1962), pp. 43-47, and André Grabar, "Deux portails sculptés paléochrétiens d'Egypte et d'Asie Mineure, et les portails romans," ibid., 20 (1970), pp. 15-28.

live the life of the Gospel. Perhaps he was alone for a considerable time before disciples discovered him; perhaps he arrived with a companion or a group of followers. At any rate, before the middle of the fifth century a small community seems to have lived at Alahan. By the use of timber beams and the adjustment of the natural caves with chisel and trowel three, or in places four, storeys for habitation were eventually established in the western outcrop there.[9] Whatever the architectural irregularity of such an arrangement, it provided shelter for a sizeable community. But in an earlier stage, to which the first space set aside for religious purposes can be assigned, the community cannot have numbered more than ten or twelve (Pl. 5-6)[10]

A small group such as this could find most of its material needs in the area in which it had settled. As was mentioned above, the natural conditions of the site provided several essentials for the physical well-being of the community. Caves in abundance offered shelter for men and animals as they do to this day. The orientation of the inhabited face kept the monks in the lee of the slope so that they were protected from *poyraz*, the prevailing and sometimes violent wind that sweeps down the pass from the Anatolian plateau.[11] Given the height and clear prospect to south and west, the site enjoyed an excellent opening to the sun, a valuable asset during the whole year when, as here, the extreme heat of the summer was tempered by the coolness of the caves.[12] There were abundant and conveniently located sources of water. Wood for minor construction as well as for cooking and heating was available on the slopes above and below the monastery. These slopes now provide pasture for goats and for a few sheep. It is reasonable to suppose that at the time of Alahan's foundation the monks found sufficient pasture for the animals needed to supply the wool and goat hair adequate to the rough clothing they were

[9] See above, pp. 76-79.

[10] For a description of the Cave Church, see above, pp. 77-79. Note that there was a separate entry to each aisle; they were completely separated by stylobate and arcade. Though the south aisle of the completed Cave Church was used for the Eucharist, it is conceivable that this was a function of the north aisle at an earlier stage. Eventually the north aisle received a burial and was possibly used as a baptistery; see below, pp. 204, 209.

[11] In the tower of the East Church the south wall is penetrated by windows but the north wall is not; see above, p. 113.

[12] In this the Alahan site had a distinct advantage over that at Al Oda where the sun could penetrate only late in the afternoon of the summer months. In winter the lower ranges of cells had no direct sunlight. On the other hand, Al Oda was well protected from the north wind and the sometimes bitter wind that came up the valley from the sea. The site beween Alahan and Al Oda (above, p. 198 n. 2) had maximum exposure to the sun but almost no shelter from the wind.

expected to wear as well as the coarse fabrics for other uses. The animal skins would also provide heavy winter covering[13] and the leathers required for the smaller items of clothing, fluid containers and other domestic utensils and parchment, which would be needed for writing on occasion when papyrus was difficult to obtain or inadequate for the scribe's purpose.[14] The same flocks could supply the monks' milk and cheese and their meagre requirements of meat.[15] Fruit trees long since gone wild are found on the site, indicating the possibility of at least modest success in their cultivation earlier.[16] There is still topsoil in the fold of the water-course by the spring furthest to the east. This and some evidence of terraces suggest that vegetables once flourished at the level and in the neighbourhood of the monastery as they do today in the settlement 300 metres below.[17] This hamlet was the likely source of cereals for bread, the staple of monastic diet and the one major item of food that the immediate area of the monastery could not provide. Wine and oil were probably brought from producing areas at lower altitudes. The former was required for the Eucharist. It was not normally part of monastic fare but would be needed at least for purposes of hospitality. The lamps of the monastery and the needs of the kitchen probably required the purchase of olive oil.

The Alahan community might have continued in the comparative obscurity and privacy that seems to have been the case at Al Oda, but a change occurred so that the site was developed to include large liturgical spaces and subsidiary buildings. Construction ceased to be a casual adjustment of caves; it came to mean splendid work, involving large structures in stone embellished with sculpture, mosaic and wall painting (Pl. 1, 4). The excavations show that Alahan became a place where large crowds gathered, that it was likely a place of pilgrimage and that the monastic community adjusted accordingly.

[13] See St. Basil, Ep. 2, in *Lettres*, ed. Courtonne, 1: 11 on the wearing of adequate clothing; cf. Festugière, *Les moines d'Orient*, 1: 42 and passim.

[14] The monk's role as scribe is not emphasized in early eastern monasticism. Yet there were many monastic authors and there is evidence of a considerable exchange of letters.

[15] On monastic diet see St. Basil, Ep. 2, in *Lettres*, ed. Courtonne, 1: 12 and Festugière, *Les moines d'Orient*, 1: 59-64.

[16] The late Dr. Hans Helbaek made a brief examination of the trees and shrubs of the Alahan site in the summer of 1962 and reported the presence of small shrub (*Styrax officinalis*) source of a sweet-scented resin. He noted that it was found on the monastic terrace but nowhere else in the district and added, "I should consider it highly probable that it was employed by the monks as a component of incense" (letter to Michael Gough of 17 September 1963).

[17] See Michael Gough, "The Church of the Evangelists at Alahan," pp. 183-184. Note Egeria's remarks on the efforts of monks at Mount Sinai to grow vegetables and fruit: *Itinerarium Egeriae*, 3.6, ed. A. Franceschini and R. Weber, Corpus Christianorum Series Latina 175 (Tournai, 1965), pp. 40-41.

As the monastery grew so that it came to include several times its original complement of monks and received guests on a regular basis and pilgrimages from time to time, the possibilities of the site had to be exploited and provision made to supply for its limitations, made all the more evident by the new demands. Some of the qualities contributing to the attractiveness of the site in the first place made its enlargement possible. The most remarkable instance of this was the exploitation of the water supply.[18] Though the spring immediately above the Cave Complex was probably the first used, two others, 240 and 340 metres to the east respectively, proved capable of most sophisticated development. Their waters, carefully collected and controlled as to rate of flow, were led along the upper shelf and thence into liturgical and residence areas below as needed.[19] There seems to have been provision for continuous flow of water through the font in the Baptistery (Fig. 62, Pl. 50, 51). Water was brought to each of the living areas and, by the use of catch-basins and cisterns, provision was made for the collection of sediment, reduction of the rate of flow and the accumulation of water at different places where it was useful. The most impressive development of water resources was at the third spring. As has been described in detail in Part Two, excavation revealed a reservoir in which water could be accumulated under conditions well suited to retain its coolness, and a vaulted area probably used as a cooling room and a small bath (Fig. 69, Pl. 68-70). This last, at first glance a suprising part of a monastic complex, given contemporary strictures on the *thermae*, was essentially a private arrangement, hygienic, not social, in its purpose.[20] It was probably reserved to members of the

[18] See above, pp. 142-147; cf. Michael Gough, "Alahan Monastery, Fifth Preliminary Report," *Anatolian Studies*, 18 (1968), pp. 165-167; idem, "Alahan Monastery – 1970," *Türk Arkeoloji Dergisi*, 19/1 (1970), pp. 96-97; idem, "Excavations at Alahan Monastery 1970," *Royal Ontario Museum Archaeological Newsletter*, NS no. 64 (Sept. 1970); and idem, "Domestic Appointments at Alahan Monastery," unpublished address to the American Institute of Archaeology, New York and to the Archaeological Institute, Ankara, 1972.

[19] For a similar arrangement at the monastery of Breiğ in Syria, constructed 550-600 on a site with problems and possibilities not unlike those of Alahan, see Georges Tchalenko, *Villages antiques de la Syrie du Nord. Le massif de Bélus à l'époque romaine*, Bibliothèque archéologique et historique 50, Vol. 1 (Paris, 1953), p. 124.

[20] H. Dumaine, "Bains," *Dictionnaire d'archéologie chrétienne et de liturgie*, 2.1 (Paris, 1925), pp. 72-82, 101-111. See Jean Lassus, *Sanctuaires chrétiens de Syrie. Essai sur la genèse, la forme et l'usage liturgique des édifices du culte chrétien, en Syrie, du IIIe siècle à la conquête musulmane*, Bibliothèque archéologique et historique 42 (Paris, 1947), p. 238; and, for the baths built 454-455 by Bishop Placcus as part of the *domus ecclesiae* of Gerasa, see Carl H. Kraeling, ed., *Gerasa, City of the Decapolis* (New Haven, 1938), pp. 265-269, 175-176.

community, though its use may have been extended to catechumens as part of their preparation for baptism.

The cliff that formed the northern face of the shelf on which the monastery grew restricted the site but also provided one of the means of its growth. In some ways it would have been easier to have built the required structures on the wide shelf immediately above the original foundation. However, once the decision had been made to exploit the level of the Cave Complex, the face had to be cut back; handsome building stone was exposed in the process. Thus, as a sufficiently wide footing for buildings and courtyards was prepared, excellent building material for the churches and other less imposing structures was provided. Partially quarried blocks in a working area contiguous to the sanctuary wall of the East Church are witness to the convenience of the source of supply.

It is reasonable to suppose that the slopes above and below the monastery were at least as well forested then as they are now. Thus timber for beams needed for gallery floors and roofs of churches and for the beams and pillars of dwelling areas, to which rows of openings in the stone bear witness, was ready to hand (Pl. 65, 67).[21] Fuel for cooking and heating would be needed in considerable quantities; it also was available on the slopes.[22]

A supply of food, adequate to the enlarged demand of the community and its guests, was beyond the productive capacity of the immediate area of the monastery;[23] it would have to become dependent on external sources. Presumably, like other religious centres of importance, Alahan was endowed with estates to provide for its needs. The settlement on a small plateau 300 m below probably became involved in the life of the monastery at least after the latter had become a place of pilgrimage and gangs of artisans and labourers as well as pilgrims made their way there.[24]

[21] See David Magie, *Roman Rule in Asia Minor to the End of the Third Century after Christ* (Princeton, 1950), 1: 266-268 and n. 20 in 2: 1141.

[22] Ovens were found in the habitation areas west of the Baptistery and east of the Necropolis; see above, pp. 136, 141. Remnants of flues that may well go back to the beginning of the monastery can be seen in the Cave Complex. There was water-heating equipment in the Spring Complex and in a bath in the area south of the retaining wall; see above, p. 142 and Michael Gough, "Excavations at Alahan, 1972," *Royal Ontario Museum Archaeological Newsletter*, NS no. 91 (Dec. 1972). A significant amount of fuel would be required for these purposes. On the use of cooked food by monks, see Festugière, *Les moines d'Orient*, 1: 59.

[23] Some pilgrims would bring their food with them.

[24] Suggested by Michael Gough in his "Domestic Appointments at Alahan Monastery." The discovery of a section of an ancient conduit bringing water down the slope from a higher, conceivably the monastic, level opens the possibility that the settlement depended on the monastery for its water supply. See above, p. 147.

Excavations in 1970 revealed a fifth-century depot for agricultural produce that, it has been suggested, was intended for monastic use.[25] On the small but flat area on the edge of the modern settlement, excellent fruit and vegetables and some light grains are grown. During the years of Alahan's flowering, it may well have been the centre of a monastic farm as well as a staging-place for travellers and supplies bound for the shrine. At any rate, from farms such as this came the oil for lights[26] and cooking, the wine and much of the fruit, vegetables and meat as well as the cereals and other foods necessary for the support of the community on the heights above.[27]

*
**

When the fully developed Alahan complex is examined, it is immediately evident that the east wall of the Basilica, and its continuation through the arch that marked the western entrance to the Colonnaded Walk and the end of the retaining wall (Pl. 53), tended to divide the site into two sets of buildings.[28] To the west was the original cave dwelling with its small church and the Basilica. Eventually the Cave Complex was developed to a considerable size (Fig. 14-17); its southern limit was set by a wall, part of the lower courses of which are still in place. This wall formed the northern side of a court at the eastern end of which was the Basilica, an arrangement sometimes found in Syrian monasteries.[29] In a sense, this group of buildings can be seen as a complete monastic unit. The Cave Complex (Pl. 6) provided dwelling areas,[30] a church with oratories above, some space for burials in the north nave of the Cave Church and in the deepest cave. Pottery found in the excavation indicates that food was prepared and served there. The Basilica provided the large liturgical space for crowds that would come on special occasions. Sharing the courtyard with the visitors to the Basilica as they did, the monks who lived in the

---

[25] Michael Gough, "Alahan Monastery – 1970," p. 97.

[26] Provision for suspended lamps can be seen in the triumphal arch of the East Church; fragments from oil lamps were found in all parts of the excavations. See above, pp. 51-52, 97, 120.

[27] Cf. Tchalenko, *Villages antiques*, 1: 173-178, and Lassus, *Sanctuaires chrétiens de Syrie*, pp. 266-267.

[28] See above, pp. 101-102, 120ff.

[29] E.g., Turmanin (Deir Manin, North Syria); see Tchalenko, *Villages antiques*, 1: 155-158.

[30] Verzone, *Alahan Monastir*, p. 14 suggested that monks inhabited several floors over the southeast pastophory of the Basilica. There are no beam sockets in the walls that remain. An arrangement of this kind might have been used over the northeast room at the end of the north aisle; it was adjacent to one of the quarried cells. See above, pp. 138-139.

Cave Complex must have suffered a serious loss of privacy. The remnant of a stair cut on the face of the cliff shows that they had direct access to the upper shelf and the open spaces to the north; perhaps they found solitude there.

The impression of the area east of the suggested division is different. The Colonnaded Walk (Fig. 55) leads directly to the East Church, drawing that part of the complex into harmonious unity. Its north wall prevented free access to the areas where the monks lived, allowing exit in that direction only at the Two-Storey Building, the Baptistery and the Necropolis.[31] Unlike the compact dwelling unit in the western section, a line of separate cells provided living quarters for the monks (Pl. 66, 67)[32] Food seems to have been prepared and eaten in the structures that exploited the quarry contiguous to the forecourt of the East Church. Thus, in this eastern section, there is once again a virtually complete set of monastic requirements, including food preparation and a place for burial, one in which privacy was more successfully preserved.[33] Habitation arrangements seem to have been more of a eremitic than of a coenobitic type.

Furthermore, while the Basilica was superior to any other building on the site in its sculptural embellishment and while there is good reason for thinking that it had decoration in mosaic and painted plaster as well, there is a certain haphazard quality in its plan that cannot be dismissed simply by reference to the difficulties of the site on which it was built. On the other hand, the part of the complex to the east of the suggested line of division, while inferior in detail, is remarkable for the quality of its design and the successful relation of its parts.

Yet one must not fail to see that there are strong indications of unity within the complex, indications that, from the point of view of design and construction, it remained under a single direction.[34] Decorative themes such as the fish and partridge are carried through Basilica, Colonnaded Walk and East Church. The synthrona of both the great churches were enlarged in a similar way. Finally, the fact that all the buildings of the site were constructed in line on a restricted shelf when, from the point of view of the engineer and probably from that of the architect, it would have

[31] This important observation was made by Verzone, *Alahan Monastir*, pp. 6-7.

[32] See above, pp. 138-139, 140-141.

[33] Experience of the interruptions of regular life that resulted from pilgrimages may have led to this improved design. Note that a church within a dwelling area does not appear in the eastern part of the complex. Forsyth remarked on the element of privacy in his "Architectural Notes on a Trip through Cilicia," p. 229.

[34] See above, pp. 32-33, 147-148.

been much easier to build on top of the uneroded part of the outcrop and along the wider shelf that extends to the east[35] points to a desire to keep the later buildings in close relation to the original foundation.[36]

More difficult of response is the question touching the continuity and unity of the group that made Alahan its home. Did the increased fame of the community result in a situation in which those monks who sought to live apart from the world found it necessary to withdraw? Were they replaced by others who provided pastoral care and served as guides to those who came to honour the memory of the first group?[37] Or did two communities live side by side during the period of the monastery's prosperity? Perhaps – to pursue the logic of the buildings set out above – one group, who served pilgrims, inhabited the comparatively public western part, the Cave Complex and the Basilica, while the other group pursued a more secluded life in the privacy afforded by the design realized in the eastern part. There are examples from Syria where different communities lived on a single site and, in her *Itinerarium* Egeria makes it clear that, about a generation before the foundation of Alahan, several groups of monks and nuns lived together at the shrine of St. Thekla less than one hundred kilometres to the south.[38] On the other hand, St. Basil was opposed to this arrangement, though he did not insist that all the monks dwell together under a single roof in the coenobia he described. In fact, he urged that novices live separately from older confreres, a disposition that could have been easily realized at Alahan.[39] Given the paucity of evidence available, it is not possible to make a firm choice of any of these alternatives, nor even to eliminate the possibility that there are others. However it is possible to set out a hypothesis that incorporates the evidence that is available and not only suggests answers to the question touching the evolution of the community but also answers more

---

[35] Buildings at this level would be more exposed to the north wind.

[36] See below, pp. 214-215.

[37] Cf. the distinction made between monks who lived near sanctuaries and those who sought more secluded places, described in *Itinerarium Egeriae*, 19.4, ed. Franceschini and Weber, pp. 59-60. See Christine Mohrmann, "Égérie et le monachisme," in *Corona gratiarum: Miscellanea patristica historica et liturgica Eligio Dekkers O.S.B. XII lustra complenti oblata*, Instrumenta Patristica 10 (Brugge/'s Gravenhage, 1975), 1: 163-180.

[38] See the "Life of St. Sabas" by Cyril of Scythopolis, ch. 32, ed. Eduard Schwartz in Schwartz, *Kyrillos von Skythopolis*, Texte und Untersuchungen 49.2 (Leipzig, 1939), pp. 117-118; trans. Festugière, *Les moines d'Orient*, vol. 3 (Paris, 1962), part 2, pp. 43-45; and *Itinerarium Egeriae*, 23.2-6, ed. Franceschini and Weber, p. 66.

[39] The *Long Rules*, q. 35 "Whether there should be several communities in the same parish," and q. 15 "At what age consecration of oneself to God should be permitted ..." in St. Basil, *Ascetical Works*, trans. Wagner, pp. 301-304, 264-268, and PG 31: 1003-1008, 951-958.

fundamental questions as to why and how the monastery grew to become a place of pilgrimage. The key is the inscription found on the principal grave of the Necropolis.[40]

In its original state, the inscription informed the reader that the sarcophagus on which it was carved contained the remains of Tarasis, of blessed memory, who died 13 February 462 (Pl. 2).[41] The arrangement of the grave and its surroundings leaves no doubt as to its importance: not only does it occupy the centre of a range of arcosolia, but the sarcophagus is much the most impressive in the tomb area. Furthermore, the monument (Shrine) on the Colonnaded Walk is placed directly in front of it (Fig. 57, Pl. 60) and the decorations of the monument's capitals suggest that it was considered to be the religious as well as the physical centre of the complex.[42] Most important of all, a grave is let into the surface of the terrace at the base of the sarcophagus. Finally, on a site where there was very little open space suitable for building or for the gathering of pilgrims, the decision to leave the large tomb area without encumbrance speaks even today of its importance. A later lapicide would add that Tarasis was the founder of "rest-houses" but, from the point of view of the evolution of the site, the phrase "μακαρίας μνήμης" is the more telling. At best it is a restrained statement of Tarasis' holiness, but the orchestration of tomb, monument and burial area reinforces the conclusion that Tarasis was considered or would come to be considered a saint. It seems reasonable to conclude that by 462 Alahan possessed a tomb to which the faithful would come on pilgrimage. It suggests that even before that there was a holy man in the monastery to which they came for advice and instruction. In its original form, however, the inscription says nothing of Tarasis' administrative activities.

If the inscription is read with its gloss: "ὁ κτίσας τὰ ἀπα(ντη)τήρια" the argument can be carried further. Given the uncertain meaning of "ἀπαντητήρια" it would not be entirely unreasonable to suppose that the reference was to the various buildings on the site and that Tarasis was considered to be the founder of the monastery.[43] Its expansion could then be explained by the growth of his fame. However, if the gloss is under-

[40] See above, pp. 22-23.

[41] The dating of Tarasis' death by the consuls of the previous year is evidence not only that the names of the new consuls were slow to reach the region but also that the inscription was composed and carved soon after his demise.

[42] See above, pp. 123, 125-126.

[43] Writing before excavation at Alahan had begun, M. Usman suggested that the large tombs in the Necropolis were those of the founders of the monastery: "I Sepolcri di Alahan," in Verzone, *Alahan Monastir*, p. 64.

stood in its more likely meaning, namely that Tarasis was the builder of "rest-houses," then it can at least be concluded that he established a hospice to provide for visitors[44] and that the monastery already enjoyed some sort of fame before Tarasis died. Of course the fame could have been derived from Tarasis himself: as a consequence he found it expedient to build a hospice for those who came to consult him. At any rate, it is unlikely that the lapicide who adjusted the inscription would have been content to refer to Tarasis as founder of a hospice when he actually established the community. Thus one is led to suggest that the original foundation was older, that the sanctity of the founder or one of his companions, or perhaps the attraction of a relic treasured there, led to visits by pilgrims for whom Tarasis eventually provided shelter. In this hypothesis the first visitors came to honour a holy man or a relic; their numbers were such that they required the building of a hospice – for which Tarasis was responsible – and a large public church, the Basilica. Tarasis himself was remembered for his holiness and the eastern part of the complex was built to honour his memory. It was designed around his grave.[45]

In this hypothesis the essential unity of the site and of the community that lived there is explained in such a way that differences of organization and quality of plan can be accommodated. By and large, the strongest argument is for the institutional continuity of the monastery at Alahan, it being understood that it became a centre of devotion for the wider Christian community and that the monastery grew in numbers and somewhat changed its outlook so as to accommodate the new situation.

The monk sought a life of seclusion and penance bearing fruit in contemplation. His desire was a common one in the early Church and led to a movement that realized itself in many forms. By the end of the fourth century, due in part to the teaching and practice of St. Basil, it was usually accepted that, whether the monk were to follow the eremitic or the cenobitic way to perfection, he should spend the initial period of his new life in community. There he first experienced the meaning of withdrawal from the world, received instructions in Christian belief and practice and learned the psalter and other modes of prayer that he would use in the

---

[44] See above, pp. 22-23.
[45] Michael Gough, "Domestic Appointments at Alahan Monastery"; cf. Semavi Eyice, *Karadağ ve Karaman Çevresinde Arkeolojik İncelemeler* (Istanbul, 1971), pp. 92-93, 222.

future.[46] It is in this context that the basin cut in the floor at the west end of the north aisle in the Cave Church (Fig. 14) may find explanation.[47] Sometimes individuals were attracted to monastic life before they became Christians. For them baptism and the assumption of the obligations of the monk were part of the same act.[48] Thus it is possible that from the earliest days of the Alahan community the basin was used as a baptismal font for the reception of its neophytes.[49]

The period of initiation completed, the young monk would join his elders in the regular cenobitic life or, in another tradition, that of the *laura*,[50] would live in a hermitage from which he would come once or twice a week to join his brethren for the Eucharist. As was remarked above, there were several cells at Alahan; they do not have the seclusion from each other that was characteristic of the *laura* in its Palestinian form. Furthermore, though there were convenient places for hermitages in grottoes above and below the level on which the monastery stands, surface inspection has yielded no sign that they were used for that purpose (Fig. 67, Pl. 65). It seems very likely that the Alahan cells were arranged with the purpose of keeping them in close proximity in so far as a rather difficult site would allow. The evidence suggests that the Alahan community evolved in the direction favoured by St. Basil, namely the life of the coenobium, consisting of a rather small group that prayed, worked and dined and took their rest together. In great centres of pilgrimage there were monks ("τάγματα") attached to the shrine whose role it was to attend

---

[46] See Festugière, *Les moines d'Orient*, 1: 41-53. On St. Sabas' instruction of novices see the "Life of St. Sabas," ed. Schwartz, p. 113; trans. Festugière, *Les moines d'Orient*, 3.2: 39-40.

[47] See above, pp. 78, 80.

[48] On the reference to monks among his catechumens by Cyril of Jerusalem, see D. J. Chitty, *The Desert a City* (Oxford, 1967), pp. 48 and 61 n. 23; cf. Robert Murray, "The Features of the Earliest Christian Asceticism" in *Christian Spirituality: Essays in Honour of Gordon Rupp*, ed. Peter Brooks (London, 1975), pp. 73-75. In the "Life of St. Euthymius" by Cyril of Scythopolis we read of the saint's cure of Terebon; moved by the miracle Terebon and a group of Saracens requested baptism. Euthymius had a font cut in the floor of his cell and, having instructed them, baptized them there. See the edition by Eduard Schwartz in *Kyrillos von Skythopolis*, pp. 18-21; trans. Festugière, *Les moines d'Orient*, 3.1: 73-74.

[49] See the discussion of the Baptistery, below, pp. 217-219.

[50] The *laura* was a semi-eremitic colony of monks who lived apart from each other but were subject to a common superior and usually came together for common prayer. They enjoyed an important development in Palestine under St. Euthymius (377-473) in the years that saw the beginning of the community at Alahan. Mar Saba, a still extant monastery between Jerusalem and the Jordan Valley, is a continuation of the *laura* founded by St. Sabas (434-532). See Festugière, *Les moines d'Orient*, 3.2: 146-147, Index s.v. "Laures."

to pilgrims and see to the provision of liturgical services, a possibility for the community at Alahan that is attractive[51] given the fact that the scanty incidental evidence afforded by the inscriptions refers to the provision of shelter for guests.[52]

Whatever form his life might assume, the monk was expected to give much of it to private and public prayer. The former was possible anywhere: oratories[53] and churches, the graves of deceased confreres, more withdrawn retreats on the mountain side where silence and the splendour of the terrain would foster contemplation – all were suitable for prayer and meditative reading. Essentially informal, such prayer could be continued during work and when travelling. But the monk's day was organized around the divine office, several periods of prayer based on the psalter and other scriptural readings.[54] Those members of the community who were present in the monastery were expected to gather for these prayers at the times appointed.[55] In the early days of Alahan's existence, the Cave Church was probably used for this purpose. We know from accounts of other places of pilgrimage that the office was recited in a public church and that at least part of it saw participation by the laity.[56] Eventually this arrangement probably obtained at Alahan.[57]

The divine office was a form of prayer open to any monk or hermit who could read or who had memorized the psalter. The Eucharist required the presence of a bishop or a priest. It is clear from patristic writings that monastic communities did not always have a priest available either from among their number or from the neighbourhood. In such cases the Eucharist was offered on special feasts when an officiating cleric was present. St. Basil recommended the reservation of the sacred species

---

[51] Ibid., 1: 41 n. 1. On the role of monks as guardians of the shrine of St. Thekla, see Basilius, bp. of Seleucia, *Vie et miracles de sainte Thècle*, ed., trans. Gilbert Dagron, Subsidia Hagiographica 62 (Bruxelles, 1978), pp. 57-58. On the diminished role of monks at shrines in episcopal centres, see Mohrmann, "Égérie et le monachisme."

[52] On the meaning of "παραμονάριος" in the inscription on the tomb of Tarasis the Younger, see above, pp. 23-24.

[53] On the oratory above the Cave Church see above, p. 79.

[54] See J. Mateos, "L'Office monastique à la fin du ive siècle: Antioche, Palestine, Cappadoce," *Oriens Christianus*, 47 (= ser. 4, vol. 11), (1963), pp. 53-88.

[55] See St. Basil, *The Long Rules*, q. 37 "Whether prayer and psalmody ought to afford a pretext ...," in *Ascetical Works*, trans. Wagner, pp. 308-311; PG 31: 1011-1016.

[56] See *Itinerarium Egeriae*, 24, ed. Franceschini and Weber, pp. 67-70.

[57] It is not known where the monks would have recited their office. If they used the eastern part of the nave in the Basilica or the East Church, there would have been room for thirty or forty and they would have been separated from but close to the laity who joined in their prayer. See above, pp. 114-115.

so that the brethren might receive when it was impossible to offer mass.[58]
Such may have been the situation at Alahan during its first years. Once it
became a place of pilgrimage, the presence of a priest was all the more
desirable. We know from the inscription in the arcosolium that was to
shelter the grave of Tarasis the Younger that he was a priest (Pl. 3) [59] Thus
it can be assumed that the monastery was assured of priestly services for
some time after 461. Under these circumstances the Eucharist can be
presumed to have been offered on Sundays and probably on Saturdays as
well as on major feasts and those associated with saints whose relics were
present in the monastery. It is possible that efforts were made to offer the
Eucharist for those who came to the monastery, even when their visit was
on a day or at a time when, under different circumstances, it would not
have been suitable to do so.[60]

Manual labour played an important role in the monastic routine. *Vitae*
of famous monks frequently refer to them working as weavers of the cloth
for their habits, tending gardens and patches of grain, working at the forge
or as carpenters and masons either by themselves or assisting professional
builders in the construction of monastery and church.[61] It was intended
that as much as possible the monk's work should supply his own needs
and those of his monastery and also that he should have extra produce to
give to those in need. In part, the fruits of his work provided for those
who came to the monastery for hospitality.

When death came the monk was buried among his brethren.[62] The
north nave of the Cave Church was converted to a burial chapel, a change
that, if the pattern discernible elsewhere were followed at Alahan,
occurred early in the life of the monastery.[63] In two cases arcosolia were
cut in the walls of cells set in the quarried face north of the main range of
buildings; here the body of the deceased may have been returned to his
earlier dwelling.[64] Eleven other tombs – sarcophagi in arcosolia as in the

[58] Ep. 93, in *Lettres*, ed. Courtonne, 1: 203-204.

[59] See above, pp. 23-24.

[60] Such was Egeria's experience: *Itinerarium Egeriae*, 3.6, ed. Franceschini and
Weber, p. 40. On the other hand, few pilgrims would receive the attention that she
enjoyed; see Christine Mohrmann, "Égérie et le monachisme," pp. 163-168 and passim.

[61] On labouring see St. Basil, *The Long Rules*, qq. 37, 38 in his *Ascetical Works*, trans.
Wagner, pp. 306-312; PG 31: 1009-1018. See Callinicos' account of the labour of St.
Hypatios of Rufiniana, in his *Vie d'Hypatios*, ed. G. J. M. Bartelink, Sources Chrétiennes
177 (Paris, 1971), pp. 100-103.

[62] See above, pp. 78, 139-140.

[63] E.g., *Vie d'Hypatios*, ed. Bartelink, pp. 287-293.

[64] St. Euthymius was buried in a chapel built in the grotto in which he had lived;
see the "Life of Euthymius" by Cyril of Scythopolis, ed. Schwartz, pp. 61-62; trans.

group around the grave of Tarasis, or graves cut downwards into the
bedrock with a great stone over the opening – are found in the Necropolis
between the Baptistery and the East Church. Several of the tombs were
found to contain multiple burials. There were many interments in the
deepest cave of the original settlement.[65] The basis of the distinction
between those buried in sarcophagi and those in the common grave is
unknown.[66] All the deceased seem to have been laid to rest facing the east
from which the light of their resurrection would come. On many of the
sarcophagus covers a Latin cross with its crossbeam to the west indicates
the arrangement of the body beneath. The anniversary of death would be
remembered in the office, possibly recited in part by the grave of the
monk commemorated. One at least of these commemorations can be
presumed to have been a celebration to which pilgrims came.

***

A tension descernible within monasticism from the beginning was
between the desire to be separated from other men, the better to concentrate on the things of God, and the obligation, if not always the desire, to
be available to help others in their need. St. Basil saw the lack of
opportunity for mutual charity and support as a weakness in the eremitic
life. He saw too that the monk had a responsibility that reached further
afield, urging them to devote some of the fruits of their labour to the poor,
even going so far as to urge that communities be established within
striking distance of towns and villages where those in need would live.[67] It
was in this assistance of the poor and helpless and in the more directly

---

Festugière, *Les moines d'Orient*, 3.1: 115-116. The account of the preparation of the tomb
mentions that other graves were made for abbots, priests and holy men within the chapel.

[65] In addition, there were five burials outside the south wall of the Basilica. Bones
from five skeletons were piled in the south aisle of the same church; they seem to have
been left by grave robbers. Finally, badly disturbed burials were found outside the
Baptistery along the north and east walls and at the southwest corner of the narthex; see
Michael Gough, "Excavations at Alahan, Second Preliminary Report," *Anatolian Studies*,
13 (1963), pp. 106, 108. It is likely tht all were of the secondary period.

[66] For Usman's suggestion that the founders of Alahan were buried in the formal
graves of the Necropolis, see above, n. 43. A similar distinction has been observed in
Syrian monasteries: Tchalenko, *Villages antiques*, 1: 19-20, 167-168, and Lassus,
Sanctuaires chrétiens de Syrie, p. 276. Lassus suggests that the monumental graves were
for the hegumens of the monastery. It will be recalled that in the two cases where there is
information about those for whom the Alahan sarcophagi were prepared, they were
persons of authority; see above, pp. 22-24.

[67] See St. Basil, *Ascetical Works*, trans. M. M. Wagner, p. xi.

pastoral function of counsel, instruction and the provision of a becoming liturgy that monks entered into relations with the wider community both Christian and pagan.

Providing hospitality for travellers was generally accepted as a role for monks.[68] In less populated areas monasteries seem sometimes to have been the only shelter available and there is reason for thinking that they were sited by routes for that purpose. The monastery at Alahan probably did not serve this function; given its difficult approach it is unlikely that the casual passer-by would seek shelter there, especially as there is a strong possibility that there would be shelter in the settlement below. It seems safe to conclude that it was for those who came to the monastery for a more spiritual purpose that Tarasis' hospice was intended.

Throughout the essay it has been presumed that one of the spiritual purposes for which visitors came to Alahan was pilgrimage. Yet, though there is reference to the reception of guests in the inscriptions, there is no specific allusion to pilgrims. Their presence has been deduced from the scale and general plan of the monastery and from the implications of details of construction revealed by excavation. The size of the main churches and the presence of the Baptistery and Colonnaded Walk are out of proportion with the needs of a community that probably rarely exceeded forty monks.[69] There were no large population centres in the

[68] See H. Leclercq, "Hôpitaux, Hospices, Hôtelleries," pt. 3, "Fondations en Orient," in *Dictionnaire d'archéologie chrétienne et de liturgie*, 6.2 (Paris, 1925), 2750-2765; Lassus, *Sanctuaires chrétiens de Syrie*, pp. 234, 267, 285; Tchalenko, *Villages antiques*, 1: 163-166.

[69] It is, of course, impossible to decide the size of the Alahan community at its zenith. As was mentioned above, St. Basil stressed the importance of the common life that was possible in the cenobium. He sought to avoid the excessively large numbers of Pachomian foundations, preferring a familial model; see Paul J. Fedwick, *The Church and the Charisma of Leadership in Basil of Caesarea*, Studies and Texts 45 (Toronto, 1979), pp. 156-165. Writing in 1913, W. K. Lowther Clarke suggested that thirty to forty monks were probably intended as the optimum number for a monastery of the type envisioned by St. Basil: W. K. Lowther Clarke, *St. Basil the Great: a Study in Monasticism* (Cambridge, 1913), p. 117. His opinion was accepted by Emmanuel Amand de Mendieta, "Le Système cénobitique basilien comparé au système cénobitique pachômien," *Revue de l'histoire des religions*, 152 (1957), pp. 31-80, esp. pp. 39-41. A number such as this is suitable for the living spaces that have been revealed at Alahan. Monks would sleep in common dormitories and, by and large, would require a small living space. The habitation areas of the Cave Complex and the cells along the quarried face in the eastern part of the monastery would easily supply space for a community of this size; see above, pp. 134-142. Unfortunately it is not possible to know whether part of the Cave Complex were given over to hospitality. Its position made it especially suitable for that purpose. In this discussion it has been presumed that the Two-Storey Building was not used by the monks: see below, p. 217.

immediate neighbourhood that might have required such structures. The implication is that the devotees for whom the buildings were designed came from further afield.[70]

Furthermore, each of the major churches was built with a large synthronon (Fig. 19, 44).[71] Both were eventually enlarged to provide more seating space. A simple test was sufficient to demonstrate that twenty ministers can be comfortably seated on the upper bench of the synthronon in the Basilica. To our present knowledge of monastic liturgy, monks did not take their place in the sanctuary unless they were clerics; ordained monks were rare. It is possible to explain the large synthrona in their first stage as the requirement of a monumental design, but the enlargements point to a demand based on usage. Thus it seems necessary to conclude that major gatherings of clergy occurred at Alahan. St. Basil mentions meetings of bishops at shrines on patronal feasts, meetings that had at once the quality of a pilgrimage and a local synod.[72] Similar reunions are mentioned in a fifth-century life of St. Thecla.[73] It is in gatherings of this sort, when many priests and deacons and possibly several bishops were present, that the explanation of the fully developed sanctuaries at Alahan must be seen.

Major gatherings of pilgrims would occur at Easter and Epiphany and on the feasts of those saints whose relics the monastery treasured. Beyond the tomb of Tarasis and the fact that the altar bases from the Baptistery and the south nave of the Cave Church contained apertures for reliquaries, nothing can be said with certainty of the relics treasured at Alahan.[74] However, there are several clues that should be set out in this regard. First, it is clear that the designer of the Basilica chose to respect the tiny apse in the south nave of the Cave Church though its presence upset

[70] The reconstruction of the west facades of both the Basilica and the East Church (see above, pp. 80-82, 104-107 and figs. 19, 24, 25, 44, 50, 51) show that there were windowed galleries over the narthex; on occasion, when large crowds had gathered, they could serve as tribunes from which those pilgrims who could not find places within the churches and had assembled in their forecourts might be addressed. Georges Tchalenko found tribunes of this sort to be typical of pilgrim churches in Syria and suggested that they served as open-air churches on special occasions: *Villages antiques*, 1: 235.

[71] See above, pp. 96-97, 116.

[72] Ep. 176, in *Lettres*, ed. Courtonne, vol. 2 (1961), pp. 112-113.

[73] See Miracle 33 in *Vie et miracles de Sainte Thècle*, ed. Dagron, pp. 376-377.

[74] On relics in altar bases, see Otto Nussbaum, *Der Standort des Liturgen am christlichen Altar vor dem Jahre 1000*, 2 vols., Theophaneia; Beiträge zur Religions- und Kirchengeschichte des Altertums 18 (Bonn, 1965), Index (p. 476) s.v. "Reliquienbehälter." At the time Nussbaum wrote this study, examples of the Alahan arrangement were found mostly in Greece and North Africa. The Alahan examples and that of Dağ Pazarı (see *Anatolian Studies*, 10 [1960], 7) were unknown to him.

the harmony of the projected narthex. At the same time, he sought to bring the Basilica as close to that apse as possible. An ancient altar base is still in the apse; there is a large circular opening in the centre of its upper suface, an opening that would make it possible for a devotee to reach down and touch the relic contained there.[75] These facts suggest the hypothesis that the earliest of the churches housed an important relic and that this relic is, at least in part, the explanation of the original pilgrimage to Alahan.

The base of the Basilica's altar did not contain an opening for a reliquary; perhaps it was understood that the new building shared in the sacred quality of the apse to which it was contiguous. But there were at least two places where important relics may have been housed within the building. The first is an intriguing possibility: because of the angle of the bedrock on which the Basilica was constructed there was an undercroft running from the south wall an unknown distance to the north.[76] Its position and entrance are similar to those of the chapel under the shrine of St. Thekla at Meriamlik, facts which lead to the question whether there were a reliquary-crypt beneath it. Unfortunately, the unstable state of the slope at that point has made further investigation impossible. The second possibility involves the pastophory at the southeast corner of the Basilica. There are indications that it received a development reminiscent of that found in some Syrian churches. In this latter group the pastophory was treated as a separate chapel, a martyrium in which relics were displayed for veneration. Remembering the size of the room, its careful decoration and the fact that there was an ante-room between it and the south aisle, there is, given the Syrian analogue, some little reason for suggesting that it was intended for special use, namely the housing of a relic.[77]

---

[75] This altar base was probably used during the secondary period of occupation, but the quality of its incised decoration indicates that it is primary; see above, p. 77. The opening may have received a column that provided a central support to the *mensa* but, given the depth of the aperture, even in that case there would have been room for a reliquary beneath. This arrangement is found in the fifth-century church at Chersonesos, Crete; see Nussbaum, *Der Standort*, 1: 165-166, 2: 86, Abb. 59. Such an altar is shown in mosaics (ca. 450) in the Orthodox Baptistery at Ravenna. See Friedrich W. Diechmann, *Ravenna Hauptstadt des spätantiken Abendlandes*, 3: *Frühchristliche Bauten und Mosaiken von Ravenna*, 2nd ed. (Wiesbaden, 1958), pls. 63, 65, and 67; cf. Giuseppe Bovini, *Die Mosaiken von Ravenna* (Wiesbaden, 1977), pl. 9.

[76] See above, pp. 29, 80.

[77] See Lassus, *Sanctuaires chrétiens de Syrie*, pp. 162-184. However, in his article "Syrie" (*Dictionnaire d'archéologie chrétienne et de liturgie*, 15.2 [Paris, 1953], col. 1878-1879) Lassus points out that no case of the placing of relics under the altar is known in Syria and continues (col. 1879): "on peut croire que le culte des martyrs s'y est developpé parallèlement à la liturgie eucharistique, et non pas, comme en Afrique et en Occident, en

The altar base in the Baptistery contained an opening for a reliquary (Pl. 50).[78] Nothing can be said with certainty about relics in the East Church. In this building, which with its vertical axis has so many of the qualities of a martyrium, there is only the mark of an altar base in the bema floor; nothing of the base itself remains.[79] Against the east wall of the south pastophory the excavators found the remains of a piece of furniture that might have been an altar.[80] It consisted of a decorated base between slots for four uprights (Pl. 47). There was no sign that an opening for a reliquary had been let into the stone. Given the rather general opinion that there should be only one altar in a church[81] and the fact that all the other Alahan altars stood well clear of the wall of the rooms in which they stood, it is prudent to think of other explanations. It may have been the base of a table used in preparing the Eucharistic elements. It is also conceivable that it was the base for a free-standing reliquary. It is clear that the Syrian analogue must not be pressed excessively, but it may be significant that the pastophory in question was at the eastern extremity of the long axis provided by the Colonnaded Walk and the south aisle of the church.[82]

It is probable that, when the complex was completed, the Basilica was used for regular Sunday and possibly the Saturday Eucharist and for public recitation of the office, while the East Church, at the heart of the more private part of the monastery, was used for the celebration of feasts associated with the saints honoured at Alahan and for the liturgies of

---

liaison intime avec elle." It should be noted that, to our present knowledge, there was no reliquary within the main liturgical area of either of the large churches at Alahan.

[78] See above, p. 132.

[79] See Michael Gough, "Excavations at Alahan: Third Preliminary Report," *Anatolian Studies*, 14 (1964), p. 186.

[80] See above, p. 117, and Michael Gough, "Alahan Monastery 1968," *Türk Arkeoloji Dergisi*, 17/1 (1968), p. 67 and pl. 3.

[81] See H. Leclercq, "Autel," *Dictionnaire d'archéologie chrétienne et de liturgie*, 1.2 (Paris, 1924), 3186, and Joseph Braun, *Der christliche Altar in seiner geschichtlichen Entwicklung* (Munich, 1924), 1: 368-369. It is possible that the south pastophory was already considered to be a separate chapel and thus a suitable place for an altar.

[82] It is impossible to identify the saints to whom these relics – real and hypothetical – are to be referred. Yet some lines of speculation are not unreasonable. The reliquary associated with Tarasis the Younger (see above, p. 24) likély contained a relic of St. Konon, one of the heroes of Isauria. It is conceivable that it had once been at Alahan and was taken to the Çirga region after the monastery was abandoned. It is not without interest that the only two inhabitants of Alahan of which there is personal information were named Tarasis; could the name indicate a personal devotion to St. Tarasis/Sozon, a native of Lycaonia martyred at Pompeiopolis ca. 304, and the presence of a relic of this saint at the monastery from an early date? See F. Halkin, *Bibliotheca hagiographica graeca*, 3rd ed. (Bruxelles, 1957), 2: 263 no. 1643 and 265 no. 1644.

Easter and Epiphany during which catechumens were received into the Church by baptism.[83]

The Baptistery is a reminder that some came to Alahan for reasons other than pilgrimage; they came that they might enter the Church there. In many cases, baptism would have been preceded by a period of instruction extending through Lent or the weeks before Epiphany. It was probably for these catechumens and for visits of shorter duration by pilgrims of some importance that the hospice was intended.[84] Excavation of the Two-Storey Building (Fig. 66, 58, Pl. 61-63) has revealed a somewhat more refined construction than that of the monks' habitation and the quality of tableware as well as hints as to the food consumed indicate that the guests of the monastery received decent hospitality during their stay.[85]

Baptism was ordinarily received as part of the liturgy of the Resurrection or on the feast of the Epiphany. Much is known of its ritual as practised at Jerusalem and Antioch during the late fourth and early fifth centuries: in broad lines it involved the candidate's abjuration of Satan followed by exorcism, the setting aside of clothing and a complete anointing, the descent into the font followed by the clothing in baptismal dress and the anointing with chrism.[86] The descriptions in question make it clear that the articulation of the monumental baptistery was intended to supply distinct and becoming spaces for the different parts of the ceremony. The Baptistery at Alahan is an excellent example of such a structure (Fig. 62, Pl. 50-52). Abjuration and exorcism probably occurred in the narthex. The laying aside of clothing and the first anointing could be given suitable ritual statement in the south nave.[87] The more elaborate

[83] See the discussion of the different liturgical uses of multiple churches in Gordana Babić, *Les chapelles annexes des églises byzantines: Fonction liturgique et programmes iconographiques*, Bibliothèque des Cahiers archéologiques 3 (Paris, 1969), pp. 9-31.

[84] The needs of most pilgrims would be simpler. They would find shelter for their brief stay in the churches and under the roof of the Colonnaded Walk. It is estimated that the latter, when completed, would provide a covered area of ca. 650 m².

[85] The best tableware on the site was exposed during the excavations of 1972. It was on the slope immediately below the Two-Storey Building. See St. Basil, *The Long Rules*, q. 20 "The rule to be followed in serving meals to guests," in his *Ascetical Works*, trans. Wagner, pp. 277-280; PG 31: 969-976. On the special dwelling for the hegumen and for priests in some Syrian monasteries see Tchalenko, *Villages antiques*, 1: 166-167.

[86] See Hugh M. Riley, *Christian Initiation* (Washington, 1974), pp. 153-154, and passim; and Sebastian Brock, "Studies in the Early History of Syrian Orthodox Baptismal Liturgy," *The Journal of Theological Studies*, NS 23 (1972), 16-64.

[87] On consignation see Riley, *Christian Initiation*, pp. 349-357. On the question as to which of the two ritual anointings was to be received in a special area, the *consignatorium*, see Massey H. Shepherd Jr., "The Formation and Influence of the Antiochene Liturgy," *Dumbarton Oaks Papers*, 15 (1961), pp. 42-43; the author argues that in the region of Antioch and areas influenced by its liturgy it was the anointing before baptism to which major importance was attached.

northern nave provided space for the actual baptism and subsequent ritual acts. It should be noted that the font was deep enough to permit the complete immersion of the candidate by the presiding bishop.[88]

Baptismal immersion was seen as a dying with Christ and the emerging from the font as the earnest of the final resurrection. Dionysius the Pseudo-Areopagite linked the anointing at baptism, a preparation for the struggle that lay ahead, with the final anointing of the dead, the sign of victory achieved.[89] Both the dead and the newly baptized looked to the east, whence their final resurrection was to come. The double symbolism was expressed in the frequent association of the font with a martyrium, a symbolism that was realized at Alahan where the Baptistery, in which the neophytes moved towards the east as they passed through the font to be received by the bishop who anointed them, was adjacent to the Necropolis, where heroes of the past looked to the east as they awaited their resurrection.

When the ceremony was completed the baptismal party went in procession to the church where the neophyte was received by the congregation and took part in the Eucharist that followed.[90] The flow of the Colonnaded Walk indicates that the procession moved to the East Church.[91]

At Alahan the north nave of the Baptistery is terminated in an apse with an altar and a small synthronon. The altar could easily be confused with a simple table. (Indeed, it may well have served such a function, providing the surface on which the baptismal robe, sacred oils, etc. were placed during the reception of the sacrament.) But its position in relation to the synthronon and the opening for a reliquary in the base leave no doubt that it was an altar. It may have been intended for use on occasions when small groups arrived who wished to offer the Eucharist after other altars had already been used for that purpose.[92] It seems more likely, however, that this is evidence of a less formal baptismal ceremony, indicating that by the early sixth century baptism was sometimes part of a less grand

[88] See the description of baptism in Theodore of Mopsuestia, *Catechetical Homilies*, 14.18-20, in *Les homélies catéchétiques de Théodore de Mopsueste*, ed., trans. Raymond Tonneau and Robert Devresse, Studi e Testi 145 (Vatican City, 1949), pp. 441-445.

[89] *Ecclesiastical Hierarchy*, 7.3 §§ 8-9, in *The Works of Dionysius the Areopagite*, trans. John Parker, part 2 (London, 1899), pp. 158-159; also in PG 3: 563-566.

[90] See *Itinerarium Egeriae*, 38.1-2, ed. Franceschini and Weber, pp. 82-83; cf. Lassus, *Sanctuaires chrétiens de Syrie*, p. 227, on the excavations at Qalat Sem'an.

[91] See the discussion of the relationship between baptism and pilgrimage in Lassus, *Sanctuaires chrétiens de Syrie*, pp. 227-228 and on processions, pp. 217-222.

[92] See Babić, *Les chapelles annexes*, pp. 9-10.

liturgy, one involving a small attendance and completed by the Eucharist offered in the Baptistery itself.[93]

*
**

In its role as a shrine to which pilgrims came to honour the saints who were their heroes and protectors, and as a place to which others came for instruction and to enter the Christian life, Alahan demonstrates two pastoral functions by which monks played an important part in the life of the Christian community. In time those functions came to an end there. The reasons for the demise of the monastery are unknown, but a few tentative suggestions in this regard can be made. Throughout the late fifth and the sixth centuries theological dispute caused division within the Empire and monasteries, much involved, were sometimes hurt in the process. It is not inconceivable that Alahan was the victim of such a quarrel.[94] There was a serious revolt in the region during the last decade of the fifth century and the general political confusion and brigandage of the years that followed were made all the worse when the Persians occupied the coast well to the west of Silifke between 617 and 632.[95] The following generations would have to live under the shadow of Islam. Under such conditions the exposure of the site may have made it untenable. There may also have been physical reasons for withdrawal: failure of the water supply, a landslide from the upper slope or an earthquake and its aftermath.[96] However uncertain these suggestions must be, it is possible to have a more definite opinion as to the manner of the community's disappearance. The excavation of the site revealed no sign that its inhabitants were surprised by disaster. Whether Alahan were eventually overwhelmed by a landslide or by plunderers, it was not occupied at the time. The monks had withdrawn earlier and in order, taking their possessions with them.

Some time later the site was occupied again. The repairs to the Cave Church, Basilica and Baptistery indicate that it was a religious community that sought shelter there.[97] The quality of the restored buildings reveals a

[93] Lassus makes a similar suggestion for Syria; *Sanctuaires chrétiens de Syrie*, p. 228.
[94] See Michael Gough, "The Emperor Zeno and Some Cilician Churches," *Anatolian Studies*, 22 (1972), pp. 199-212. On the situation in Isauria, see Ernest Honigmann, *Évêques et évêchés monophysites d'Asie antérieure au vɪᵉ siècle*, Corpus Scriptorum Christianorum Orientalium 127, Subsidia 2 (Louvain, 1951), pp. 84-97.
[95] See C. Mango, "Isaurian Builders," in *Polychronion. Festschrift Franz Dölger zum 75. Geburtstag*, ed. Peter Wirth (Heidelberg, 1966), pp. 358-365; and Clive Foss, "The Persians in Asia Minor and the End of Antiquity," *English Historical Review*, 90 (1975), pp. 721-747.
[96] See above, p. 149.
[97] See above, pp. 149-153.

diminished capacity for embellishment and design and the fact that much smaller liturgical spaces were required. Repair of the East Church, less seriously damaged from the point of view of structure, seemed to have been beyond the capacities of the monks and probably beyond their needs as well. In time the new community was to withdraw. Its dwellings and chapels were buried beneath the debris of the mountain side but the East Church remained virtually as before.

Appendix 1

Ricordi di un Breve Soggiorno di Studi ad Alahan

Paolo Verzone

Nei tre giorni dal 31 maggio al 2 giugno 1955 nel corso di un viaggio di studio effettuato coll'appoggio della Mimarlik Fakultesi dell'Università tecnica di Istanbul, di cui allora ero professore, effetuai uno studio delle rovine del monastero di Alahan Monastir. Mi accompagnavano l'Arch. Erdoğan Yalkın e la Dr. Mukerrem Usman, miei assistenti.

La località era completamente deserta ed i ruderi erano raggiunti a piedi dalla sottostante strada dove lasciavamo la jeep che ci aveva condotti collà ed il percorso attraverso a prati e boschi era incantevole; nei tre giorni di lavoro febbrile io e l'arch. Yalkın rilevammo le rovine e personalmente le fotografai con un vecchio apparecchio Zeiss; ritornati ad Istanbul necessitava un controllo di qualche misura incerta e l'arch. Yalkın si recò nuovamente nel sito accompagnato da un altro architetto che però, non volle procedere nella montagna per timore di eventuali orsi; l'arch. Yalkın dovette far tutto da solo e, dopo una visita con qualche misura, riprese la via del ritorno.

La Turchia d'allora era ben differente da quella attuale: l'albergo di Mut dove passavamo la notte, recandoci poi colla jeep ogni mattina ad Alahan, era quanto di più semplice si può immaginare, ed i residenti erano contadini di passagio: la Dr. Usman non aveva potuto ottenere una camera ma solo un fondo di corridoio, separato da una tenda dagli altri ospiti assiepati nel corridoio. Essa passò una notte bianca perchè due di questi, al di là della tenda contrattavano ad alta voce, a partire dalle due di notte, non so quale prodotto dei loro campi; la richiesta era di sei lire turche al chilogrammo e l'offerta di cinque: l'accordo fu concluso dopo tre ore di animata discussione a cinque e mezza.

Quando noi effettuamo le nostre visite il complesso monumentale dell'antico monastero si presentava nel modo più suggestivo nel quadro incantevole delle montagne dell'Isauria: nella roccia che l'accompagnava sul lato a notte una serie di grotte evocavano il sacrificio dei monaci che anticamente vi abitavano. Una prateria animata da gruppi di alberi discendeva dalla parte opposta: una sorgente d'acqua gelata situata a qualche centinaio di metri di distanza (deliziosa per chi riusciva a vincere l'antipatia per gli innumerevoli grossi insetti neri che turbinavano in essa) giustificava la scelta del sito per la comunità.

Le strutture delle unità abitative dei monaci dovevano essere molto fragili e provvisorie e non ne restava pressochè nulla: fra di esse vi erano inserite tombe ad arcosolio con semplici sarcofagi.

Il luogo dove sorgeva il monastero non interessava solo i monaci votati alla vita contemplativa ed alle preghiere: esso sovrastava la valle del Kalycadnus fra l'attuale Karaman, l'antica Laranda e Selefke (Seleucia), che era percorsa da molti viaggiatori che volevano attraversare i monti del Tauro senza passare dalle porte cilicie. Il percorso doveva essere difficile e ciò spiega la presenza di un centro religioso d'assistenza per i viaggiatori e fu ancora seguito dai crociati di Federico Barbarossa nel 1190, già provati dalle precedenti privazioni; i dignitari ed i soldati germanici soffrirono incredibilmente in questa marcia che doveva concludersi tragicamente coll'annegamento del Sovrano a Selefke.

Il cronista Ansberto descrive la pietosa odissea di essi fra questi monti del Tauro: i vescovi, i principi ed i signori procedevano aiutandosi coi piedi e con le mani come dei quadrupedi: illustri cavalieri malati erano portati su letti a dorso di cavallo: gli scudieri col viso coperto di sudore, portavano i loro signori, affranti e languenti sugli scudi.

Prima di noi il complesso era stato visitato dal conte di Laborde che ne aveva offerto due suggestive tavole litografiche nel suo libro di viaggi in Asia Minore, un'opera che per il lusso e lo spirito informatore si legava ancora ai "Voyages pittoresques" della fine del settecento, e poi dal rev. A. C. Headlam accompagnato dal Ramsay e dal Dr. Hogarth: la pubblicazione che ne seguì constituì per molti anni l'illustrazione "standard" del monumento. Esso era stato distinto, fino allora col nome leggendario di "Koca Kalesi," il castello del Vecchio, a lui attribuito da contadini locali: più esattamente E. Herzfeld, che visitò il sito nel corso di un viaggio in Cilicia insieme a S. Guyer nel 1906, gli attribuì quello effettivo locale di Alahan, da un han di cui restano le rovine nelle vicinanze.

Una breve notizia in un numero dell'"Illustrated London News" del 1946 riprodusse poi qualche aspetto inedito del complesso monumentale. L'illustrazione che io preparai del monumento coi rilievi effettuati e colle fotografie riportate dalla nostra breve permanenza fu pubblicata nel settembre del 1955 in lingua turca nella serie promossa dall'Università Tecnica: alcuni disegni erano opera dell'arch. E. Yalkin, un'illustrazione delle iscrizioni del prof. E. Bean, ed un capitolo sui sepolcri della prof. M. Usman: esso uscì contemporaneamente al primo articolo del prof. M. Gough: l'anno seguente seguì l'edizione italiana della monografia. All'epoca della nostra breve permanenza il complesso monumentale di Alahan presentava la chiesa occidentale interrata dai rottami delle distrutte strutture e si riconoscevano solo il portale centrale, coi suoi meravigliosi stipiti scolpiti, parte del muro sud e resti della chiesa più recente ad una sola navata (ricostruzione della basilica ipostile primitiva che venne rimessa alla luce dagli scavi operati dal prof. M. Gough); era però riconoscibile l'abside maggiore che da noi fu puntualmente rilevata.

Lo scavo della basilica no. 1[1] ha ricostituito il quadro cronologico della vita del monastero in armonia con la degradazione della vita e della civiltà in Anatolia dopo le affermazioni politiche e militari degli Omeiadi di Siria; la costruzione di una piccola chiesa a volte inattaccabile dagli incendi, nel sito di una basilica a tre navi copertura lignea è ormai un dato acquisito per l'evoluzione della civiltà in Anatolia nell'Alto Medio Evo.

Il lungo porticato che consentiva ai pellegrini un rifugio ed assicurava ad essi non solo una sosta al riparo dalle intemperie ma un esaltante spettacolo della natura e del paesaggio fu da noi rilevato coi dislivelli che suggerivano l'antica presenza di scalee intermedie: questo nobile portico ipostile, già percorso dalle processioni dei monaci, (l'endicola intermedia ne costituiva verosimilmente una stazione) risultò effettivamente una delle più nobili realizzazioni del genio architettonico tardo-romano non solo in Isauria ma in tutto l'Impero d'Oriente.

Della chiesa mediana[2] che dagli scavi risultò un battistero (il che sta a provare i frequenti pellegrinaggi e la presenza di pagani fra i visitatori del monastero) ben poco emergeva dal suolo.

La chiesa orientale (no. 3)[3] risultava già nel 1955 ben conservata col pavimento coperto da un sottile strato di rottami: le strutture delle navate erano intatte ed in particolare era, ed è ben conservato, il tamburo della cupola coi suoi raccordi angolari.

Questo monumento, forse un martyrium dedicato ad un santo a noi ignoto, e la sua struttura con cupola in mezzo alla nave (che sembra una via di mezzo fra la basilica ed il martyrium – tomba di martire) e la datazione da me proposta vent'anni fa, l'ultimo quarto del v secolo, sembra corrispondere a questa tipologia: lo sfoggio di colonne sembra pure suggerito da una sensibilità ancora legato all'eredità classica. La cupola a scheletro ligneo a manto di piombo che coronava il monumento e di cui sono rimasti miracolosamente intatti i pennachi angolari a colonette et semicolonette è una preziosa testimonianza di strutture del genere.

Ma il maggior pregio del monumento è tuttavia la meravigliosa decorazione a rilievi che purtroppo sfugge a determinazioni sicure. Anzitutto i capitelli delle colonne del tipo a foglie d'acanto finemente dentellate ("feingezahnter Akanthus" di Kautzsch) sono del tipo creato dagli artisti del Mar di Marmara e diffuso dalla Corte a Costantinopoli ed in Grecia. Quelli tipici dell'Acheropitos di Salonicco risultano databili, come ha provato M. Vickers, nel periodo in cui fu attivo Hormisdas, Prefetto del pretorio d'Oriente fra il 448 ed il 450. Essi trovano rispondenza in quelli della non lontana chiesa di Dağ Pazarı con un disegno generale diverso ed in quelli del Martyrium di Meriamlik, probabilmente del vi secolo. E' probabile che questi raffinati lavori siano stati eseguiti in Isauria ed in Cilicia da artisti inviati dal Mar di Marmara: essi comunque non corrispondono

---

[1] The Basilica; the number is that used by Professor Verzone in his own monograph. [Ed.]

[2] The Baptistery. [Ed.]

[3] The East Church. [Ed.]

alla tipologia più semplice delle chiese della Cilicia e nemmeno a quella dei monumenti religiosi della Siria, da cui la Cilicia culturalmente dipendeva: valga a quest'ultimo proposito il grandioso santuario di Qal'at Si'man, costruito nell'ultimo quarto del v secolo, che nei suoi capitelli offre foglie mosse dal vento oppure di tipo normale ma sempre lavorato a striature e non a forellini di trapano e minute dentellature.

L'elemento salienta della decorazione delle chiese di Alahan non è tuttavia costituito dai capitelli ma dai rilievi trabeazioni, degli stipiti e delle fasce decorative che presentano una problematica di eccezionale interesse sia per l'originalità dei motivi che per la raffinatezza d'esecuzione.

Non si trovano parole adatte per mettere in evidenza la genialità creativa che ha guidato la mano degli artisti e la maestria dell'esecuzione dei rilievi venuti alla luce in questi ultimi anni: solo qualche frammento del S. Polieuctos di Costantinopoli possono competere con quelli ancora in sito di Alahan.

Per quanto riguarda l'iconografia lasciano stupefatti le sequenze di pesci guizzanti che si sviluppano negli sguanci del portale laterale della facciata della chiesa a cupola con varietà di dimensioni, forme ed atteggiamenti. Anche la tecnica di esecuzione è diversa ed alterna effetti plastici e pittorici.

Ma gli ornamenti zoomorfici non si limitano ai pesci: uccelli bezzicanti fra i racemi oppure isolati sono scolpiti a forte rilievo, nei cassetoni di certe cornici o negli sfondi della edicola del portico che forse offriva, nell'arcate centrale della nicchia, l'etimasia. Anche la decorazione di racemi è lussureggiante ed offre tralci di vite con grappoli, fogliami uscenti da cornucopie, fascette di foglioline lobate variamente.

Tutto questo repertorio lascia sconcertati; la decorazione zoomorfa a pesci e uccelli si sviluppò nei manoscritti di età merovingia nelle Gallie ma invano ne ho cercati esempi del v o vi secolo. Anche le decorazioni a racemi regolari a vite e grappoli si sviluppò e diffuse specialmente a partire dal vii secolo (Khisbat a Mafiar, Rotonda della Roccia a Gerusalemme, tempietto di Cividale, S. Salvatore di Brescia).

Anche la tecnica raffinatissima dell'esecuzione lascia sconcertati al pari della genialità dell'invenzione degli elementi ornamentali; si sarebbe tentati, da certi pezzi traforati con lo scalpello, a proporre per il monumento una data più recente dell'ultimo quarto del v secolo cioè la metà del secolo seguente ma proprio in questo tempo noi ritroviamo accanto ai raffinati capitelli della S. Sofia di Costantinopoli quelli estremamente rozzi del S. Giovanni d'Efeso ricostruito proprio per munificenza dello stesso Giustiniano nel cuore della civilissima Ionia.

In realtà la storia dell'arte decorativa in età bizantina è ancora da scrivere ed a renderne ardua la ricerca stanno gli incredibili squilibri fra le diverse regioni e le diverse scuole di una stessa età: valga tuttavia a compensarci delle dolorose incertezze che ci trovagliano in questi studi l'emozione di un monumento di incomparabile bellezza come il monastero di Alahan, ora restituito in tutti i suoi resti alla contemplazione degli amanti dell'arte dagli scavi del compianto Prof. M. Gough e dei suoi collaboratori.

Appendix 2

Sequence of Excavation, 1955-1972

Michael Gough first visited Alahan in 1952, returning in 1953. He began excavation there in 1955 and resumed work in 1961. Excavation continued until 1972. A summary list of activities by season is as follows.

1955. First excavation of the eastern and western sectors of the Basilica and of the southern part of the Baptistery; small sounding in the East Church; excavation of the rock-cut church at Al Oda. Reported in *Anatolian Studies*, 7 (1957), 153-161[1] and *Anatolian Studies*, 12 (1962), 173-184.

1961. Main excavation of the Basilica. Reported in *Anatolian Studies*, 12 (1962), 173-184.

1962. Completion of the Basilica excavation and the main excavation of the Baptistery. Reported in *Anatolian Studies*, 13 (1963), 105-115.

1963. Excavation of the nave, apse and narthex of the East Church; removal of secondary building in the Baptistery; excavation of the areas west of the Baptistery (The Two-Storey Building) and west of the East Church (domestic quarters). Reported in *Anatolian Studies*, 14 (1964), 185-190.

1965. Excavation of the Colonnaded Walkway; further work in the nave of the East Church; excavation of the funerary area northeast of the Baptistery; further excavation of the Two-Storey Building; excavation of the Cave Church. Reported in *Anatolian Studies*, 17 (1967), 37-47.

1967. Removal of secondary walls in the Basilica and Baptistery; further excavation of the Colonnaded Walkway; excavation of the Spring Complex. Reported in *Anatolian Studies*, 18 (1968), 159-167.

1968. Excavation of the north aisle and the southeast chamber of the East Church. Reported in *Türk Arkeoloji Dergisi*, 17/1 (1968), 67-68.

1970. Completion of the Spring Complex excavation and study of the water supply and distribution; sounding in the late Roman *mansio* below the monastery. Reported in *Türk Arkeoloji Dergisi*, 19/1 (1972), 95-98.

1972. Excavation of the Lower Terrace. Reported in *Royal Ontario Museum Archaeological Newsletter*, NS no. 91 (Dec. 1972), 4 pp.

---

[1] The excavation at Al Oda was undertaken at the same time as the first excavation at Alahan for convenience, due to the proximity of the two sites. No connection has been established between Alahan and Al Oda and the excavation of the latter is only mentioned here because of the coincidence of the excavation dates.

Bibliography

Alpözen, T. O. "Bodrum Müzesi Ticarı Amphoraliarı." *Türk Arkeoloji Dergisi*, 22/2 (1975), 5-32.

Amand de Mendieta, Emmanuel. "Le Système cénobitique basilien comparé au système cénobitique pachômien." *Revue de l'histoire des religions*, 152 (1957), 31-80.

Babić, Gordana. *Les Chapelles annexes des églises byzantines: Fonction liturgique et programmes iconographiques*. Bibliothèque des Cahiers archéologiques, 3. Paris, 1969.

Basil, Saint. *Lettres*. Ed. Yves Courtonne. 3 vols. Paris, 1957-1966.

———. *The Long Rules*. In *Ascetical Works*, trans. M. M. Wagner, pp. 223-337. The Fathers of the Church. New York: 1950.

———. *The Long Rules*. In PG 31: 905-1052.

Basilius, Bp. of Seleucia. *Vie et miracles de sainte Thècle*. Ed., trans. Gilbert Dagron. Subsidia Hagiographica, 62. Brussels, 1978.

Bass, G. F., ed. *A History of Seafaring Based on Underwater Archaeology*. London and New York, 1972.

———. "Underwater Excavations at Yassi Ada: A Byzantine Shipwreck." *Archäologischer Anzeiger*, 77 (1962), 537-564.

Bellinger, A. R. *Catalogue of the Byzantine Coins in the Dumbarton Oaks Collection ...*, 1: *Anastasius I to Maurice. 491-602*. Washington, DC, 1966.

Boardman, J., and J. W. Hayes. *Excavations at Tocra 1963-1965*, 2: *The Archaic Deposits II and Later Deposits*. British School of Archaeology at Athens, Supplementary Volume 10/ Society for Libyan Studies. London, 1973.

Bovini, Giuseppe. *Die Mosaiken von Ravenna*. Wiesbaden, 1977.

Braun, Joseph. *Der christliche Altar in seiner geschichtlichen Entwicklung*. 2 vols. Munich, 1924.

Brock, Sebastian. "Studies in the Early History of Syrian Orthodox Baptismal Liturgy." *Journal of Theological Studies*, NS 23 (1972), 16-64.

Brooks, E. W. "The Emperor Zenon and the Isaurians." *English Historical Review*, 8 (1893), 209-238.

Bury, J. B. *History of the Later Roman Empire from the Death of Theodosius I to the Death of Justinian*. 2 vols. London, 1923.

Callinicos. *Vie d'Hypatios*. Ed. G. J. M. Bartelink. Sources chrétiennes, 177. Paris, 1971.

Catling, H. W. "An Early Byzantine Pottery Factory at Dhiorios in Cyprus." *Levant*, 4 (1972), 1-82.

———, and A. I. Dikigoropoulos. "The Kornos Cave: An Early Byzantine Site in Cyprus." *Levant*, 2 (1970), 37-62.

Chitty, D. J. *The Desert a City*. Oxford, 1967.

Clarke, W. K. Lowther. *St. Basil the Great: A Study in Monasticism*. Cambridge, 1913.

Corpus Inscriptionum Graecarum. 4 vols. Berlin, 1828-1877.

Dalton, O. M. *Catalogue of the Finger Rings in the British Museum. Early Christian, Byzantine, Teutonic, Mediaeval and Later*. London, 1912.

Deichmann, Friedrich W. *Ravenna, Hauptstaat des spätantiken Abendlandes*, 3: *Frühchristliche Bauten und Mosaiken von Ravenna*. 2nd ed. Wiesbaden, 1958.

Delougaz, Pinhas, and Richard C. Haines. *A Byzantine Church at Khirbet al-Karak*. University of Chicago Oriental Institute Publications, 85. Chicago, 1960.

Dionysius the Areopagite. *Ecclesiastical Hierarchy*. In *The Works of Dionysius the Areopagite*, trans. John Parker, pt. 2, pp. 67-162. London, 1899.

———. *Ecclesiastical Hierarchy*. In PG 3: 369-584.

Dumaine, H. "Bains." In *Dictionnaire d'archéologie chrétienne et de liturgie*, vol. 2.1 (Paris, 1925), col. 72-117.

Dumbarton Oaks. *Handbook of the Byzantine Collection*. Washington, DC, 1967.

Evagrius Scholasticus. *The Ecclesiastical History*. Ed. J. Bidez and L. Parmentier. Amsterdam, 1964.

Eyice, Semavi. *Karadağ ve Karaman Çevresinde Arkeolojik Incelemeler*. Istanbul, 1971.

Fedwick, Paul J. *The Church and the Charisma of Leadership in Basil of Caesarea*. Studies and Texts, 45. Toronto, 1979.

Festugière, A.-J. *Les moines d'Orient*. 7 parts in 4 vols. Paris, 1961-1965.

Fıratlı, N. "Un trésor du vie s. trouvé à Kumluca, en Lycie." In *Akten des VII. Internationalen Kongresses für Christliche Archäologie. Trier ... 1965*, pp. 523-525. Vatican City and Berlin, 1969.

Forsyth, George H. "Architectural Notes on a Trip through Cilicia." *Dumbarton Oaks Papers*, 11 (1957), 223-236.

Foss, Clive. "The Persians in Asia Minor and the End of Antiquity." *English Historical Review*, 90 (1975), 721-747.

Gill, M. "The Small Finds." In R. M. Harrison, *Excavations at Saraçhane in Istanbul*. Princeton, forthcoming.

Gilson, A. G. "A Group of Roman Surgical and Medical Instruments from Corbridge." *Saalburg Jahrbuch*, 37 (1981), 5-9.

Gough, Michael. "Alahan Monastery 1968." *Türk Arkeoloji Dergisi*, 17/1 (1968), 67-68.

———. "Alahan Monastery – 1970." *Türk Arkeoloji Dergisi*, 19/1 (1970), 95-98.

———. "Alahan Monastery, A Masterpiece of Early Christian Architecture." *The Metropolitan Museum of Art Bulletin*, 26 (June 1968), 455-464.

———. "Alahan Monastery, Fifth Preliminary Report." *Anatolian Studies*, 18 (1968), 159-167.

——. "Alahan Monastery, Fourth Preliminary Report." *Anatolian Studies*, 17 (1967), 37-47.

——. "Alahan Monastery: The Final Season." *Royal Ontario Museum Archaeological Newsletter*, NS no. 101 (Oct. 1973).

——. "The Church of the Evangelists at Alahan, a Preliminary Report." *Anatolian Studies*, 12 (1962), 173-184.

——. "A Church of the Iconoclast (?) Period in Byzantine Isauria." *Anatolian Studies*, 7 (1957), 153-161.

——. "Dağ Pazarı. The Basilian Church 'Extra muros'." In *Studies in Memory of David Talbot Rice*, ed. Giles Robertson and George Henderson, pp. 147-163. Edinburgh, 1975.

——. "Domestic Appointments at Alahan Monastery." Unpublished address given under the auspices of the American Institute of Archaeology at various centres, notably at the Institute for Advanced Study, Princeton.

——. *The Early Christians*. London, 1961.

——. "The Emperor Zeno and some Cilician Churches." *Anatolian Studies*, 22 (1972), 199-212.

——. "Excavation of Alahan Monastery 1970." *Royal Ontario Museum Archaeological Newsletter*, NS no. 64 (Sept. 1970).

——. "Excavations at Alahan 1967." *Türk Arkeoloji Dergisi*, 16/1 (1967), 95-97.

——. "Excavations at Alahan, 1972." *Royal Ontario Museum Archaeological Newsletter*, NS no. 91 (Dec. 1972).

——. "Excavations at Alahan Monastery 1970." *Royal Ontario Museum Archaeological Newsletter*, NS no. 64 (Sept. 1970).

——. "Excavations at Alahan Monastery, Second Preliminary Report." *Anatolian Studies*, 13 (1963), 105-115.

——. "Excavations at Alahan Monastery, Third Preliminary Report." *Anatolian Studies*, 14 (1964), 185-190.

——. "A Fifth Century Silver Reliquary from Isauria." *Byzantinoslavica*, 19 (1958), 244-250.

——. "Notes on a Visit to Mahras Monastery in Isauria." *Byzantine Studies/ Études byzantines*, 1 (1974), 65-72.

——. *The Origins of Christian Art*. London, 1973.

——. "Some Recent Finds at Alahan (Koja Kalessi)." *Anatolian Studies*, 5 (1955), 115-123.

——. "A Thurible from Dağ Parazı." *Anadolu Araştırmaları*, 2 (1965), 231-235.

Grabar, André. "Deux portails sculptés paléochrétiens d'Egypte et d'Asie Mineure, et les portails romans." *Cahiers archéologiques*, 20 (1970), 15-28.

Grierson, P. *Catalogue of the Byzantine Coins in the Dumbarton Oaks Collection ...*, 2: *Phocas to Theodosius III. 602-717*. 2 parts. Washington, DC, 1968.

——. *Catalogue of the Byzantine Coins in the Dumbarton Oaks Collection ...*, 3: *Leo III to Nicephorus III. 717-1081*. 2 parts. Washington, DC, 1973.

Halkin, F. *Bibliotheca hagiographica graeca*. 3rd ed. 3 vols. Brussels, 1957.

Harrison, R. M. "Churches and Chapels in Central Lycia." *Anatolian Studies*, 13 (1963), 117-151.

——. "The Emperor Zeno's Real Name." *Byzantinische Zeitschrift*, 74 (1981), 27-28.

——. "The Monastery of Mahras Dağ in Isauria." In *Yayla. Third Report of the Northern Society for Anatolian Archaeology*, pp. 22-24. Newcastle-upon-Tyne, 1980.

——, and Nezih Fıratlı. "Excavations at Saraçhane in Istanbul: Fifth Preliminary Report." *Dumbarton Oaks Papers*, 22 (1968), 195-203.

——, and ——. "Excavations at Saraçhane in Istanbul: First Preliminary Report." *Dumbarton Oaks Papers*, 19 (1965), 231-236.

——, and ——. "Excavations at Saraçhane in Istanbul: Fourth Preliminary Report." *Dumbarton Oaks Papers*, 21 (1967), 273-278.

——, and ——. "Excavations at Saraçhane in Istanbul: Second and Third Preliminary Reports." *Dumbarton Oaks Papers*, 20 (1966), 223-238.

Hayes, J. W. "Excavations at Saraçhane in Istanbul: Fifth Preliminary Report; A Seventh-Century Pottery Group." *Dumbarton Oaks Papers*, 22 (1968), 203-216.

——. *Late Roman Pottery*. London: British School at Rome, 1972.

——. "A New Type of Early Christian Ampulla." *The Annual of the British School at Athens*, 66 (1971), 243-248.

Headlam, Arthur C. *Ecclesiastical Sites in Isauria (Cilicia Trachea)*. Society for the Promotion of Hellenic Studies, Supplementary Papers, 1. London, 1893.

Hill, P. V., and J. P. C. Kent, and R. A. G. Carson. *Late Roman Bronze Coinage. AD 324-498*. London, 1960.

Hill, Stephen. "The Early Christian Church at Tomarza, Cappadocia." *Dumbarton Oaks Papers*, 29 (1975), 151-164.

——. "Dağ Pazarı and its Monuments. – A Preliminary Report." In *Yayla. Second Report of the Northern Society for Anatolian Archaeology*, pp. 8-12. Newcastle-upon-Tyne, 1979.

——. "Sarı Kilise." In *Yayla. [First] Report of the Northern Society for Anatolian Archaeology*, pp. 16-20. Newcastle-upon-Tyne, 1977.

Honigmann, Ernest. *Évêques et évêchés monophysites d'Asie antérieure au VIe siècle*. Corpus Scriptorum Christianorum Orientalium, 127, Subsidia 2. Louvain, 1951.

Itinerarium Egeriae. Ed. A. Franceschini and R. Weber. Corpus Christianorum Series Latina, 175, pp. 27-90. Tournai, 1965.

Kitzinger, Ernst. "A Pair of Silver Book Covers in the Sion Treasure." In *Gatherings in Honor of Dorothy E. Miner, ed. Ursula E. McKracken, et al.*, pp. 3-17. Baltimore, 1974.

Kraeling, Carl H., ed. *Gerasa. City of the Decapolis*. New Haven, 1938.

Krautheimer, Richard. *Early Christian and Byzantine Architecture*. 2nd ed. Pelican History of Art. Harmondsworth, 1975.

Laborde, Léon de. "Église d'Aladja dans le Taurus." *Revue archéologique*, 4 (1847-1848), 172-176.

——. *Voyage de l'Asie Mineure* [Voyage en Orient, 1.] Paris, 1838.

Lassus, Jean. *Sanctuaires chrétiens de Syrie. Essai sur la genèse, la forme et l'usage liturgique des édifices du culte chrétien, en Syrie, du IIIe siècle à la conquête musulmane.* Bibliothèque archéologique et historique, 42. Paris, 1947.

——. "Syrie." In *Dictionnaire d'archéologie chrétienne et de liturgie*, 15.2 (Paris, 1953), col. 1855-1942.

Leake, William M. *Journal of a Tour in Asia Minor.* London, 1824.

Leclercq, H. "Autel." In *Dictionnaire d'archéologie chrétienne et de liturgie*, 1.1 (Paris, 1924), col. 3155-3189.

——. "Hôpitaux, Hospices, Hôtelleries." In *Dictionnaire d'archéologie chrétienne et de liturgie*, 6.2 (Paris, 1925), col. 2748-2770.

McKay, Pierre A. "The First Modern Visitor to Alahan." *Anatolian Studies*, 21 (1971), 173-174.

Magie, David. *Roman Rule in Asia Minor to the End of the Third Century after Christ.* 2 vols. Princeton, 1950.

Mango, C. "Isaurian Builders." In *Polychronion. Festschrift Franz Dölger zum 75. Geburtstag*, ed. Peter Wirth, pp. 358-365. Heidelberg, 1966.

Mateos, J. "L'Office monastique à la fin du IVe siècle: Antioche, Palestine, Cappadoce." *Oriens Christianus*, 47 (= ser. 4, vol. 11), (1963), 53-88.

Mattingly, H., and E. A. Sydenham, and Percy H. Webb. *The Roman Imperial Coinage*, vol. 5.1. London, 1927.

Milik, J. T. *Gli Scavi del "Dominus Flevit" (Monte Oliveto Gerusalemme)*, 1: *La necropoli del periodo romano.* Pubblicazioni dello Studium Biblicum Franciscanum, 13. Jerusalem, 1958.

Mitford, T. B. "Some New Inscriptions from Early Christian Cyprus." *Byzantion*, 20 (1950), 105-175.

Mohrmann, Christine. "Égérie et le monachisme." In *Corona gratiarum: Miscellanea patristica historica et liturgica Eligio Dekkers O.S.B XII lustra complenti oblata*, 1: 163-180. Instrumenta Patristica 10. Brugge and 's Gravenhage, 1975.

Monumenta Asiae Minoris Antiqua, 3: *Denkmäler aus dem rauhen Kilikien.* Ed. Joseph Keil and Adolf Wilhelm. Publications of the American Society for Archaeological Research in Asia Minor. Manchester, 1931.

Murray, Robert. "The Features of the Earliest Christian Asceticism." In *Christian Spirituality: Essays in Honour of Gordon Rupp*, ed. Peter Brooks, pp. 63-77. London, 1975.

Napoleone-Lemaire, J., and J. Ch. Balty. *Fouilles d'Apamée de Syrie*, 1.1: *L'Église à atrium de la grande colonnade.* Brussels, 1969.

Nussbaum, Otto. *Der Standort des Liturgen am christlichen Altar vor dem Jahre 1000.* 2 vols. Theophaneia; Beiträge zur Religions- und Kirchengeschichte des Altertums, 18. Bonn, 1965.

Ramsay, W. M. *The Historical Geography of Asia Minor.* Royal Geographical Society, Supplementary Papers, 4. London, 1890.

Riley, Hugh M. *Christian Initiation*. Washington, DC, 1974.

Russell, J. "Byzantine *Instrumenta Domestica* from Anemurium: The Significance of Context." In *City, Town and Countryside in the Early Byzantine Era*, ed. R. L. Hohlfelder, pp. 133-154. New York, 1982.

Saller, Sylvester John, ed. *The Memorial of Moses on Mount Nebo*. 3 parts. Publications of the Studium Biblicum Franciscanum, 1. Jerusalem, 1941-1950.

Schwartz, Eduard. *Kyrillos von Skythopolis*. Texte und Untersuchungen, 49.2. Leipzig, 1939.

Shepherd, Massey H., jr. "The Formation and Influence of the Antiochene Liturgy." *Dumbarton Oaks Papers*, 15 (1961), 23-44.

Strzygowski, Josef. *Kleinasien, ein Neuland der Kunstgeschichte*. Leipzig, 1903; rpt. New Rochelle, NY, 1980.

Tchalenko, Georges. *Villages antiques de la Syrie du Nord. Le massif de Bélus à l'époque romaine*. 3 vols. Bibliothèque archéologique et historique, 50. Paris, 1953-1958.

Theodore of Mopsuestia. *Les homélies catéchétiques de Théodore de Mopsueste*. Ed., trans. Raymond Tonneau and Robert Devresse. Studi e Testi, 145. Vatican City, 1949.

Thierry, N. "Notes sur l'un des bas-reliefs d'Alahan Manastırı, en Isaurie." *Cahiers archéologiques*, 13 (1962), 43-47.

——, and J.-M. Thierry. "Le Monastère de Koca Kalesi en Isaurie." *Cahiers archéologiques*, 9 (1957), 89-98.

Verzone, Paolo. *Alahan Monastir: Un Monumento dell'arte Tardo-Romano in Isauria*. Turin, 1956.

——. *Alahan Manastırı mimarisi üzerinde bir inceleme*. Istanbul, 1955.

Waagé, F. O. *Antioch-on-the-Orontes*, 4.1: *Ceramics and Islamic Coins*. Princeton, London and The Hague, 1948.

Ward-Perkins, J. B. "The Italian Element in Late Roman and Early Medieval Architecture." *Proceedings of the British Academy*, 33 (1947), 163-183. .

Williams, Caroline. "A Byzantine Well-Deposit from Anemurium (Rough Cilicia)." *Anatolian Studies*, 27 (1977), 175-190.

Winlock, H. E., and W. E. Crum. *The Monastery of Epiphanios at Thebes*. 2 vols. Metropolitan Museum of Art Egyptian Expedition, 3-4. New York, 1926; rpt. New York, 1973.

Wright, Denis. "The Lost Monastery of Alahan: Christian Remains in Roman Cilicia." *Illustrated London News*, vol. 208 (5 Jan. 1946), pp. 24-25.

Zgusta, Ladislav. *Kleinasiatische Personennamen*. Prague, 1964.

Index

PLATE 2. – *above* Grave inscription of the elder Tarasis

PLATE 3. – *below* Grave inscription of the younger Tarasis

PLATE 4. – *above* Alahan Monastery: General view from the southeast

PLATE 5. – *below left* The Cave Complex

PLATE 6. – *below right* The Cave Church

The Basilica

PLATE 7. – *left* The Evangelists` Door and south corner of the narthex from the west

PLATE 8. – *above* The south facade of the south pastophory

PLATE 9. – *below* General view from the northeast

The Basilica

PLATE 10. – *above left* Cornice of Evangelists' Door

PLATE 11. – *above right* Moulding of string course

PLATE 12. – *right* Narthex voussoir

PLATE 13. – *below left* Dolphin corbel on west facade

PLATE 14. – *below right* Moulding on west faces of jambs of Evangelists' Door

The Basilica

The Basilica: The Evangelists' Door

PLATE 19. – *top* West face of lintel

PLATE 20. – *above* Underside of lintel

PLATE 21. – *left* Inner face of north jamb, St. Gabriel

PLATE 22. – *right* Inner face of south jamb, St. Michael

PLATE 23. – *above left*
The Basilica:
Pilaster capital from
main arcade

PLATE 24. – *above right*
The Basilica:
Column capital from
main arcade

The Basilica

PLATE 25. – *above* South arcade from east to west

PLATE 26. – *below* Moulding on interior of main arcade stylobate

The Basilica:
Fragments of screens from main arcade

PLATE 27. – *right* Part of single panel screen of interlocking roundels with a bead and reel frame (Screen No. 6)

PLATE 28. – *below left* Solid screen in four panels. Pomegranate motif in egg and dart frame (Screen No. 11)

PLATE 29. – *above right* Pierced screen in two or four panels of small roundels with flower insets in oak leaf frame

PLATE 30. – *right* Solid screen in four parts: aisle panel contained in frame of flowing vine scroll (Screen No. 5)

PLATE 31. – *above* The East Church: General view from the southeast

PLATE 32. – *below* The East Church: The west facade

PLATE 33. – *above* The East Church: The interior of the tower

PLATE 34. – *below* The East Church: General view from the north

PLATE 35. – *above* The East Church: Central door entablature

The East Church

PLATE 36. – *left* Central door console

PLATE 37. – *right* South door console

PLATE 38. – *below left* South door: north jamb, interior face

PLATE 39. – *below right* South door: south jamb, interior face

PLATE 40. – *below* South door from the west

The East Church

PLATE 41. – *above left* Squinch arch console

PLATE 42. – *above right* Squinch arch console

PLATE 43. – *left* Interior below tower from the south west

PLATE 44. – *below* Column capital from main arcad

The East Church

PLATE 45. – *above left* The bema and the apse

PLATE 46. – *above right* An "eagle" capital

The East Church

PLATE 47. – *below left* The south pastophory: Base of table set against the east wall

PLATE 48. – *below right* The northeast pedestal

PLATE 49. – The East Church: The interior looking west

The Baptistery

PLATE 50. – *above left* The font from the east

PLATE 51. – *above right* The apse

PLATE 52. – *below* General view from the northeast

PLATE 53. – *above* Colonnaded Walk: The West Gate from the east

PLATE 54. – *above* Colonnaded Walk: Pilaster Complex No. 2 from the east

PLATE 55. – *above* Colonnaded Walk: General view the from northwest

PLATE 56. – *left* The Baptistery: The narthex from the southwest

57. – *above* Colonnaded Walk: Transverse voussoir

58. – *above* Colonnaded Walk: Column base the north

PLATE 59. – *left* Colonnaded Walk: Columns from southeast

PLATE 60. – *above* Colonnaded Walk: The Shrine from the north

PLATE 61. – *above* The Two-Storey Building: General view from the northeast

PLATE 62. – *below left* The Two-Storey Building: The grain store

PLATE 63. – *below right* The Two-Storey Building: The cistern

PLATE 64. – *above left* The Two-Storey Building: The eastern end

PLATE 65. – *above right* Living quarters north of the Basilica

PLATE 66. – *below left* Living quarters west of East Church: The baking oven

PLATE 67. – *below right* Living quarters west of East Church

PLATE 68. – *above* The Spring Complex: General view from the south

PLATE 69. – *below left* The Spring Complex: Well House interior and cistern

PLATE 70. – *below right* The Spring Complex: Well House access passage

PLATE 71. – *above left* The Spring Complex: Bath and hot water tank

PLATE 72. – *above right* The Spring Complex: The aqueduct leading to the monastery

PLATE 73. – *below left* The Lower Terrace: General view from the east

PLATE 74. – *below right* The Lower Terrace: General view from the southwest

The Pottery

The Pottery

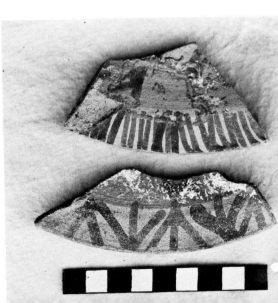

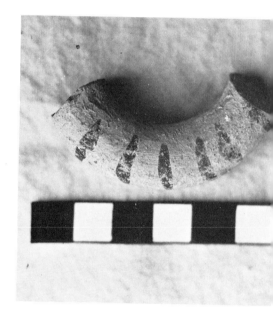

The Pottery

PLATE 85. – *above left* Catalogue No. 47

PLATE 86. – *above right* Catalogue No. 45

PLATE 87. – *right* Catalogue No. 50

PLATE 88. – *below left* For the type see Catalogue No. 38

PLATE 89. – *below left* Catalogue No. 52 (right hand sherd)